First World War
and Army of Occupation
War Diary
France, Belgium and Germany

52 DIVISION
Divisional Troops
Royal Army Medical Corps
1/3 Lowland Field Ambulance
17 April 1918 - 31 May 1919

WO95/2894/3

The Naval & Military Press Ltd
www.nmarchive.com
Published in association with The National Archives

Published by

The Naval & Military Press Ltd

Unit 10 Ridgewood Industrial Park,

Uckfield, East Sussex,

TN22 5QE England

Tel: +44 (0) 1825 749494

www.naval-military-press.com

www.nmarchive.com

This diary has been reprinted in facsimile from the original. Any imperfections are inevitably reproduced and the quality may fall short of modern type and cartographic standards.

© Crown Copyright
Images reproduced by permission of The National Archives, London, England, 2015.

Contents

Document type	Place/Title	Date From	Date To
Heading	WO95/2894-3		
Miscellaneous			
Heading	War Diary of 1/3rd Lowland Field Ambulance RAMC (T) from 14th April 1918-To 30th April 1918 Volume (3).		
War Diary	Marseilles.	17/04/1918	17/04/1918
War Diary	Musso.	18/04/1918	19/04/1918
War Diary	Noyelles.	21/04/1918	22/04/1918
War Diary	Array.	22/04/1918	29/04/1918
War Diary	Rue	29/04/1918	29/04/1918
War Diary	Airie.	30/04/1918	30/04/1918
War Diary	Cohem.	30/04/1918	30/04/1918
Miscellaneous	R.A.M.C. Administrative Instructions No. 1. Appendix I.	27/04/1918	27/04/1918
Miscellaneous	155th Infantry Brigade. Administrative Instructions No. 4. Appendix I.	27/03/1918	27/03/1918
Heading	War Diary of 1/3rd Lowland Field Ambulance RAMC (T) From 1st May 1918 to 31st May 1918 (Volume 3).		
War Diary	Cohem	01/05/1918	06/05/1918
War Diary	Ref Map Maroeuil 1/20,000	07/05/1918	07/05/1918
War Diary	Aire Maroeuil.	07/05/1918	07/05/1918
War Diary	Mont St. Eloy.	08/05/1918	25/05/1918
War Diary	Aux Rietz	25/05/1918	31/05/1918
Operation(al) Order(s)	155 Infantry Brigade Order No. 89. Appendix II		
Miscellaneous	A.D.M.S. No. S.R.2. Appendix II.	01/05/1918	01/05/1918
Miscellaneous	3rd Lowland Field Ambulance. Appendix II	04/05/1918	04/05/1918
Miscellaneous	To:- 3rd Low. Fld. Amb. Appendix III	03/05/1918	03/05/1918
Operation(al) Order(s)	R.A.M.C. Operation Order No. 1 By Colonel A.J. MacDougall A.D.M.S. 52nd Division. Appendix III	04/05/1918	04/05/1918
Miscellaneous	Time Table For Entraining.	05/05/1918	05/05/1918
Miscellaneous	Transport and Mounted Personnel March Table.		
Operation(al) Order(s)	155th Inf. Brigade Order No. 90. Appendix III	04/05/1918	04/05/1918
Operation(al) Order(s)	After Order 52nd Divisional Train Order No. 21 Appendix III	05/05/1918	05/05/1918
Operation(al) Order(s)	52nd Divisional Train Order No. 21.	05/05/1918	05/05/1918
Miscellaneous	155th Infantry Brigade Administrative Instructions No.5. Appendix III	05/05/1918	05/05/1918
Miscellaneous	Table Of Reliefs "A" Appendix III.	07/05/1918	07/05/1918
Operation(al) Order(s)	155 Infantry Brigade Order No. 91.	07/05/1918	07/05/1918
Miscellaneous	A.D.M.S. No. Sr 27 Appendix III	08/05/1918	08/05/1918
Miscellaneous	Corps No. 1, G. 537. 52nd Div. No. G.R. 8/4/29. Appendix III	05/05/1918	05/05/1918
Miscellaneous	Summary Of Medical Arrangements XVIII Corps In The Event of A Hostile Attack. Appendix III	09/05/1918	09/05/1918
Miscellaneous	Addendum To Summary of Medical Arrangements, XVIII Corps In The Event of A Hostile Attack. D/9/5/18. Appendix III.	09/05/1918	09/05/1918
Miscellaneous	O.C. 3rd Low. Fld. Amb.	09/05/1918	09/05/1918
Miscellaneous	Addressed 2nd L.F.A. copy to 3rd L.F.A. for information.	09/05/1918	09/05/1918

Miscellaneous	O.C. 3rd L.F.A.	09/05/1918	09/05/1918
Miscellaneous	O.C., 3rd L.F.A. Appendix III	09/05/1918	09/05/1918
Miscellaneous	In The Event of a Hostile Attack. Appendix III	10/05/1918	10/05/1918
Miscellaneous	M1037/18. Appendix III.	10/05/1918	10/05/1918
Miscellaneous	O.C. 3rd L.F.A. Appendix III.	10/05/1918	10/05/1918
Miscellaneous	O.C. 1st Low. Fld. Amb. Appendix III.	10/05/1918	10/05/1918
Miscellaneous	M1070/18 Appendix III	11/05/1918	11/05/1918
Miscellaneous	S.R. 45. Appendix III	11/05/1918	11/05/1918
Miscellaneous	S R 42 O.C., 3rd Lowland Field Ambce. Appendix III	11/05/1918	11/05/1918
Miscellaneous	Reference 52nd Division Order No. 105. Appendix III	14/05/1918	14/05/1918
Miscellaneous	Medical Arrangements No. 3. 52nd (Lowland) Division. Appendix III	26/05/1918	26/05/1918
Miscellaneous	Medical Arrangements No. 2 52nd (Lowland) Division. Appendix III	17/05/1918	17/05/1918
Miscellaneous	Medical Arrangement In The Event Of Active Operations 52nd (Lowland) Division. Appendix III	17/05/1918	17/05/1918
Miscellaneous	A.D.M.S. 52nd Division. No. SR 64. Appendix III.	22/05/1918	22/05/1918
Miscellaneous	Arrangements in the event of a severe Gas Attack. (Cancelling S.R.45 d/11/5/18.) Appendix III	20/05/1918	20/05/1918
Operation(al) Order(s)	52nd Division Standing Order No. 1. Battle. Appendix IV.	04/05/1918	04/05/1918
Miscellaneous	52nd (Lowland) Division. Administrative Circular Memorandum No. 1. Transport. Appendix V.	07/05/1918	07/05/1918
Miscellaneous	Headquarters 52nd Division. R 212/2 Appendix VII	03/05/1918	03/05/1918
Miscellaneous	52nd (Lowland) Division Administrative Circular Memorandum No.2 Baths. Appendix VIII.	12/05/1918	12/05/1918
Miscellaneous	D.G., S.393/37/3. D.M.S. No. 1498/6. Appendix IX	12/05/1918	12/05/1918
Miscellaneous	A.D.M.S. 52nd Div. No. R 105/4 Appendix X.	16/05/1918	16/05/1918
Miscellaneous	To:- O.C. 3rd Lowland Field Ambulance. Appendix XI	17/05/1918	17/05/1918
Miscellaneous	R.A.M.C. Operation Order No. 3. by A.D.M.S. 52nd (Lowland) Division. Appendix XII.	23/05/1918	23/05/1918
Operation(al) Order(s)	155th Inf. Brigade Order No. 96.	23/05/1918	23/05/1918
Miscellaneous	Amendment to 155 Inf. Bde. Order No. 96. Appendix XIII.	25/05/1918	25/05/1918
Miscellaneous	A.D.M.S. 52nd Divn. No S.R. 78. Appendix XIV	26/05/1918	26/05/1918
Miscellaneous	A.D.M.S. 52nd Div. No. SR 82 Appendix XIV	30/05/1918	30/05/1918
Miscellaneous	M 1367/18	31/05/1918	31/05/1918
Miscellaneous	Appendix XV		
Heading	War Diary of 1/3 Lowland Field Ambulance R.A.M.C. (T) from 1st June to 30th June 1918 (Volume 3).		
War Diary	Aux Rietz (A. 8. C 4.6.)	01/06/1918	05/06/1918
War Diary	Aux Rietz.	06/06/1918	30/06/1918
Miscellaneous	Officer Commanding 1/3rd Lowland Field Ambulance. (Appendix 1.)	08/06/1918	08/06/1918
Miscellaneous	M1502/18. (Appendix 1.)	09/06/1918	09/06/1918
Operation(al) Order(s)	157th Infantry Brigade Order No. 106. Appendix 2.		
Miscellaneous	Use of Morphia. Appendix 3.	18/06/1918	18/06/1918
Miscellaneous	Summary Of Medical Arrangements XVIII Corps Appendix 4.	16/06/1918	16/06/1918
Miscellaneous	Officer Commanding 3rd Lowland Field Ambulance. Appendix 5.	29/06/1918	29/06/1918
Operation(al) Order(s)	R.A.M.C. Operation Order No. 4. By Colonel A.J. Macdougall A.M.S. A.D.M.S. 52nd. (Lowland) Division.	29/06/1918	29/06/1918
Heading	War Diary for 1/3rd Lowland Field Amblce R.A.M.C. (T) from 1st July to 31st July 1918 (Volume 3)		

War Diary	Aux Rietz (A.8.c.4.6)	01/07/1918	02/07/1918
War Diary	Mont St Eloi (F.q.c)	02/07/1918	04/07/1918
War Diary	Mont St Eloi.	04/07/1918	22/07/1918
War Diary	Fresnicourt Q.26.a.0.5. Ref Map Line 1/20,000.	23/07/1918	23/07/1918
War Diary	Fresnicourt.	23/07/1918	31/07/1918
Miscellaneous	Medical Arrangements 1/3rd Lowland Field Ambulance. Appendix I.	07/07/1918	07/07/1918
Miscellaneous	Summary Of Medical Arrangements. 52nd (Lowland) Division.	04/07/1918	04/07/1918
Miscellaneous	Addendum To Medical Arrangements In The Event Of A Hostile Attack-52nd Division.	04/07/1918	04/07/1918
Miscellaneous	Medical Arrangements 52nd (Lowland) Division In The Event Of A Hostile Attack.		
Miscellaneous	A.D.M.S. 52nd Division. No S.R. 18 Appendix 2.	07/07/1918	07/07/1918
Operation(al) Order(s)	R.A.M.C. Operation Order No. 5 by Colonel A.J. Macdougall. A.M.S. A.D.M.S. 52nd Division. Appendix 3.	14/07/1918	14/07/1918
Miscellaneous	A.D.M.S. 52nd Division No S.R. 143/1. Appendix 4.	18/07/1918	18/07/1918
Miscellaneous	Warning Order. O.C., 1/3rd Lowland Field Ambulance. Appendix 4.	19/07/1918	19/07/1918
Miscellaneous	S.R. 57 Appendix 4.	19/07/1918	19/07/1918
Miscellaneous	155th Infantry Brigade. Administrative Instructions No 6. Appendix 4.	20/07/1918	20/07/1918
Operation(al) Order(s)	R.A.M.C. Operation Order No. 6. by Lieut-Colonel J.W. Leitch, D.S.O. A/A.D.M.S. 52nd (Lowland) Division. Appendix 4.		
Miscellaneous	In continuation of Administrative Instruction No 6 dated 20th July 1918:- Appendix 4.		
Miscellaneous	S.R. 58. Appendix 4.	21/07/1918	21/07/1918
Miscellaneous	S.R. 57. Appendix 4.	21/07/1918	21/07/1918
Operation(al) Order(s)	155th Inf. Brigade Order No.104. Appendix 4.		
Miscellaneous	March Table.		
Miscellaneous	Ref. Map Lens. 1/100,000. Sheet 11a Appendix 5.	23/07/1918	23/07/1918
Miscellaneous	Ref. Map. 1/40,000 Sheet 44b (old 36b). Ref. O.1/2. dated 23/7/18.		
Miscellaneous	S.R. 143/17. Appendix 5.	23/07/1919	23/07/1919
Miscellaneous	List Of Contents Of "B" Section Limber Wagon. Appendix 5.		
Miscellaneous	List Of Contents of "C" Section Limber Wagon. Appendix 5.		
Operation(al) Order(s)	Ammendment to R.A.M.C. Operation Order No. 7. by Lieut-Colonel, J.W. Leitch, D.S.O. A/A.D.M.S. 52nd Division.		
Operation(al) Order(s)	R.A.M.C. Operation Order No. 7 by Lieut-Colonel J.W. Leitch D.S.O. A/A.D.M.S. 52nd Division.	30/07/1918	30/07/1918
Heading	War Diary of 1/3rd Lowland Field Ambulance, R.A.M.C. (J) from 1st August to 31st August 1918 (Volume 3)		
War Diary	E.1.c.4.4.	01/08/1918	22/08/1918
War Diary	Ref Map Lens Ed2 1/100,000	22/08/1918	23/08/1918
War Diary	Ref Map Sheet 51c.	23/08/1918	23/08/1918
War Diary	Barly.	23/08/1918	23/08/1918
War Diary	Gouy-En Artois.	23/08/1918	25/08/1918
War Diary	Le Fermont.	25/08/1918	26/08/1918
War Diary	M.31.b.2.8.	26/08/1918	27/08/1918
War Diary	Mercatel.	27/08/1918	27/08/1918

War Diary	Henin.	27/08/1918	28/08/1918
War Diary	Mercatel.	28/08/1918	30/08/1918
War Diary	T.1.c.5.5.	30/08/1918	31/08/1918
Miscellaneous	D.M.S. First Army No. 770/124. Appendix I.	14/08/1918	14/08/1918
Operation(al) Order(s)	R.A.M.C. Operation Order No. 8. by Colonel A.J. Macdougall, A.M.S. A.D.M.S. 52nd (Lowland) Division. Appendix 2.	15/08/1918	15/08/1918
Miscellaneous	A.D.M.S. 52nd Division. No. SR 178 d/ 17/8/18. Appendix 3.		
Miscellaneous	A.D.M.S. SR 182 20th August 1918 Appendix 3.	20/08/1918	20/08/1918
Miscellaneous	Wire to 1/1st, 1/2nd and 1/3rd Lowland Fld. Ambces. SR 182/1 Appendix 3.	20/08/1918	20/08/1918
Miscellaneous	A.D.M.S. SR 181 20th August 1918 Appendix 3.	20/08/1918	20/08/1918
Miscellaneous	XVII Corps Medical Arrangements No. 10. Appendix 3.	19/08/1918	19/08/1918
Miscellaneous	Appendix No. 1 to XVII Corps Medical Arrangements No.10 dated 19th August 1918.	19/08/1918	19/08/1918
Miscellaneous	VI Corps Medical Arrangements No. XIV. (Operations.).		
Miscellaneous	VIth Corps Medical Arrangements No. XIV. (Operations).	13/07/1918	13/07/1918
Miscellaneous	1/3rd Lowland Fld. Amb. No. SR 64 d/ 20-8-18 Appendix 3.		
Miscellaneous	O.C., 1/3rd Lowland Field Ambulance. Appendix 3.	21/08/1918	21/08/1918
Miscellaneous	D.D.M.S. XVII Corps No. 8/36. Appendix 3.	21/08/1918	21/08/1918
Miscellaneous	A.D.M.S. SR181 Appendix 3.	21/08/1918	21/08/1918
Operation(al) Order(s)	R.A.M.C. Operation Order No. 9 by Colonel A.J. Macdougall, A.M.S. A.D.M.S. 52nd (Lowland) Division. Appendix 3.	22/08/1918	22/08/1918
Operation(al) Order(s)	155th Inf. Brigade Order No. 109. Appendix 3.	22/08/1918	22/08/1918
Miscellaneous	March Table. Issued with 155th Infantry Brigade Order No 109.		
Miscellaneous	O.C. 1/3rd Lowland Field Ambulance. Appendix 3.		
Operation(al) Order(s)	R.A.M.C. Operation Order No. 10 by Colonel A.J. Macdougall, A.M.S. A.D.M.S. 52nd (Lowland) Division. Appendix 4.	23/08/1918	23/08/1918
Miscellaneous	Officer Commanding 1/3rd Lowland Field Ambulance. Appendix 4.	23/08/1918	23/08/1918
Operation(al) Order(s)	R.A.M.C. Operation Order No. 11. by Colonel A.J. Macdougall, A.M.S. A.D.M.S. 52nd (Lowland) Division. Appendix 5.	24/08/1918	24/08/1918
Operation(al) Order(s)	R.A.M.C. Operation Order No. 12. by Colonel A.J. Macdougall, A.M.S. A.D.M.S. 52nd (Lowland) Division. Appendix 5.	25/08/1918	25/08/1918
Miscellaneous	Wire to S.E.B.O. W 616 dated 26/8/18. Appendix 5.		
Miscellaneous	O.673/18. Appendix 5.	27/08/1918	27/08/1918
Miscellaneous	O.C. 1/3rd Lowland Field Ambulance. Appendix 5.	26/08/1918	26/08/1918
Miscellaneous	Wire to 1/3rd Lowland Field Ambulance. Appendix 6.	27/08/1918	27/08/1918
Miscellaneous	Wire to S.E.B.O No. W 643 dated 27/8/18 Appendix 6.		
Miscellaneous	A.D.M.S. 52nd (Lowland) Division. Appendix 6.		
Miscellaneous	XVII Corps Medical Arrangements No. 12 Appendix 7.	27/08/1918	27/08/1918
Miscellaneous	No. M.O. 48/ Appendix 8.	30/08/1918	30/08/1918
Miscellaneous	XVII Corps Medical Arrangements No. 13. Appendix 9.	30/08/1918	30/08/1918
Heading	1/3rd Lowland Fa Sept 1918		

Heading	War Diary of 1/3rd Lowland Field Ambce RAMC (T) From 1-9-18 to 30-9-18 (Volume 3)		
War Diary	T.1.c.5.5.	01/09/1918	06/09/1918
War Diary	U 25.	06/09/1918	30/09/1918
War Diary	J.3.c.	30/09/1918	30/09/1918
War Diary	F.20.c.29.	30/09/1918	30/09/1918
War Diary	J.3.c.	30/09/1918	30/09/1918
Miscellaneous	O.C. 1/3rd Lowland Field Ambulance. Appendix I.	01/09/1918	01/09/1918
Miscellaneous	O.C. 1/3rd Lowland Field Ambulance. Appendix I.	02/09/1918	02/09/1918
Miscellaneous	Wire to S.E.B.O. No. W591 dated 4/9/18 Appendix II.	04/09/1918	04/09/1918
Miscellaneous	Wire to S.E.B.O W 540 dated 2/9/18 Appendix II.		
Operation(al) Order(s)	R.A.M.C. Operation Order No. 16 by A.D.M.S., 52nd (Lowland) Division. Appendix 4.	06/09/1918	06/09/1918
Miscellaneous	O 800/18 Appendix 4.	06/09/1918	06/09/1918
Miscellaneous	D.D.M.S., XVII Corps No. 6/100 A.D.M.S. 52nd Divn. No. Mo/192. Appendix 5.	11/09/1918	11/09/1918
Miscellaneous	Suggested improvements in Organization and Equipment. Appendix 5.	12/09/1918	12/09/1918
Miscellaneous	A.D.M.S. 52nd Divn. No. S.R. 218/7 Appendix 6.	14/09/1918	14/09/1918
Operation(al) Order(s)	R.A.M.C. Operation Order No. 17 by A.D.M.S., 52nd (Lowland) Division. Appendix 6.	14/09/1918	14/09/1918
Miscellaneous	No. B. 23 Ref. Map France, 57c N.E. Appendix 6.	17/09/1918	17/09/1918
Miscellaneous	O.C., 1/3rd Lowland Field Ambulance. Appendix 6.	18/09/1918	18/09/1918
Miscellaneous	Evacuation Of Wounded From R.A.Ps. Appendix 7.	21/09/1918	21/09/1918
Miscellaneous	B.45. Appendix 6.	21/09/1918	21/09/1918
Miscellaneous	Appendix 8.	23/09/1918	23/09/1918
Miscellaneous	O.C. 1/3rd Lowland Field Ambulance. Appendix 9.	24/09/1918	24/09/1918
Diagram etc	Trolley Post Horsed Ambulance Post.		
Operation(al) Order(s)	R.A.M.C. Operation Order No 18 by A.D.M.S. 52nd (Lowland) Division. Appendix 9.	25/09/1918	25/09/1918
Miscellaneous	Resume of Information contained in 52nd Division Administrative Instructions No. A.F. 41 of 24th September, 1918. Appendix 9.	25/09/1918	25/09/1918
Miscellaneous	O 935 26/9/18. Appendix 9.		
Miscellaneous	Wire to R.I.B.O No. W 815 dated 26/9/18 Appendix 9.		
Miscellaneous	A.D.M.S., 52nd Divn. No. SR/234 Appendix 10	29/09/1918	29/09/1918
Miscellaneous	O 955 Appendix 10.	29/09/1918	29/09/1918
Heading	War Diary of 1/3rd Lowland Field Ambulance, R.A.M.C. (T) From 1st October 1918 to 31st October 1918 Volume III.		
War Diary	J. 3. C.	01/10/1918	07/10/1918
War Diary	Vaux Vraucourt	07/10/1918	07/10/1918
War Diary	L.I.G.N.Y. Reference Map Line.	08/10/1918	08/10/1918
War Diary	Ambrines	08/10/1918	19/10/1918
War Diary	Reference Bully Grenay 11. & 1.	19/10/1918	19/10/1918
War Diary	Bully Grenay.	19/10/1918	19/10/1918
War Diary	(J.1) Lievin.	19/10/1918	19/10/1918
War Diary	Lievin.	20/10/1918	22/10/1918
War Diary	(K.I) Fouquieres.	22/10/1918	22/10/1918
War Diary	(A.2) Auby	22/10/1918	23/10/1918
War Diary	Auby.	23/10/1918	23/10/1918
War Diary	(B.1) Raches.	24/10/1918	25/10/1918
War Diary	Raches	26/10/1918	28/10/1918
War Diary	(D I) Landas.	28/10/1918	28/10/1918
War Diary	Landas.	28/10/1918	31/10/1918

Miscellaneous	Special Order Of The Day by Lieut-Colonel J. Young, Commanding 1/3rd Lowland Field Ambulance, R.A.M.C., T. Appendix I.	08/10/1918	08/10/1918
Miscellaneous	Routine Order by Major General F.J. Marshall, C.M.G., D.S.O., Commanding 52nd (Lowland) Division. Appendix 2.	18/10/1918	18/10/1918
Miscellaneous	Dear Mc Dougall, Appendix 3.	25/10/1918	25/10/1918
Heading	War Diary of 1/3rd Lowland Field Ambulance, R.A.M.C. (T.F.) from 1st November 1918 to 30th November 1918 Volume III.		
War Diary	H.28.a.8.4. (Landas).	01/11/1918	04/11/1918
War Diary	H.28.a.8.4.	04/11/1918	05/11/1918
War Diary	O.16.c.9.9 (La Vallee).	06/11/1918	09/11/1918
War Diary	P.9.c.9.8. (St. Amand)	09/11/1918	10/11/1918
War Diary	Harchies (G.29. Sheet 45).	10/11/1918	10/11/1918
War Diary	Harchies.	10/11/1918	11/11/1918
War Diary	D.26.a.6.9. (Sheet 45.)	12/11/1918	12/11/1918
War Diary	D.26.a.6.9.	12/11/1918	23/11/1918
War Diary	V.28.a.3.4. (Lens) Sheet 38.	23/11/1918	30/11/1918
Miscellaneous	Wire to O.C., 1/3rd Low. Fld. Amb. No W. 216. dated 4th Nov. 1918. Appendix 1.		
Operation(al) Order(s)	R.A.M.C. Operation Order No. 22 by A.D.M.S., 52nd (Lowland) Division. Appendix 1.	04/11/1918	04/11/1918
Miscellaneous	A.D.M.S., 52nd Divn. No. S.R. /18. Appendix 2.	04/11/1918	04/11/1918
Miscellaneous	Wire to O.C., 1/3rd Low. Fld. Amb. Appendix 3.		
Operation(al) Order(s)	R.A.M.C. Operation Order No. 23 by A.D.M.S., 52nd (Lowland) Division. Appendix 3.	06/11/1918	06/11/1918
Operation(al) Order(s)	R.A.M.C. Operation Order No. 24 by A.D.M.S. 52nd (Lowland) Division. Appendix 3.	09/11/1918	09/11/1918
Miscellaneous	A.D.M.S., 52nd Divn. No. S.R. 118/3 Appendix 4.	09/11/1918	09/11/1918
Miscellaneous	Wire to O.C. 1/3rd Low. Fld. Amb. No. W 283 dated 9th Nov. 1918 Appendix 5.		
Miscellaneous	O.C., 1/3rd Low. Fld. Amb. Appendix 5.	09/11/1918	09/11/1918
Miscellaneous	Wire to O.C., 1/3rd Low. Fld. Amb. No. W 289 dated 10th November 1918 Appendix 6.		
Miscellaneous	Wire to 1/3rd Lowland Fld. Amb. No. W 299 dated 10th Nov. 1918 Appendix 7.		
Miscellaneous	O.C., 1/3rd Low. Fld. Amb. Wire No. W 309 dated 11th Nov., 1918 Appendix 8.		
Miscellaneous	Wire to O.C., 1/3rd Low. Fld. Amb. Appendix 9.		
Miscellaneous	Wire to O.C. 1/3rd Low. Fld. Amb. No. W 338 dated 12th Nov., 1918 Appendix 9.		
Miscellaneous	A.D.M.S., 52nd Divn. No. R. 467/1 Appendix 9.	18/11/1918	18/11/1918
Miscellaneous	R. 467/1 Appendix 9.	16/11/1918	16/11/1918
Miscellaneous	A.D.M.S., 52nd Div. R 465/5 Appendix 9.	16/11/1918	16/11/1918
Miscellaneous	A.D.M.S., 52nd Div., No. R 497/1 Appendix 9.	18/11/1918	18/11/1918
Heading	War Diary of 1/3rd Lowland Field Ambulance, R.A.M.C. (T) From 1st December 1918 to 31st December 1918 Volume IV.		
War Diary	V.28.a.34. (Sheet 38).	01/12/1918	04/12/1918
War Diary	V.28.a.34.	04/12/1918	04/12/1918
War Diary	Mons.	04/12/1918	06/12/1918
War Diary	V.28.a.3.4.	06/12/1918	11/12/1918
War Diary	Mons.	12/12/1918	31/12/1918

Heading	War Diary of 1/3rd Lowland Field Ambulance, R.A.M.C. (J) from 1st January 1919 to 31st January 1919 Volume 4.		
War Diary	Mons.	01/01/1919	31/01/1919
Heading	War Diary of 1/3rd Lowland Field Ambulance, R.A.M.C. (J) from 1st February 1919 to 28th February 1919 Volume 4.		
War Diary	Mons.	01/02/1919	28/02/1919
Miscellaneous			
Heading	War Diary of 1/3rd Lowland Field Ambulance, R.A.M.C. (T) from 1st March 1919 to 31st March 1919 Volume 4.		
War Diary	Mons.	01/03/1919	21/03/1919
War Diary	Soignies.	22/03/1919	31/03/1919
Heading	War Diary of 1/3rd Lowland Field Ambulance R.A.M.C. (T) from 1-4-19 to 30-4-19 (Volume 4)		
War Diary	Soignies.	01/04/1919	30/04/1919
Heading	1/3rd Lowland Field Ambulance R.A.M.C. (T) War Diary from May 1st to May 31st 1919 Volume No 4.		
War Diary	Soignies.	01/05/1919	31/05/1919

way/16cm 28g

War Diary

of

1/3rd Lowland Field Ambulance RAMC(T)

From 1st April 1918 — To 30th April 1918

Volume (3)

MARSEILLES 17/4/18 Arrived Marseilles.

Strength - officers: Lieut T.D. FERGUSON evacuated to hospital sick.
sick.

Unit disembarked
Officers 7
Other Ranks 188
A.S.C. (H.T.) 45.

Sheet No. 3

WAR DIARY
or
INTELLIGENCE SUMMARY.

Army Form C. 2118.

Place	Date	Hour	Summary of Events and Information	Remarks and references to Appendices
MARSEILLES	17/4/18		Unit proceeded to No 3 Rest Camp, Musso	WWG
MUSSO	18/4/18		Nil	WWG
"	19/4/18		Unit entrained PRINC.	WWG
NOYELLES	20/4/18		Unit detrained NOYELLES and camped in Rest Camp there.	WWG
"	22/4/18		Unit marched to ARRAY	WWG
ARRAY	"		Headqrs and Transport established in the Chateau d'ARRAY B. C. Section billetted in the village	
	"		Received A.D.M.S. instruction it was 1st Line Transport at ABBEYVILLE — all vehicles to be marked with Divisional Identifich sign.	
	"		Hospital Opened. Admitted 2 Evacuated 2	
	23/4/18		A.D.M.S. R 35/4 instr. Capt. MURRAY to take over 53rd Sanitary Section 1 O.R. to hospital sick.	WWG
	24/4/18		2 O.Rs posted to Reserve Army Training School for duty.	WWG
"	"		Received A.D.M.S. W 23 — Yo. to be prepared to move on 28/4/18.	

WAR DIARY or INTELLIGENCE SUMMARY

Army Form C. 2118.

Sheet No 4

Place	Date	Hour	Summary of Events and Information	Remarks and references to Appendices
FRY	24/4/18		1st Line Transport as under drawn from Advanced (HT) Depot ABBEVILLE	WWG
			Vehicles Ambulance Wagons MK VI — 3 Animals	
			GS Wagons — 6 LD Horses 15	
			Limbered G.S. — 4 HD — 18	
			Water Carts — 3	
			Mallet Carts — 1	
			Bicycle — 1	
			Admitted 7 Discharged 1 Evacuated 6 Remaining Sick	
			Received A.D.M.S. instruction to draw remounts from ABBEVILLE	
"	25/4/18		Strength — Officers Captain R. STANSFELD (MO) joined for duty	WWG
			from 1/1st Low. Fld. Amb.	
			1 O.R. to hospital	
			Strength – A.S.C. (H.T.)	
			Admitted 5 Evacuated 5	
"	26/4/18		Remounts as under drawn from No 2 adv. Remount Squadron, ABBEVILLE	WWG
			Riding Horses — 8	
			L.D — " — 2	
			H.D — " — 2	
			Admitted 11 Evacuated 9 Remaining 2.	
"			Recvd ADMS W 34 — 1 officer + 2 O.Rs to proceed as Billeting	
			Party + later over billets in AIRE	

Sheet No. 5 WAR DIARY or INTELLIGENCE SUMMARY.

Army Form C. 2118.

Place	Date	Hour	Summary of Events and Information	Remarks and references to Appendices
R.R.V.	7/4/18		Admitted 3 Evacuated to Remaining 1.	WWG
"	"		1 Officer & 2 O.Rs despatched to AIRIE as Billeting Party	
"	"		Received R.D.M.S. Administrative Instructions No 1.	Appendix No 1.
"	"		" " " No 4.	
"	"		155 BGU	
"	"		Strength - R.A.M.C. 1 O.R. to hospital sick	
"	"		Strength - A.S.C.(M.T.) 1 O.R. returned to H.T. & S. Base Depot	
"	28/4/18		Admitted 9 Evacuated 7 Remaining 3	WWG
"	"		Strength - R.A.M.C. 1 O.R. to hospital sick	
"	29/4/18		Admitted 9 Evacuated 12 Remaining Nil	WWG
"	"		Hospital closed.	
"	"		Billets vacated and handed over to le Maire d'ary	
"	"		Unit marched to RUE	
RUE	"		Unit entrained	
AIRIE	30/4/18		Unit detrained and marched to billets in COHEM.	WWG
			Mechanical Transport & Ambulance Cars & 8 A.S.C.(M.T.) joined for duty from 25 th Motor Ambce. Convoy	

Army Form C. 2118.

Sheet No 6

WAR DIARY
or
INTELLIGENCE SUMMARY.

(Erase heading not required.)

Instructions regarding War Diaries and Intelligence Summaries are contained in F. S. Regs., Part II. and the Staff Manual respectively. Title pages will be prepared in manuscript.

Place	Date	Hour	Summary of Events and Information	Remarks and references to Appendices
O H F M	30/4/18		Strength - A.S.C. (M.T.) 1 O.R. to hospital sick	WWG
			Admitted 8 Discharged - Evacuated 6 Remaining 2	
			Strength	
			Officers 8	
			O. Rs. 183	
			A.S.C. (H.T.)	
			O. Rs. 42	
			A.S.C. (M.T.)	
			O. Rs. 8	
			Animals	
			Riders 8	
			L. D. Horses 17	
			H. D. -- 20	

WW Greer. Captain.
for Lieut. Colonel.
(Absent on leave).
O. C. 133rd Scotland Field Ambulance.

SECRET.   Copy No. 3.

R.A.M.C. ADMINISTRATIVE INSTRUCTIONS No. 1.

Appendix I

I. **MOVE.** Field Ambulances will move by rail on April 28th in accordance with attached time-table on transfer from Reserve to First Army. On arrival in new area the Division will come under orders of XI Corps.

II. **ENTRAINMENT.** Entraining Stations will be as under:-

   1st Lowland Field Ambulance at RUE.
   2nd Lowland Field Ambulance at NOYELLES.
   3rd Lowland Field Ambulance at RUE.

III. **BILLETS.** On arrival in the new area Ambulances will be billeted as follows:-

   1st L.F.A. in 156th Bde. Area.
   2nd L.F.A. in 157th Bde. Area.
   3rd L.F.A. in 155th Bde. Area.

IV. All transport and animals will arrive at Entraining Stations 3 hours before the train leaves. Personnel to entrain will arrive 1 hour before the train leaves.

V. **TRANSPORT.** Supply vehicles of the train will entrain with units to which they are affiliated. One man per train vehicle will be detailed by units to act as supply loader. On arrival in new Area these men will remain attached to the Train until further orders.

VI. **SUPPLIES.**

   (a) Railhead up to 28th inst. inclusive, RUE. From 29th inst. a new railhead will be allotted in First Army area.

   (b) On Entrainment, 28th inst, supply situation will be as follows:-

   Rations for 28th inst. with Units.
   - " - " 29th "   on supply vehicles of train.
   - " - " 30th "   drawn from Railhead by M.T.

VII. **WATER CARTS.** All water carts will entrain full.

VIII. **STATES.** Movement Orders shewing the number of personnel, vehicles, and animals proceeding by each train, will be handed by Units to the R.T.O. on arrival at Entraining Station.

IX. **MEDICAL.** O.C., 3rd Lowland Field Ambulance will detail a Medical Officer to be on duty at RUE Station during entraining of troops.

O.C., 2nd Lowland Field Ambulance will detail a Medical Officer to be on duty at NOYELLES Stn. during entrainment of 157th Brigade Group.

Two Motor Ambulance Cars will be detailed for duty at each Station, from this Office. On completion of entrainment, these Ambulance Cars should be given written instructions to report to A.D.M.S. ABBEVILLE.

X. Acknowledge.

(Sgd). A. J. MacDougall, Colonel, A.M.S.,

27/4/18.   A.D.M.S., 52nd Division.

SECRET.   Copy No. 14.

155th Infantry Brigade.

Administrative Instructions No. 4.

27th March, 1918.

1. Train Time Table.

Trains will leave RUE Station with loads as under:-
29th inst.

Train No.	Marche.	Departe.	Loads.
5	T.16	0014	155th Bde. H.Q., Bde. Supply Sect. Signal Sect., L.T.M. Bty., one Company with Cooker and team of 1/5th R.S.F., one Company with Cooker and Team 1/4th K.O.S.B.
7.	T.19	0254	1/5th R.S.F. less one Company, with Cooker and Team.
9	T.22	0544	1/4th K.O.S.B. less one Coy., with Cooker and Team.
11	T. 1	0844	1/5th K.O.S.B. less one Coy., with Cooker and Team.
13	T. 4	1134	218th Coy. A.S.C. 1 Coy. with Cooker and Team 1/5th K.O.S.B.
15	T. 7	1424	1/3rd L.F.A.
17	T.10	1744	H.Q. Divnl. Train., 412 Fd. Coy. R.E.
19	T.13	2034	No. 1 Coy. A.S.C.

2. Loading Party.

Loading Party 1 Officer and 100 men referred to in para 5 of Administrative Instructions No. 3, will be detailed from 1/5th K.O.S.B.   It will arrive at RUE Station at 1400 tomorrow reporting to R.T.O.

3. Entraining Officer.

Sec. Lieut. A. McBRYDE, 1/5th K.O.S.B. will report to R.T.O. RUE Station at 1530 tomorrow.

4. Detraining Officer.

Lieut. H. O'C. Jones, 1/4th K.O.S.B. will travel to Station of detrainment by train No. 1 leaving RUE at 1744.   He will report to the R.T.O. on arrival at destination.

5. Motor Lorries.

Motor Lorries will transport second blankets and any spare kit for which there is accommodation tomorrow 28th inst., to RUE Station in accordance with following table.

No. 1 LORRY.

Units.	Time of Loading.	Place.	Time of Departure.
Bde. H.Q.) Supply Sect.) Signal Sect.) 1/5th R.S.F.)	0900.	Brigade H.Q.	0930.

Appendix 1

- 2 -

No. 1 Lorry. (Continued).

Units.	Time of Loading.	Place.	Time of Departure.
1/5th R.S.F.) L.T.M. Bty.)	0900	Brigade H.Q.	0930.
4th K.O.S.B.	1200	FAVIERES.	1230.

On completion of above two runs No. 1 Lorry will report to 5th L.T.M. Bty. at PONTHOILE as transport for its move.

No. 2 Lorry.

Units.	Time of Loading.	Place.	Time of Departure.
5th K.O.S.B.	0930	FOREST MONTIERS.	1000.
3rd L.F.A.) 412 Fd. Coy. R.E.) No. 1 A.S.C. Coy.)	1300	ARRY.	1330.
H.Q. Divnl. Train.) 218 A.S.C. Coy.)	1500	LANBOY.	1530.

On completion of above No. 2 Lorry will rejoin 52nd. Divnl. M.T. Coy.

In addition to above all Units will arrange for two journeys of 1st Line Transport, if necessary, to RUE Station. They will be responsible for forming and guarding their own Dumps.

In the event of above Motor Lorries arriving more than half an hour late at loading point Unit concerned will report same by Cyclist Orderly to this office.

6. Field Cookers.

Battalions will take steps to have best use made of Field Cookers during the journey. They will detail cooks to travel with each kitchen and fuel etc., will be carried.

7. Detached Unit.

Following Transport will be left by Division for carriage of supplies etc., of 4th Bn. R.S.F. remaining at NOUVION, one 3 ton lorry, 2 supply wagons, 4 baggage wagons.

The lorry will be sent 74th Divnl. M.T. Coy., at NEUVILLE FOREST MONTIERS on 28th inst., Supply and baggage wagons have been delivered today. Pending the arrival of 74th Division 1/4th R.S.F. will be administered by Reserve Army Headquarters.

8. Acknowledge.

(Sgd). H. A. Pollok, Major,
Staff Captain, 155th Inf. Brigade.

Vol 2

140/1983

War Diary
of
1/3rd Lowland Field Ambulance RAMC(T)

from 1st May 1918 To 31st May 1918

(Volume 3)

COMMITTEE FOR THE
MEDICAL HISTORY OF THE WAR
Date 9 JUL 1918

Army Form C. 2118.

WAR DIARY
or
INTELLIGENCE SUMMARY.
(Erase heading not required.)

Confidential

War Diary
of
1/3rd Lowland Field Ambulance RAMC(T)

From 1st May 1918 To 31st May 1918

(Volume 3)

Sheet No. I

WAR DIARY
of
INTELLIGENCE SUMMARY.
(Erase heading not required.)

Army Form C. 2118.

Place	Date	Hour	Summary of Events and Information	Remarks and references to Appendices
COHEM	1/5/18			Appendix I (cont.)
	2/5/18		Transport - Mechanical. 2 Motor Cycles received from 52nd (Lowland) Division M T Company. Admitted 2 x. Discharged -. Evacuated 3. Remaining 1. x indices wounded -. Diarrhoea -. Received 155 Brigade Order No. 89. - Nurolus prison for 155 Brigade section of 6/2 line Received A.D.M.S. 52nd Division, S.R. 2. - Arrangements to be made on receipt of order "Man Battle Stations". Admitted 5 x. Discharged -. Evacuated 6. Remaining 1. x indices Wounded -. Diarrhoea 1.	W49 Appendix II W49 Appendix II
	3/5/18		Received A.D.M.S. 52nd Division S.R. 9. - Warning Order that Division will be transferred to XVIII Corps. Strength R.A.M.C. 1 Other Rank rejoined from Leave in U.K. 1 Other Rank to Hospital sick Strength A.S.C. (HT) 1 Other Rank to Hospital sick	W49 Appendix III

WAR DIARY or INTELLIGENCE SUMMARY

Army Form C. 2118.

Sheet N° 2.

Place	Date	Hour	Summary of Events and Information	Remarks and references to Appendices
COHEM	3/5/18		**Strength N.C.R.** R.A.M.C. Officers. 10. A.S.C. (H.T.) Other Ranks 41. Other Ranks. 183. A.S.C. (M.T.) Other Ranks. 8. Admitted 15x. Discharged -. Evacuated 12. Remaining 4. x Wounded -. Diarrhoea 2.	WWW
	4/5/18		**Strength - Officers.** Lieut. Colonel J. YOUNG took over command of unit, on returning from leave in U.K. Received A.D.M.S. 52nd Division Standing Order N° 1 - "Battle." Received A.D.M.S. 52nd Division, R.A.M.C. Operation Order N° 1 - Relief of 4th Canadian Division in MERICOURT SECTOR of line. Move to move to MONT ST ELOY on 7th inst and be in reserve with 155 Brigade. Received 155 Brigade Order N° 90. - Reference above move. Captain R.G. WALKER reconnoitred to examine area THIENNE - STEENBECQUE 1a BAS - BOIS d'AMONT with a view to selection of sites for Bearing Stations and works for evacuation of casualties. Received Report from Captain R.G. WALKER, M.C. Report on above. Above Report forwarded to A.D.M.S. 52nd Division. Admitted 7x. Discharged -. Evacuated 3. Remaining 8. x Wounded -. Diarrhoea 1.	Appendix IV. Appendix III. Appendix II. JY.

Sheet No. 3.

Army Form C. 2118.

WAR DIARY
or
INTELLIGENCE SUMMARY.

Place	Date	Hour	Summary of Events and Information	Remarks and references to Appendices
COHEM.	5/5/18		Received 52nd Divisional Train Order No. 21 and 155 Brigade Administrative Instructions No. 5 - reference transfer of 52nd Division from XI Corps to XVIII Corps.	Appendix III
			Received A.D.M.S. 52nd Division S.R. 11 - Sending copy of Medical arrangements at present existent in 9th Canadian Division	
			Move:- Advance party of 1 Officer and 2 Other Ranks left for MONT ST. ELOY.	
			Admitted 2.2. * Discharged 1. Evacuated 15. Remaining 13. X Wounded - Diarrhœa 2.	
			Strength A.S.C. (H.T.) 1 Other Rank to Hospital sick.	
			Transport Mechanical. 2 Motor Ambulance Cars received from 52nd Division M.T.Coy.	
			Strength A.S.C.(M.T) 2 Other Ranks arrived for duty from 52nd Division M.T.Coy.	
	6/5/18		Received 155 Brigade Wire B 68. - Warning Order that 155 Brigade will go into line to relieve 13 regime of 51st Division on night 8th/9th.	J.M.

Sheet No. 4.

Army Form C. 2118.

WAR DIARY
INTELLIGENCE SUMMARY.
(Erase heading not required.)

Instructions regarding War Diaries and Intelligence Summaries are contained in F. S. Regs., Part II. and the Staff Manual respectively. Title pages will be prepared in manuscript.

Place	Date	Hour	Summary of Events and Information	Remarks and references to Appendices
COHEM.	6.5.18.		Move - Following personnel, with all H.T. vehicles and animals, left COHEM to join 155 Brigade Train for move to MONT ST. ELOY. - R.A.M.C. - Officer 1. Other Ranks 2. - A.S.C (H.T.) Other Ranks 40.	
			Admitted 15 x. Discharged 1. Evacuated 27. Remaining - x Wounded - Sickness -	J.Y.
Ref Map 1/40,000 (MAROEUIL) AIRE.	7.5.18.	0600	Move. "A" and "B" Sections left COHEM for AIRE.	
		1130.	Above Sections entrained, and at	
MAROEUIL.		1645	Detrained and moved to MONT ST. ELOY, where they occupied Billets.	
		1615	"C" Section left COHEM, and at	
		2100	entrained at AIRE.	
			Received 52 ry Division Administrative Circular Memorandum N°1.	Appendix V.
			Received 155 Inf. Brigade Order N° 91. - Relief of 153rd Inf Brigade by 155th Brigade on night 8th/9th.	Appendix III
			Transport following wagons damaged on route to MONT ST. ELOY: - 1 G.S. wagon - Battery spring cut. 1 Ambulance wagon - Broken canvas hood.	
			Admitted 21 x. Discharged - Evacuated 21. Remaining - x Wounded - Diarrhoea 1.	J.Y.

Sheet N° 5.   Army Form C. 2118.

WAR DIARY
of
INTELLIGENCE SUMMARY.
(Erase heading not required.)

Instructions regarding War Diaries and Intelligence Summaries are contained in F. S. Regs., Part II. and the Staff Manual respectively. Title pages will be prepared in manuscript.

Place	Date	Hour	Summary of Events and Information	Remarks and references to Appendices
MONT ST. ELOY.	8/5/18	0500	"C" Section detrained MAROEUIL, and joined main body in MONT ST. ELOY.	
			A.D.M.S. informed of completion of move.	
			Received A.D.M.S. S.R. 27 — Advanced Dressing station to be opened at Aux RIETZ.	Appendix III.
			Received 52nd Division Memorandum — S.O.S. in event of hostile attack.	Appendix IV
			Received Summary of Medical Arrangements, XVIII Corps, in the event of a hostile attack.	Appendix V
			Application made to A.D.M.S. for use of a Sheet Disinfector, or 2 Serbian Barrels, for use in disinfecting clothing etc. of patients. Reply received that these could not be supplied, application to No. 2 and No. 3 Canadian Sanitary Sections.	
			No. 2 and No. 3 Canadian Sanitary Sections approached on this subject but without success.	
			Strength :— A.S.C. (H.T.)	
			1 Other Rank to Hospital sick.	
			Move. Following personnel proceeded to Aux RIETZ, and established Dressing Station (82. J. 0. 3.2.0.) — R.A.M.C. 1 Officer, 21 Other Ranks.	

Sheet No. 6.

WAR DIARY
or
INTELLIGENCE SUMMARY.

Army Form C. 2118.

Place	Date	Hour	Summary of Events and Information	Remarks and references to Appendices
MONT ST. ELOY.	8/5/18		Admitted 21 x. Discharged -. Evacuated 20. Remaining 1. x Wounded - Diarrhoea -	J.V.
	9/5/18		Received A.D.M.S., S.R. 28. - Hospital to be cleared, and transport packed, ready to move at short notice.	Appendix III.
			Received A.D.M.S. B.R. 32 - Further in regard to above.	
			Received A.D.M.S. S.R. 33 - Sick DDMS XVIII Corps instructions regarding division of unit into two echelons.	
			Received A.D.M.S. S.R. 36 - A.D.S. at AUX RIETZ to be utilised as Walking	Appendix III.
			Wounded Collecting Post, in the event of active operations. O.C. A.D.S. informed accordingly.	
			On instructions of A.D.M.S., Lieut. J.F. LINDSAY proceeded to No. 8 C.C.S. for temporary duty.	
			Admitted 55 x. Discharged 3. Evacuated 11. Remaining 42. x Wounded - Diarrhoea - Scabies 24.	J.V.
	10/5/18		Received from A.D.M.S. 15 pairs of gloves for dealing with gassed cases.	
			Transport, Mechanical. Two Motor Ambulance Cars attached from No. 8 M.A.C., for evacuation of cases from M.D.S. to C.C.S. - also 2 Drivers.	

Army Form C. 2118.

Sheet No 7.

WAR DIARY
or
INTELLIGENCE SUMMARY.
(Erase heading not required.)

Instructions regarding War Diaries and Intelligence Summaries are contained in F. S. Regs., Part II. and the Staff Manual respectively. Title pages will be prepared in manuscript.

Place	Date	Hour	Summary of Events and Information	Remarks and references to Appendices
MONT ST. ELOY.	10/5/18		Received A.D.M.S. BR 42 - arrangements in the event of Hostile attack.	Appendix III.
			Observation made to A.D.M.S. & reply above.	Appendix III.
			Reply thanks from A.D.M.S.	Appendix III.
			Received S.R. 44 from A.D.M.S. - arrangements in the event of having gas attack.	Appendix III.
			Strength:- A.S.C. (H.T.)	
			1 Other Rank to hospital sick.	
			Transport - Mechanical.	
			1 Ford Ambulance Car received from 52nd Division M.T. Coy = with Driver.	
			Following posted to A.D.S:-	
			R.A.M.C. 1 Other Rank (cyclist with cycle) - 2 Other Ranks A.S.C. (H.T.)	
			3 L.D. Animals :- 1 Limbered G.S. wagon, and 1 cluster cart.	
			Admitted 48 x . Discharged - . Evacuated 88 . Remaining 2.	
			x Wounded - . Diptheria - . Scabies 7.	J.M.
	11/5/18		Strength :- Officer.	
			On instructions of A.D.M.S. - Captain J. M. MITCHELL posted to 1/5th Royal Irish Regiment (Pioneer Battalion) vice Lieut. SULLIVAN, wounded.	

Sheet No. 8.

WAR DIARY
INTELLIGENCE SUMMARY.
(Erase heading not required.)

Army Form C. 2118.

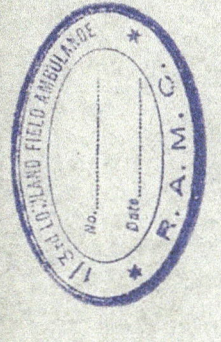

Place	Date	Hour	Summary of Events and Information	Remarks and references to Appendices
MONT ST ELOY.	11/5/18		Report on interview with Light Railway authorities re removal of walking wounded - forwarded to A.D.M.S.	Appendix III
			On instructions of A.D.M.S. :-	
			1 Other Rank posted to Divisional Baths, BERTHONVAL FARM, to work Thresh Disinfector.	
			Received A.D.M.S., S.R. 46 - Removal of sick within the Division to be carried out by Horsed Ambulance wagons.	
			O.C. A.D.S. informed accordingly.	
			Received A.D.M.S., S.R. 45 - Revised arrangements in the event of enemy gas attack.	Appendix III
			Received 62nd Division Memorandum on 1st Line Baggage Vehicles.	
			Received A.D.M.S., S.R. 42 - Orderly to be placed in charge of each train of walking wounded.	
			Application made to A.D.M.S. for further supply of gloves for dealing with "Mustard" gassed cases.	
			Transport :- A.S.C. (H.T.)	
			1 L.D. Animal evacuated from Mobile Veterinary Section.	
			Admitted 56 x. Discharged - . Evacuated 28. Remaining 10.	
			x Wounded - . Diarrhoea - . Scabies 7.	

Sheet No. 9.

WAR DIARY
INTELLIGENCE SUMMARY.
(Erase heading not required.)

Army Form C. 2118.

Place	Date	Hour	Summary of Events and Information	Remarks and references to Appendices
MONT ST. ELOY. 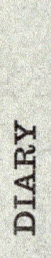	11/5/18		Unit Strength:- R.A.M.C. Officers. 9. Other Ranks. 183. — A.S.C. (HT) Other Ranks 36. A.S.C. (MT) Other Ranks. 11.	
	12/5/18		Received A.D.M.S. R.212/2 — Sanitary arrangements. Received 52nd Division Administrative Circular Memorandum No.2. — Baths. On instructions of A.D.M.S. all second shirts and third pair of socks withdrawn from personnel & forwarded to Divisional Baths. Admitted 64 x. Discharged 2. Evacuated 22. Remaining 29. x wounded —. Diarrhoea —. Scabies 9. Received A.D.M.S. S.R.42 — Refuse evacuation by Light Railway. Received from A.D.M.S. an additional supply of 44 pairs of gloves for treatment of gassed cases.	J.J. Appendix VII Appendix VIII J.J. Appendix III
	13/5/18		Strength:- A.S.C. (HT). 1 Other Rank rejoined from hospital. " 2 Horsed Ambulances, with teams and personnel, attached to A.D.S. for duty.	

Sheet No. 10.

Army Form C. 2118.

WAR DIARY
INTELLIGENCE SUMMARY

Place	Date	Hour	Summary of Events and Information	Remarks and references to Appendices
MONT ST ELOY	13/5/18		Admitted 51 x. Evacuated 76. Remaining 76. Discharged — x Wounded — Diarrhoea — Scabies 1,5.	J.Y.
	14/5/18		Received A.D.M.S. S.R.53 - Evacuation of wounded prisoners of war.	Appendix III
			Received A.D.M.S. 52nd Division S.R.52 - Medical arrangements for units in Divisional line.	
			Admitted 55 x. Evacuated 27. Discharged — Remaining 33. x Wounded — Diarrhoea 1. Scabies 10.	J.Y.
	15/5/18		On instructions of A.D.M.S. - 20 bearers attached to 1/2nd Lowland Field Ambulance in order that they may become familiar with the route of evacuation in the trenches. A relief to be sent every third day.	
			Received A.D.M.S. R 395/17 - Arrangements regarding sick and wounded of U.S. Army.	Appendix IX
			Admitted 42 x. Evacuated 71. Discharged — Remaining 4. x Wounded — Diarrhoea — Scabies 5.	J.Y.
	16/5/18		Received A.D.M.S. R.105/4 - 5 Motor Ambulance Cars with personnel, to be sent to 77th American Division.	Appendix X
			Admitted 61 x. Evacuated 42. Discharged — Remaining 23. x Wounded — Diarrhoea 1. Scabies 4.	J.Y.

Sheet No. 11.   Army Form C. 2118.

WAR DIARY

INTELLIGENCE SUMMARY

(Erase heading not required.)

Place	Date	Hour	Summary of Events and Information	Remarks and references to Appendices
MONT ST. ELOY.	16/5/18	21.30	In compliance with A.D.M.S. instructions – 1 Sgt. and 9 Drivers left, in charge of an officer, to proceed to 77th American Divison, with Ambulance Cars. A.D.M.S. informed thereof. Informed by A.D.M.S. that, pending arrival of cars to replace those sent away, cars from 1/3 8 M.A.C. will be sent above. 12 Other Ranks posted to A.D.S. for duty. Admitted 61. x Evacuated 42. Discharges – Remaining 23. x Wounded – Sick 1. 4.	fy.
	17/5/18		Received from A.D.M.S. S.R.60. – Altered arrangements N° 2. New arrangements in the event of gas alarm, drawn up by Captain R. STANSFIELD, M.C. Transport – Mechanical. Arrived from N° 8 M.A.C. – 5 cars and 7 personnel. Attached from 52nd Division M.T. Coy 2 Other Ranks. Strength: - R.A.M.C. 1 Other rank to hospital sick. Admitted 42. x Evacuated 45. Discharged 1. Remaining 19. x Wounded – Sick 7.	Appendix III. Appendix XI. fy.

WAR DIARY

INTELLIGENCE SUMMARY

Sheet No. 12

Place	Date	Hour	Summary of Events and Information	Remarks and references to Appendices
MONT ST. ELOY.	18/5/18		**Strength - Officers.** Captain R. STANSFELD, M.C. posted to 1/2nd Lowland Field Ambulance for temporary duty. - Authority A.D.M.S. 52nd Division. Lieut. & Qr.Mr. D.H. McDONALD to hospital sick. **Strength A.S.C. (HT)** 1 Other Rank rejoined from hospital. **Other.** 20 Bearers sent to 1/2nd Lowland Field Ambulance to relieve the 20 at present with that Unit. Relief party rejoined unit. Admitted 55 x. Evacuated 61. Discharged -. Remaining 17. x Wounded 1. Diarrhoea 1. Scabies 9. **Unit Strength.** R.A.M.C. Officers 8 A.S.C. (HT) 37. Other Ranks 182. A.S.C. (MT) 4.	M.
	19/5/18		**Exchange of Duties - Officers.** Lieut. P.T.J. O'FARRELL posted to 1/5th K.O.S.B. in temporary relief of Captain A.J.G. HUNTER, M.C. returned to unit. - Authority A.D.M.S. Instructions received from A.D.M.S. 52nd Division to place motor ambulance cars and one G.S. wagon at disposal of O.C. 2nd Lowland Field Ambulance	M.

Army Form C. 2118.

Sheet No. 13.

WAR DIARY
or
INTELLIGENCE SUMMARY.
(Erase heading not required.)

Place	Date	Hour	Summary of Events and Information	Remarks and references to Appendices
MONT ST ELOY.	19/5/18		Instructions referred to in previous entry complied with. Inspections. D.D.M.S. XVIII Corps visited A.D.S. Admitted 51. x Evacuated 24. Discharged 10. Remaining 34. x wounded - Diarrhoea - Scabies 10.	J.Y.
	20/5/18		Captain W. W. GREER, M.C. posted to A.D.S. to take over command. Inspections. D.M.S. visited A.D.S. Admitted 34. x Evacuated 40. Discharged 18. Remaining 10. x wounded - Diarrhoea - Scabies 7. Received A.D.M.S., S.R 64 - Arrangements in the event of enemy gas attack. Also 20 bearers sent to 1/2nd Lowland Field Ambulance in relief of those at present with that unit. Relieved bearers rejoined unit. Transport - mechanical.	Appendix III. J.Y.
	21/5/18		Received from O/C 8 M.A.C. — 2 cars and 2 drivers. Billets fairly heavily shelled - 1 horse slightly wounded. Admitted 56. x Discharged - Evacuated 36. Remaining 30. x wounded - Diarrhoea - Scabies 1.	J.Y.

Sheet N° 14.   Army Form C. 2118.

WAR DIARY
or
INTELLIGENCE SUMMARY.
(Erase heading not required.)

Place	Date	Hour	Summary of Events and Information	Remarks and references to Appendices
MONT ST. ELOY.	22/5/18		Transport – Mechanical. 7 Drivers and 5 Motor Ambulance Cars returned to 2 of 8 M.A.C. Reported from 52nd Divisional M.T. Company – 12 other Ranks 4 cars. Received A.D.M.S. Amendment to S.R. 64.	Appendix III. J.Y.
	23/5/18		Admitted 46.x. Evacuated 43. Discharged 10. Remaining 20. x Wounded –. Diarrhoea 3. Scabies 3. Received A.D.M.S. S.R. 72 – R.A.M.C. Operation Order N° 3 – Receipt of 1/27 Scotland Field Ambulance, by unit, on night 25/26 inst. O.C. A.D.S. informed of above. Admitted 71.x. Evacuated 62. Discharged 1. Remaining 28. x Wounded 11. Diarrhoea 1. Scabies 1.	Appendix XII. J.Y.
	24/5/18		Exchange of Duties – Officers. Captain A.J.G. HUNTER, M.C. returned to 1/5th K.O.S.B. and Lieut P.T. J. O'FARRELL rejoined unit – authority A.D.M.S. Above. 40 Other Ranks posted to A.D.S. Admitted 49.x. Evacuated 66. Discharged 1. Remaining 11. x Wounded –. Diarrhoea 2. Scabies 6.	J.Y.
	25/5/18		Above. M.D.S. MONT ST ELOY handed over to 1/2nd Lowland Field Ambulance and M.D.S. at Aux RIETZ taken over from them by us. 2 Cars and 3 Drivers of 2 of 8 M.A.C. handed over to 1/2nd Lowland Field Amb. with M.D.S.	

Sheet No. 15.

Army Form C. 2118.

WAR DIARY
or
INTELLIGENCE SUMMARY.
(Erase heading not required.)

Place	Date	Hour	Summary of Events and Information	Remarks and references to Appendices
Aux RIETZ	25/5/18	1800	Move (continued). - 1 car and 6 O.R. taken over from 1/2nd Low. Fld. Amb. at M.D.S. 4 Other Ranks posted to "Scottish Rifles Bearer Post" and 6 Other Ranks posted to "Artillery Bearer Post", in relief of 1/2nd Lowland Field Ambulance.	
			Posting. 1 Other Rank posted to 52nd Divisional Trains as Bakers.	M.
			Received 155 Inf. Bde. Order No 96. - Contemplated Projector Gas attack.	Appendix XIII.
			Strength:- Officers. Captain R. STANSFELD, M.C. rejoined from temporary duty with 1/2nd Lowland Field Ambulance.	
			Strength - R.A.M.C. 1 Other Rank rejoined from hospital. Admitted 61 x Evacuated 51. Discharged - Remaining 21. x wounded - Diarrhoea - Scabies 4.	M.
	26/5/18		Move. Report received from Captain W.W. GREER, M.C. that VIMY A.D.S. and its affiliated Relay and Regimental Aid Posts have now been taken over from 1/2nd Lowland Field Ambulance. Similar Report received from Captain R.G. WALKER, M.C. regarding A.D.S. CHAUDIERE, and its affiliated Relay and Regimental Aid Posts.	

Sheet No. 16.

WAR DIARY
INTELLIGENCE SUMMARY.

Place	Date	Hour	Summary of Events and Information	Remarks and references to Appendices
Aux RIETZ.	26/7/18		A.D.M.S. notified that relief now complete. Received A.D.M.S. - Medical Arrangements No 3. Casualty.	Appendix III
			1 Other Rank wounded (H.E.) at A.D.S. VIMY and evacuated to Hospital.	
			Inspections of D.M.S. 52nd Division visited M.D.S. Admitted 20 x. Evacuated 40. Discharged 1. Remaining x Wounded - Diarrhoea - Scabies -	
			Unit Strength. R.A.M.C. Officers 7 - A.S.C.(H.T.) 38 } Other Ranks. Other Ranks. 182. - A.S.C.(M.T.) 13	
			Received A.D.M.S. S.R. 78 - Reserve Rations to be held at A.D.Ss and Relay Posts.	Appendix XIV
			Received A.D.M.S. S.R. 77 -	Appendix XIII
	27/7/18		Bearer Sub-division of 1 Sgt. and 36 bearers arrived from 1/1st Lowland Field Ambulance to reinforce unit bearers - Authority A.D.M.S. Above Sub-division posted to A.D.Ss.	g.y.
			Strength - A.S.C.(H.T.)	
			1 Other Rank to hospital acds. Admitted 8 x. Evacuated 7. Discharged 7. Diarrhoea -. Remaining 1 Scabies -.	g.y.

Sheet 17.

WAR DIARY
or
INTELLIGENCE SUMMARY.
(Erase heading not required.)

Army Form C. 2118.

Place	Date	Hour	Summary of Events and Information	Remarks and references to Appendices
Aux RIETZ	28/7/16		Strength :- A.S.C. (H.T)	
			1 Baker Driver joined from 219 Coy A.S.C.	
			Admitted 57 x. Evacuated 56. Discharged - Remaining 1.	
			x. Wounded 57; Dixtheen. Scabies.	
	29/7/16		Admitted 20. Evacuated 6. Discharged - Remaining 1.	Y.
			x. Wounded 7. Dixtheen - Scabies -	Y.
	30/7/16		Admitted 17. Evacuated 9. Discharged - Remaining 7.	Y.
			x. Wounded 10. Dixtheen - Scabies -	} Appendix XIV
			Received A.D.M.S. S.R. 82 - New form to be established.	
	31/7/16		Report on above sent to A.D.M.S.	
			Admitted 10 x. Evacuated 9. Discharged Remaining	Appendix XV.
			x. Wounded. Dixtheen. Scabies.	Y.
			Disposition of Unit - Sections of - after relief of 1/2nd Lowland Field Ambce appendix	
			Unit Strength :-	
			R.A.M.C. Officers 7.	
			Other Ranks 122.	
			A.S.C. (H.T) Other Ranks 38.	
			A.S.C. (M.T) Other Ranks 13.	

Lieut. Colonel
R.A.M.C. (T)
O.C. 1/3rd Lowland Field Ambulance.

SECRET.   Appendix II   Copy No. 7

155 Infantry Brigade Order No. 89.

Ref: Map FRANCE, 1/40,000 Sheet 36 A.

1. In continuation of 155 Infantry Bde. Order No. 88, the nucleus garrison for 155th Bde. Section of the line will be furnished by 1/5 R.S.F. and 155th L.T.M. Batty. with 2 Coys. and 6 Stokes Guns in the line the remainder in immediate support.

2. The remaining Battalions will be disposed in reserve as follows :-

   1/4th K.O.S.B.   In Western Edge of BOIS d' AMONT,   about I 30.a.
   1/4th R.S.F.   - do -   - do -   about I. 23.d.
   1/5th K.O.S.B.   About I.10.d.

3. One Section 1/3rd Lowland Field Ambulance will form Collecting Stations.
   (a) On Light Railway Track about I.24. central.
   (b) At I.12.b.2.6., about 200 yards South West of LE BAS.
   and Advanced Dressing Station at I.16.a.3.1. immediately N. of Cross Roads

4. The following routes will be used by units to their Battle Stations

   (a) 1/5th R.S.F. via BOESEGHEM, THIRNNE, TANNAY.
   (b) Via BOESEGHEM, THIRNNE, and Southern bank of Canal De La NIEPPE.
   (c) Via ANCIERE, VOIERONINE, STEENBECQUE, LE BAS.

   155 L.T.M. Batty.) Via NEUFPRE, PECQUEUR, HOULERON and PLAINE BAS.
   1/4th K.O.S.B.   ) Bridge at Ferry I.23.d.

   1/5th K.O.S.B. Via PT. TOURNANT, (I.11.d.) BOESEGHEN and PLAINE BAS.

   1/4th R.S.F. will follow 1/5th K.O.S.B. as far as PLAINE BAS thence across Railway and Canal at I.22.b.

5. Bde. H.Q. will be established at I.16.a.6.5.

6. These moves will be carried out on receipt of the Order "MAN BATTLE STATIONS".
   The routes referred to in para 4 will be thoroughly reconnoitred
   The 2 Coys. 1/5th R.S.F. detailed as nucleus garrison will march off immediately on receipt of the order, without waiting for the assembly of the remainder of the Battalions.

7. ACKNOWLEDGE.

(Sgd) W.M. Burkett, Captain
Bde. Major,
155th Infantry Brigade.

Appendix II

SECRET. A.D.M.S. No. S.R.2.

O.C.,
3rd Lowland Field Ambulance.
----

1.   With reference to G.S. Circular Memorandum No 57 on receipt of the order "MAN BATTLE STATIONS" the following arrangements will be made :-

G.O.C.
Br.Gen. R.S. ALLAN
    D.S.O.
155 Inf. Bde.
155 L.T.M. Batty.
1 Sec. 3rd L.F.A.

Troops as per the margin will move to occupy the BUSNES - STEENBECQUE line from Southern edge Bois d' AMONT to junction with XV CORPS at J.1.b.5.1. and will be responsible for maintaining touch with troops on both flanks.

2.   With reference to above, please make a reconnaissance and render a report as early as possible to this office giving suitable sites for collecting and A.D. Stations, showing road suitable for vehicles and canal crossings.

1/5/18

                       (Sgd.) A.T. MacDougall, A.M.S.
             A.D.M.S.   52nd (Lowland) Division.

Appendix II

O.C.,
3rd Lowland Field Ambulance.   M 967/18.
----------------   4-5-18.

    I have been over the Area THIENNE - STEENBECQUE, LA BOIS, d'
AMONT and find :-

    There is being erected by the 13th Field Ambulance a Field
Dressing Station in I 17.c.8.2. to which a Branch of the Light Railway
is being laid.   The site suggested in I.24. central, though better
situated regards troops in the line, is much more difficult of access
and there is no ground immediately alongside that Light Railway Track
suitable for Advanced Dressing Station work.   I would suggest a very
modified, small collecting post there, opposite one of the tracks running
North and South through the wood and the utilsing, if possible, of the
huts mentioned in I.17.c.

    To the North of CANAL DE LA NIEPPE at STEENBECQUE LA BAS a
collecting Post can be established on the road running N.E. and S.W.
across the top left hand corner of I.12.b; and South of main Railway
Line.   There are alternative roads along both sides of main railway
track suitable for evacuation by wagon or Motor Ambulance from Collecting Post to Main Dressing Station, in THIENNE.   This would be better
if situated at the ESTAMINET in D.16.c.2.2. (at the cross roads) than
as proposed by Brigade in I.16.a.4.1. (also at cross roads).

    The difficulty of lateral communication between the proposed
Collecting Posts exists, but foot bridges over the Canal de la NIEPPE
can be used by foot messengers.

    The road between Canal de la NIEPPE and the BOIS d' AMONT is
good for any wheeled traffic any many tracks from it to the Light
Railway running through I.24. central and fit for wheel traffic exist.

    The only place for crossing the la NIEPPE CANAL is in I22.b.2.6.

4-5-18   (Sgd) R.G.Walker, Captain   1/3rd Low. Fld. Amb.

<u>Wire</u>   Appendix III

SECRET

To:- 3rd Low. Fld. Amb.

No. SR 9   dated 3-5-18.

Following wire received from 52nd D.H.Q. AAA begins WARNING ORDER AAA Division less R.A. will be transferred to 18th Corps by tactical trains on 6th, 7th and 8th May and will complete the relief of 4th Canadian Division on night 7th-8th May AAA Acknowledge.

From A.D.M.S. 52nd Division.

          (Sgd.) A.MacDougall, Colonel A.M.S.

SECRET   Appendix III   A.D.M.S. 52nd Div SR 9

R.A.M.C. OPERATION ORDER No. 1
BY
Colonel A.J. MacDougall
A.D.M.S. 52nd Division.

4th May 1918

1. **INFORMATION.** The 52nd Division will move from AIRE on 6th, 7th and 8th inst. and take over the MERICOURT SECTOR of the Line from the 4th Canadian Division.

2. Personnel will proceed in tactical trains, details to be notified later. Transport and mounted personnel and horses will move by road under O.C. Train in accordance with attached march table.

3. 157th Inf. Bde. Group (including personnel 2nd Low. Fld. Amb) will move by tactical train on 6th inst. to NEUVILLE ST. VAAST Camp.

4. 157th Inf. Bde. will relieve 11th Canadian Brigade of 4th Canadian Division in Line from T.23.c.5.0. to Northern Boundary of 4th Canadian Division at T.3.b.4.0. on night 7th/8th inst.

5. 155th Inf. Bde. (including personnel 3rd Lowland Fld. Amb.) will be in reserve in ST.ELOY arriving by tactical train on 7th inst.

6. 156th Inf. Bde. (including personnel 1st Low. Fld. Amb.) will be in support in NEUVILLE ST VAAST arriving by tactical train on 8th inst.

7. Divisional Headquarters will close at AIRE at 1700 on 6th inst and reopen at CHATEAU d'ACQ (3/4 Mile S.W. of VILLERS AU BOIS)

8. G.Os.C. Inf. Bde. Groups will detail order of entrainment of their Units and arrival at entrainment Station.
   On arrival at detraining Station Units will be met by guides from billeting parties and led to billeting Areas.

9. As much kit as possible will be sent by Baggage Wagons on the day preceeding entrainment. Minimum Officers' Kits, 2nd Blankets, and a proportion of cooking utensils can be taken in the tactical train. Lorries to take these and one days extra Rations for personnel to entraining Station will be provided as below (para.11)

10. (a) Railhead up to May 6th inclusive - AIRE.
              from May 7th inclusive - ST. ELOY.
    (b) Transport moving by road 5th, 6th and 7th inst will take two days Rations for men and animals with them.
    (c) Personnel entraining will do with Rations for the day following entrainment in addition to current days Rations.
    (d) All detached parties proceeding by lorry etc., will take 3 days rations with them.
    (e) Rations for 156th Inf. Bde. Group will be drawn on 7th inst from R.S.O. AIRE.

11. Lorries (referred to in para;10.)
    6th inst. - 2 Lorries at H.Q. 157th Inf. Bde. at 6 a.m.
    7th inst. - 2   "   " " 155th Inf. Bde. " 6 a.m.
    8th inst. - 2   "   " " 156th Inf. Bde. " 6 a.m.

12. Billeting Parties. Orders already issued.

13. O.Cs. Ambulances will detail a proportion of their Motor Ambulances to attend at the entraining Station till their Bde. Group has entrained, the remainder being sent forward in time for them to be at the detraining station on the arrival of the first train of their Bde. Group. The Cars doing duty at the entraining station will on completion of entraining of Bde. Group rejoin their Ambulances in the billeting Area.

14. **AREA STORES** All Area Stores which may have been drawn in present area will be handed in to sub-area commandants who will give receipts for them.

15. **STATES.** A Movement Order showing the number of personnel proceeding by each train will be handed by Units to the R.T.O. on arrival at the entraining Station.

(Sgd.) A.T.MacDougall, Colonel,
A.M.S.
A.D.M.S. 52nd Division.

SECRET.

A.D.M.S. SR 9

TIME-TABLE FOR ENTRAINING.

No of Train	Time of Dept're	Date	Unit	Entrain	Detrain	Date of Arrival
1.	0908	May 6th.	157 Inf.Bde.Group.	AIRE	MAROEUIL	1347
2.	0958	May 6th.	157 Inf.Bde.Group	AIRE	MAROEUIL	1352
3.	1908	May 6th.	Divnl. H.Q. } counting as part of 157th Inf. Bde. Group.	AIRE	ACQ	2327
			H.Q., R.E. }			
			M.G. Bn. }			
			Pioneer Bn. }			
			Div. Sig. Coy.)			
4.	0908	May 7th	155 Inf.Bde.Group	AIRE	MAROEUIL	1347
5.	1908	May 7th	155 Inf.Bde.Group	AIRE	MAROEUIL	2327
6.	0908	May 8th	156 Inf.Bde.Group	AIRE	ACQ	1312
7.	1808	May 8th	156thInf.B.Group	AIRE	ACQ	2212

The journey should take approx. 4 hours.

(Sgd) A.MacDougall, Colonel, A.M.S.
A.D.M.S. 52nd Division.

5/5/18

Transport and Mounted Personnel March Table.

(Note: No traffic to proceed through BRUAY.)

Date.	Formation.	From.	To.	Route.	Under Orders.	Remarks.
May 5th.	157th Inf. Bde. Group 2nd Low. Fld.Amb.	AIRE AREA.	DIVION	No restrictions:- Suggested - ST. HILAIRE FERFAY.	O.C. Train.	Billets from Town Major DIVION.
5th	Divnl. Headquarters	-do-	-do-	-do-	-do-	-do-
6th	157th Inf. Bde.Group	DIVION	NEUVILLE ST. VAAST	No restrictions:- Suggested - HOUDAIN ESTREECAUCHIE	-do-	Camp and rejoin formation.
6th	Divnl. Headquarters	-do-	-do-	-do-	-do-	-do-
6th	155 Inf. Bde.Group 3rd Low. Fld. Amb.	AIRE AREA.	DIVION.	No restrictions:- Suggested - ST. HILAIRE FERFAY.	-do-	Billets from Town Major DIVION.
7th	-do-	DIVION	MONT ST. ELOI.	No restrictions:- Suggested - HOUDAIN ESTREECAUCHIE	-do-	Camp and rejoin formation.
7th	156th Inf.Bde.Group (1st Low. Fld. Amb)	AIRE AREA.	DIVION.	No restrictions :- Suggested - ST HILAIRE Ferfay	-do-	Billets from Town Major DIVION.
8th	-do-	DIVION	NEUVILLE ST.VAAST.	No restrictions :- Suggested - HOUDAIN ESTREECAUCHIE	-do-	Camp and rejoin formation.

SECRET. Copy No. 7

155th INF. BRIGADE ORDER No. 90.

4th May 1918.

Ref: Map BELGIUM 1/100,000 HAZEBROUCK
  "   " FRANCE   -do-   LENS.

Appendix III

1. (a) The 52nd Division will move from AIRE on 6th 7th and 8th inst and take over the MERICOURT SECTOR of the Line from the 4th Canadian Division, from T.23.c.5.0. to the present Northern boundary of the Canadian Corps line at T.3.b.4.0.

(b) 157th Inf. Bde., 155 L.T.M. Batty., 412th Field Coy. R.E. and personnel 2nd Low. Fld. Amb. will move by tactical train on 5th inst. to NEUVILLE ST VAAST Camp, and and will relieve 11th Canadian Infantry Brigade of 4th Canadian Division. in line as above on night 7th/8th.

(c) 156th Inf. Bde., 156th L.T.M. Batty., 412th Field Coy., R.E. 1st Low. Fld. Amb. will be in support in NEUVILLE ST VAAST, arriving by tactical trains on 8th inst.

(d) The front of the Sector will be covered by 242nd and 65th Army F.A. Bdes. under orders of C.R.A. 52nd Division from 6 a.m. on May 7th.

(e) The Command of the Sector will pass from G.O.C. 4th Canadian Division to G.O.C. 52nd Division at 6 a.m. on May 7th. Divisional Headquarters at CHATEAU d' ACQ W.30.b.2.4.

2. Personnel will proceed to the new area in tactical train. Transport and mounted personnel will move by road.

3. 155th L.T.M. Batty. is placed under orders B.G.C. 157th Inf. Bde. from 1700 on the 6th inst.
157th L.T.M. Batty. having arrived in this country is placed under orders B.G.C. 155th Inf. Bde. from 0500 on 5th May.

4. 155th Inf. Bde. with 410th Coy. R.E. 1/3rd Low. Fld. Amb. attached will move by tactical train, details of which will be issued later to arrive at St. ELOY on the 7th inst. where it will be in reserve.

5. Transport and mounted personnel of all units of the 155th Inf Bde. Group will rendezvous at the GRANDE PLACE, AIRE (Fronting Town Hall) on the 6th inst, at a time to be notified later, and will proceed in charge of Captain J. Stewart, 1/4th K.O.S.B. Brigade Transport Officer, under orders of O.C. Divisional Train to MONT St. ELOY in two stages as under :/

Date.	From	To	Route	Remarks.
(a) 6th May	AIRE	DIVION	ST. HILAIRE - FERFEY	Billeted by Town Major DIVION
(b) 7th May	DIVION	MONT ST. ELOY	HOUDAIN-ESTREEGAUCHIE	Camp and rejoin Formation.

These routes may be modified.
There will be no traffic through BROUAY.

6. ACKNOWLEDGE.

(Sgd) W.M. Burkett, Captain,
Brigade Major,
155th Infantry Brigade.

SECRET.  Copy No. 7

AFTER ORDER 52ND DIVISIONAL TRAIN ORDER No.21

Para. 9 DISCIPLINE, add -

One brakesman is to be detailed to each H.T. Vehicle on the march. These men will march immediately in rear of their vehicle and will take special care tp operate brakes up and down hills.

The workingof brakes is to be inspected by Officers i/c Sections of the column before the column moves off.

The order regarding unauthorised men riding on vehicles is to be strictly enforced by all officers and Transport N.C.Os. on duty with the column, irrespective of the Unit to which they belong.

(Sgd) B.E. Randall, Capt & Adjt.,
52nd Divisional Train.

5-5-18.

SECRET.   Copy No. 7.

52nd DIVISIONAL TRAIN ORDER No. 21.

Ref: Maps HAZEBROUCK 1/100,000 Sheet 5A
     LENS   1/100,000 Sheet 11.

1. **MOVE.** All Transport and Mounted Personnel of undermentioned Units will move by march route from AIRE area to MONT ST. ELOY on 6th inst. and 7th inst., halting for night 6/7th at DIVION.
   155th Infantry Brigade Group.
        155th Infantry Brigade
        410th Field Co. R.E.
        3rd Lowland Field Ambulance.
        218 Coy. A.S.C. (Complete)
        52nd. Divisional Train Headquarters.
        Remainder of H.Q.Coy.52nd.Divisional Train.
        Mobile Veterinary Section.

2. **RENDEZVOUS.** All Units mentioned in 1 will rendezvous at road junction S.E. 7.6.(Ref.Map.HAZEBROUCK sheet 5A) at 1100 hours on 6th.inst.

3. **STARTING POINT.** Head of column will pass starting point level crossing on AIRE - ST.HILAIRE road S.E. 7.5-5 at 1130 hours.

4. **COMMAND.** O.C.218 Company A.S.C. will be in command of the whole column.

5. **ROUTE.** May 6th. Starting Point - ST.HILAIRE - FERFAY - DIVION.

    May 7th. DIVION - HOUDAIN - BARAFFLE - ESTREE CAUCHIE - CAMBLAIN - L'ABBAYA - MONT ST ELOY.

6. **MIDDAY HALT** The column will halt to water and feed at MAZINGHEM.

7. **SUPPLY SECTION.** Supply wagons of 155th. Brigade Group will be sent to report to Units at 1800 hours on 5th.inst., and will march with Units loaded with 1 days supplies for men an animals moving by road.
    Supply wagon of Mobile Veterinary Section will be sent to Refilling Point 157th. Brigade, AIRE at 1500 hours on 5th.inst., and when loaded will report to O.C.218 Company A.S.C.
    Company supplies will be drawn from S.O. 157th. Brigade AIRE at 1500 hours.

8. **BAGGAGE SECTION.** Baggage wagons will be sent to report to Units at 1800 hours and will march with Units.

9. **DISCIPLINE.** The strictest attention is to be paid to march discipline 100 yards is to be left between each Unit's Transport. No man, except the driver, is to ride on any vehicle without a pass signed by O.C. Column.

10. **MOTOR TRANSPORT.** One motor lorry will march with the column and will rendezvous with remainder of column at 1100 hours.

11. **BILLETING PARTIES.** O.C.Column will detail Billeting parties from each Unit in charge of an Officer. The part will proceed to DIVION in advance of the column and the Officer in charge will be informed of the strength of the respective Units.
    O.i/c Party will take over such billets as he requires from rear party of 157th. Brigade Column.

12. **REFILLING.** Supply Section Wagons will refill at DIVION at 0830 hours on 7th.inst.

13. The column will march from DIVION at 1000 hours on the 7th.inst., under orders to be issued by O.C.Column. It should arrive MONT ST ELOY at 1600 hours.
    O.C.Column will leave at DIVION a rear party to hand over billets to 156th. Brigade Column.

                                            Continued:-

Para 13 continued

He will send on an Advance Party to get in touch with Divisional Billeting Party in new area.

14 ACKNOWLEDGE.

(Sgd.) B.E. Randall, Capt&Adjt.
52nd Divisional Train.

5-5-18

Appendix III

SECRET.   Copy No. 13

Ref: BELGIUM 1/100,000
     HAZEBROUCK.
     FRANCE 1/100,000
     LENS.

155th INFANTRY BRIGADE ADMINISTRATIVE INSTRUCTIONS No. 5.

Issued with reference to 155th Brigade Order No. 90.
                                                    5th May 1918

1. **MOVES.**

52nd Division (less artillery) will be transferred on May 5th, 6th, 7th and 8th from XIth CORPS to XVIIIth CORPS and will move as follows:-

(a) Dismounted personnel by tactical trains Nos. 4 and 5 as follows:-

No. 4 Train		No. 5 Train	
Departs	Brigade H.Q.	Departs AIRE	4th R.S.F.
AIRE 0908	5th K.O.S.B.	1908 on 7th	5th R.S.F.
on 7th inst.	4th K.O.S.B.	inst.	410th Fld. Co., R.E.
	1/3rd Low. Fld. Amb.		157th T.M. Batty.
	(less 1 Section)		1 Section 1/3rd L.F.A.

Units will entrain in above order.

(b) All Horse Transport and Riding Mules will proceed by march route in accordance with instructions already issued in 155th Brigade Order No. 90.

2. **ENTRAINING OFFICER.**

Lieut. A.B. BAIN 1/4th R.S.F. will act as Brigade entraining Officer. He will report to R.T.O. at AIRE Station by 0700 on morning of 7th inst.
He will supervise all entraining of 155th Brigade Group and will travel by No. 5 Train on completion of his duties.

3. **DETRAINING OFFICER.**

Lieut. G. FAIR 1/4th K.O.S.B. will act as detraining Officer He will travel by No. 2 Train leaving AIRE Station at 0908 on the 6th inst. and on arrival at his destination will report to R.T.O. MAROEUIL. He will supervise the detraining of all personnel and baggage of 155th Brigade Group and will take steps to clear the station as quickly as possible after arrival of each train. On completion of his duties in connection with No. 5 Train he will rejoin his Unit.

4. **ENTRAINING AND DETRAINING.**

(a) The first Unit in each train will arrive two hours before the hour at which the train is due to start. The remaining units will arrive at intervals of ten minutes thereafter, the last unit being ready to entrain at least one hour before the train is timed to leave.

(b) On arrival at detraining Station Units will be met by Guides from Billeting party and led to their respective areas.

5. **LOADING PARTY.**

O.C. 1/4th R.S.F. will detail a loading party of 1 Officer and 50 Other Ranks to report to entraining Officer at AIRE Station by 0700 on the 7th. The Officer i/c this party will be responsible that all baggage of 155th Bde. Group is loaded on Trains 4 and 5 at least half an hour before the train is due to leave.
O.C. 1/4th K.O.S.B. will detail 1 Officer and 50 Other Ranks

- 2 -

to proceed with No. 4 Train.   This party will be responsible
for off-loading all baggage of 155th Bde. Group arriving at
Station of detrainment on Trains 4 and 5 and for giving every
possible assistance to detraining Officer in clearing the Station
of baggage.   On completion of its duties this party will rejoin its Unit.

6. SUPPLIES.
 (a) Present refilling point will be cleared on the evening of
the 5th after rations for the 7th have been drawn, Rations for
the 8th will be drawn at the open Space South West of AIRE Station
about H.22.c.78. at 1600 on the 6th.   Units will send Ration
Parties to draw;at that time and place and to remain there in
charge of the rations until entraining on the 7th.
 (b) Units and parts of Units proceeding by road will not draw
as above, but will receive Rations and Forage for the 8th at
DIVION on the 7th inst.   They will carry Rations and Forage for
the 6th and 7th with them.
 (c) Personnel proceeding by Trains 4 and 5 will carry
Rations for 7th and 8th.

7. TRANSPORT.
 O.C. 218th Coy. A.S.C., will arrange for his baggage Wagons
to join Units for loading on night of the 5th inst.   Units will
arrange to send forward by road all Lewis Guns, S.A.A., Tools, etc.,
and all baggage which it is possible to send.   Transport on the
7th will be available for only the minimum amount of stores from
each Unit, made up of 2nd Blankets, a proportion of cooking
utensils, Medical Equipment and minimum Officers' Kit.   One or two
bicycles may also be taken on the train, not more than three.
 Lorries will be available for this baggage on the 7th inst
in accordance with the following time-table :-

	Date.	Hour.	Unit.	Place.	Departs.
No.1 Lorry. -	7th	0505	1/5th K.O.S.B.	WITTES.	0630.
	7th	0535	155 Bde. H.Q.	WITTES.	0700.
	Arrives AIRE Station 0730?				
No.2 Lorry. -	7th	0600	1/3rd Low. F.Amb	COHEM	0625
	7th	0700	1/4th K.O.S.B.	AIRE	0725
	Arrives AIRE Station 0740.				
No.3 Lorry -	7th	1600	1/3rd Low. F.Amb	COHEM	1640
	7th	1650	1/4th R.S.F.	WARNE	1720
	7th	1750	410th Fld.Co.R.E.	AIRE	1810
	Arrives AIRE Station 1825				
No.4 Lorry -	7th	1600	1/5th R.S.F.	LES OISEAUX	1630
	7th	1750	157 T.M.B.		1740
	Arrives AIRE Station 1815				

8. AREA STORES.
 Any Area Stores which may have been drawn in present Area
will be handed over to sub-Area Commandant who will give receipts
for them.
 All Tents and Shelters not forming part of authorised Unit
equipment will be handed in to XIth CORPS TROOPS at the French
Barracks close to the Church of AIRE.

9. STATES.
 Movement Order showing the number of personnel proceeding by
each Train will be handed by Units to the R.T.O. on arrival at
the entraining Station.
 All Billeting Certificates and Claims for Damages must be
completed before Units leave this Area.

10. DISCIPLINE
 O.C. 1/4th K.O.S.B. will be O.C. No. 4 Train.
 O.C. 1/5th R.S.F. will be O.C. No. 5 Train.
 The strictest Train Discipline will be maintained throughout
the journey.

11. SANITATION
 All Billets and Areas must be left in a Sanitary condition.
All Latrines will be closed and pits filled in.

12. ACKNOWLEDGE.
                              (Sgd) H.A. Pollock, Major, St. Captain,
                                        155 Infantry Brigade.

Appendix III

TABLE OF RELIEFS "A"

Relieving Unit	Unit to be relieved	Location	Bn. H.Q. to be established at
1/5th K.O.S.B.	2 Coys 7th Gordon Hghrs. 2 Coys. 7th Black Watch	Front line & Support (left of Bn. Sub-Sect) Right of intermediate (post) Line. Right of reserve (Brown) line.	Durham Post B.9.b.3.3.
1/4th K.O.S.B.	6th Black Watch	Left of Bn. Sub-Section.	Beehive T.27.d.3.6.
1/5th R.S.F. (less 2 coys)	2 Coys 7th Black Watch	Left of intermediate (post) Line. Left of reserve (brown) line.	Mersey Alley T.26.d.2.2.

2 Coys 1/(th R.S.F. will be located in THELUS Post B.7.a/

1/4 Bn. R.S.F. will remain in Brigade reserve at Hill Camp NEUVILLE ST. VAAST .... A.2.a.9.5. until further oders.

Inter-Battalion boundary will run from B.5.a.7.7. - B.4.b.0.6. (our front line) - B.4.a. 4.2. - B.3.d.7.7.

7th May 1918

(Sgd.) W.M. Birkett, Captain,
Bde. Major 155th Infantry Brigade.

SECRET.   Copy No. 10;

155 INFANTRY BRIGADE ORDER No. 91.

Ref: Map 1/20,000 MAROEUIL.   7th May 1918

1. (a) 155 Inf. Bde Group (155th Bde., 157th L.T.M. Batty., 410th
Fld. Coy. R.E., and 1/3rd Low. Fld. Amb.) will relieve 153rd Inf Bde
Group in the line from B.10.a.central (TIRED ALLEY inclusive) to
T.20.3.c.50 (HUDSON TRENCH inslusive) on night 8th /9th inst.

   (b) 410th Fld. Coy. R.E. with attached Intantry Pioneer Coy. will
take over R.E. duties of this Section under arrangements to be made
between respective C.R.Es. coming under orders of G.O.C. 155th Inf.
Bde. from 1700 on 7th inst.

   (c) 1/3rd Low. Fld. Amb. willl take over Medical Arrangements of
the corresponding formation of the 153rd Inf Bde Group under
instructions of A.D.M.S.

   (d) 52nd M.G. Bn. will relieve M.Gs 51st Division in this Section
of the line on night 9th/ 10th inst.

2. Reliefs under para(a) will be as laid down in the attached table
"A" and will be completed by 0600 on 9th inst. Immediate details
will be arranged direct between C.Os. concerned.   Instructions for
the move forward for the relief will be issued later.

3. Attention is drawn to 52nd Division Standing Orders No. 1., para 1
as to the personnel to go into the line. Personnel detailed there-
in to remain behind will for the present be accommodated with the
first line Transport.   Casualties can be replaced from this
personnel as they occur, But that referred to in S.S. 135 Sect?XXX
paras 2 ii is not to be considered as available for this purpose.

4. Existing communications will be taken over together with maps
of the line, Maps of "No Man's Land", Defence Scheme, Aeroplane Photos
log books, R.E. and Area Stores.   Attention is drawn to the
instructions re Gas contained in part 13 of the Defence Scheme of the
Section.

5. 1 Officer, N.C.O., Lewis Gunner and Signallers per Coy., from
each relieving Bn., also Bn. Intelligence Officers, and Bn. Gas N.C.O.
will go forward into the line on the morning of the 8th inst., to
acquaint themselves of the various duties to be taken over.   Guides
will meet these parties at 153rd Bde. H.Q. at 1400. A party from
each Unit will also be sent forward by day under an Officer to take
over trench and area stores.
   1/4th R.S.F will detail 2 N.C.Os. and 12 men to take over Bde.
H.Q. observation Posts under the supervision of the Bn. Intelligence
Officer.

6. Command of Bn. Sube Sections and Bde. Section will be assumed as
the successive reliefs are completed.

7. Completion of reliefs will be reported Proirity to Bde. H.Q.

8. In the evnt of an alarm during relief Units on the move will
halt and send an Officer to the nearest Bde. H.Q. to report their
position and receive orders.

9. Bde. H.Q. will open at A.6.c.6.9 (500 yds. N. of THELUS) at
1800 on 8th inst.

10. ACKNOWLEDGE.

                                       (Sgd.) W.M. Burkett, Captain,
                                                       Bde. Major,
                                          155th Infantry Brigade.

Appendix III

A.D.M.S. No. SR 27

O.C.,
   3rd Low. Fld. Amb.

   Open an Advanced Dressing Station at the old 4th Canadian Division Headquarters AUZ RIETZ - LENS 2J.0320. O.C. 2nd Low. Fld. Amb. will point out site and huts to you, he has personnel in the latter to occupy them for you.
   Sick of the Division in the Neighbourhood irrespective of Unit will be admitted to the A.D.S. and sent to your M.D.S. A Tent Sub-Division will be sufficient, but if your accommodation for personnel at ST ELOI is limited you may send up a Section.
   Wounded will be admit-ed to 2nd Low. Fld. Amb

8/5/18

(Sgd) A.T. MacDougall, Colonel
A.M.S.
A.D.M.S. 52nd Division.

Appendix III

52nd Division.　　　　　　　　　　　　　Corps No 1. G. 537.
　　　　　　　　　　　　　　　　　　　52nd Div. No. G.R.8/4/29.

1.　In order to add another means of giving early warning of an
S.O.S. in the event of a hostile attack, the following system has
been arranged with the Corps Squadron R.A.F.

　　In the event of a hostile bombardment being being of such
a nature that an attack may be expected, the Squadron will on receipt
of orders from the Corps, send out a contact control machine with
the object of watching the enemy lines, concentration areas, etc.

　　If the bombardment is followed by an infantry attack, the
plane will as soon as it observes hostile infantry leave their
trenches, drop a red smoke flare and fly back in the dirrection of
the batteries dropping red smoke flares at intervals.

　　A demonstration of this will be carried out on each Divisional
front on the first day fit for flying after the 7thn inst,
commencing on the 24th Divisional front. The actual time and date
of the demonstration will be wired to Divisional Headquarters six
hours previously to enable all batteries and infantry Units to be
warned.

2.　The Corps Squadron is equipped with R.N. 8 Machines, the
distinguishing feature of which is that the top planes are larger
than the bottom ones;

　　The contact patrol machines have a streamer made of black
wood 2' by 1' attached to the rear edge of each bottom plane.
There is also one black band under the bottom wing

Intelligence.　　　　　　　　　　　　　(Sgd.) C/G/ King, Major,
5th May 1918　　　　　　　　　　　　　General Staff XV111 Corps.

SECRET.   D.D.M.S. No. 2999

Appendix IV

SUMMARY OF MEDICAL ARRANGEMENTS XVIII CORPS IN THE EVENT OF A HOSTILE ATTACK.

1. **AT THE FRONT.**
   (a) Wounded will be evacuated under Divisional Arrangements as far as Main Dressing Stations and Walking Wounded Collecting Posts by R.A.M.C. and Regimental Stretcher Bearers, aided by specially allotted Divisional Stretcher Bearers, hand carriage, wheeled stretchers, tram trolleys, horse ambulance wagons and motor ambulances.
   (b) It is very important that the avoidance of re-dressing cases unnecessarily at different stages in their progress, be impressed on all concerned.

2. **FROM M.D.S. AND W.W.C.Ps.**
   Cases requiring evacuation will be evacuated to C.C.S. under Corps arrangements by Motor Ambulance Cars and Motor Lorries.

3. **SLIGHTLY WOUNDED**, will be kept in Divisional Units e.g. in Rest Stations and Field Ambulances and conveyed there by Divisional Trans'pt. This particularly applies to lightly gassed cases - especially of the Mustard Gas variety.

4. **EVACUATION FROM M.D.S. TO C.C.S.**
   (a) These will be carried out by O.C. No. 8 M.A.C.
   (b) The present Main Dressing Stations are situated as follows:-
   24th Division   FOSSE 10 (R 8. central)
   20th Division   ABLAIN - ST NAZAIRE (X.10.a.8.8.
   52nd Division   AUX RIETZ (A 8.c.4.6)
   (c) The O.C. No 8 M.A.C. will definately allot a total of 10 Ambulance Cars to each Division to report at the Main Dressing Stations to clear and continue cases from M.D.S. to C.C.S. The remainder of the M.A.C. Cars will remain as a mobile reserve under O.C., M.A.C. at OHLAIN (P 24.b. central 36.b)
   (d) Cars relay Posts will be established on all circuits from A.D.S. to M.D.S. and M.D.S. to C.C.S. and as each loaded Car proceeds backward and reaches a Car Relay Post the N.C.O. in charge of Relay Post will at once send a Car forward to take its place.
   As the position, size and importance of these Car Relay Posts will vary with the varying circumstances of the action alterations will be made locally and communicated to all concerned.
   (e) The O.C., M.A.C. will arrange petrol dumps for ambulance cars at Main Dressing Station.

5. **EVACUATIONS FROM W.W.CC.P. TO C.C.S.**
   (a) These evacuations will be carried out by O.C., No. 8 MA.C.
   (b) The present Walking Wounded Collecting Posts are situated as follows:-
   24th Division.   FOSSE 11.M.8.b.1.2.
   20th Division.   JENKS SIDING, SOUCHEZ (S.2.c.8.3.)
   52nd Division.   AUX RIETZ A.8.c.4.6.
   (c) The A.D.s.M.S. will keep at least one Ambulance Car at each W.W.C.P. or at a Car Relay Post near to W.W.C.P. in order that lying cases may be dealt with if they occur.
   (d) 15 Motor Lorries will be placed at the disposal of O.C. No.8 M.A.C.
   O receipt of information of hostile attack these will proceed to H.Q., No. 8 M.A.C. to report for duty under command of O.C., No.8 M.A.C.
   O.C., No. 8 M.A.C. will definitely allot 5 lorries to report to O.C. each W.W.C.P. to clear and continue to clear cases from W.W.C.P to C.C.S.
   (e) LIGHT RAILWAY SERVICE should be used to the maximum extent to evacuate walking wounded from W.W.C.Ps as far back as possible.

6. **CLERICAL ARRANGEMENTS**
   (a) A.F.W 3210 will normally be made out at Main Dressing Station to be recorded in D. & D. Books in the adjoining A.& D. Room.

CLERICAL ARRANGEMENTS continued.
    (b) A.Fs W 3210 will be made out at A.D.Ss for the following cases only:-
        (1) Cases sent direct from to C.C.S. from A.D.S.
        (2) Cases dying in Medical Units
        (3) Returned to Duty.
    Those A.F. W.3210 will be despatched to A& D books Room at M.D.S. to be recorded in A & D Books there.
    (c) Field Medical Cards will be made out at A.D.Ss, noted added if required at M.D.Ss, and will invairably be stamped with the official rubber stamp of the Unir into whose A & D book the name of the patient is to be entered.

7. CAUTIONS.
    (a) Extracts from G.R.O.3756 is republished for information and action:-
"Wherever a message reporting the withdrawal of other troops or an order to retire is brought to a party of men the bearer whatever his rank is to be taken to the Officer in Command on the spot. The latter will not act on the faith of the message, or in compliance with the order until he has satisfied himself both as to the bona-fides of the bearer and as to the genuiness of the origin of the message or order. If he finds the messengers conduct to be unjustified he will detain him in arrest."
    (b) A.DsM.S. and O.C. No 8 M.A.C. will ensure that no driver of a lorry for walking wounded or of an ambulance Car will proceed on a journey without written instructions as to his duties also an definite statement that "the driver has instructions on no account to take orders from any officer other than his own".
        to
8. The C.C.Ss will be used for XVIII Corps evacuations are situated as below:-
    RERNES-LOZINGHEM Group for Northern portion of Corps.
    AUBIGNY-LIGNY Group for Southern portion of Corps.

9. In the event of its being necessary to retire Dressing Stations may have to remove back to:-

VILLERS AU BOIS	CACOURT
DE LA HAIE	FRESNICOURT
LES 4 VENTS	HERSIN
CAMBIGNEUL	BARLIN
AUBIGNY	RUITZ
ESTREE CAUCHIE	RANCHICOURT
	HOUDAIN.

These places must be recoinnoitred beforehand and at once.

10. ACKNOWLEDGE.

                        Sgd D.JOBSON SCOTT, Captain,
                            for Colonel,
XVIII Corps 9/5/18.   D.D.M.S.

D.D.M.S. No 2999.

Appendix III

ADDENDU TO SUMMARY OF MEDICAL ARRANGEMENTS, XVIII Corps IN THE EVENT OF A HOSTILE ATTACK. D/ 9/5/18.

1. ADDENDUM PARA 5.(e)

A Light Railway Service of Trains for Walking Wounded will be started at once, on application to the nearest Light Railway Control Box to Light Railway Central Controls.

Cases should be sent from Northern portion of Corps Area to BARLIN and from Southern portion to SAVY.

The A.D.M.S. 52nd Division will forthwith send a party to form a detraining centre at SAVY Light Railway Station and A.D.M.S. 20th Division will send a similatr party to BARLIN Light Railway Sta

A party will consist of 1 Officer 1N.C.O. and 9 Privates and will arrange re-accommodation, light refreshments etc.

2. Ammendment to Para (d)

Last sentence should read " O.C. No 8 M.A.C. definite allot One Lorry to report to each O.C. W.W.C.P.

O.C. No8 M.A.C. will detail four lorries to report to O.C detraining centre, Light Railway Station SAVY and 8 to O.C. Detraining Centre, Light Railway Centre Station BARLIN.

Sgd D. JOBSON SCOTT, Captain,
For D.D.M.S.

XVIII Corps, 9th May 1918.

Urgent. Secret.   S.R. 28.

O.C., 3rd Low. Fld. Amb.

    Evacuate all cases under charge of an N.C.O. to C.C.S. Aubigny. You should have your transport packed to leave at short notice.

                                       (Sgd) A. MacDougall, Colonel, A.M.S.

9/5/18.   A.D.M.S. 52nd Division.

Copy.

Secret.

S.R. 32.

Addressed 2nd L.F.A.   copy to 3rd L.F.A. for information.

You will keep your M.D.S. as empty of patients as possible. Any sick that come in should be evacuated by or transferred to 3rd Low. Fld. Amb. and wounded evacuated.

All heavy equipment including panniers and all transport, (horse) not immediately needed will be kept sent to park with the 1st Lowland Field Ambulance at Villers au Bois.

The amount of transport and equipment at Aux Reitz will be kept mobile.

Acknowledge.

(Sgd) A. MacDougall, Colonel, A.M.S.
A.D.M.S. 52nd Division.

9/5/18.

O.C.   3rd L.F.A.   S.R.33.   Secret.

   With reference to attached have your Unit kept ready, one part mobile, the other containing heavy equipment.
   Your present location need not be changed meantime.

                    (Sgd) F.W.C.Brown, Capt.
                    for Colonel, A.M.S.
9/5/18.   A.D.M.S. 52nd Division.

Copy.   Secret.   Appendix III   S.R.36.

O.C.,

    3rd L.F.A.
----

1. In the event of active operations your A.D.S. at Aux Reitz will be used as a Collecting Station for walking wounded and you should organise it as such, making provision for admission, anti-tetanic serum injections, dressings, feeding, and retention till evacuated.

2. Evacuations will be by means of either (a) motor lorries, (b) or Light Railway, of which intimation will be given you.

3. Normally, the sick of the locality will be admitted into your A.D.S. and evacuated into your M.D.S.

4. A sufficient supply of dressings and equipment to carry out the duty should be kept at the A.D.S. but only material that can be quickly removed.

5. I may have to call on you if necessary to send up a bearer Section, and additional Officers to assist 2nd Low. Fld. Amb. in which case you will receive further orders.

                                            (Sgd) A. MacDougall, Colonel, A.M.S.

9/5/18.   A.D.M.S. 52nd Division;

Copy.   Secret.   S.R. 42.

Appendix III

In the Event of a Hostile Attack.

With reference to D.D.M.S. No. 2899 sent to Field Ambulances.

1. O.C. 3rd L.F.A. will reinforce 2nd L.F.A. with the bearers of the 3 Sections of his Ambulance. They will work under the orders of the O.C. 2nd L.F.A. who will supply guides and allot the ground that each Section will work over so that no ground occupied by the Division is missed.

O.C. 3rd L.F.A. will detail 2 Officers to assist at the Main Dressing Station of the 2nd L.F.A.

O.C. 1st L.F.A. will send his bearers under 1 Officer up to Aux Reitz. They will be held in reserve.

2. Walking wounded will be admitted to the A.D.S of the 3rd L.F.A. O.C. 3rd L.F.A. will make all arrangements as to the times of running of the trains on the Light Railway for walking wounded to Zivy, these may be made through the nearest Traffic Control Box to Light Railway Central Control.

3. O.C. 1st L.F.A. will detail 1 Officer, 1 N.C.O. and 9 Other Ranks to proceed to Zivy Light Railway Station to form a detraining centre. Four lorries will report to the O.C. Detraining Centre at Sivy.

O.C. 3rd L.F.A. will retain 1 car at the walking wounded centre (3rd L.F.A. A.D.S.) and place the remainder at the disposal of the O.C. 2nd L.F.A. for evacuation from A.D.S. 2nd Low. Fld. Amb.

5. O.C. 2nd L.F.A. will arrange car relay posts between A.D.S. and M.D.S. and all concerned will be informed.

6. All horse Ambulance Wagons of the three Field Ambulances will be placed at the disposal of the O.C. 2nd L.F.A. for evacuating to A.D.S.

7. Cautions. (a) G.R.O. 3756 will be strictly adhered to.
(b) No driver of a lorry for walking wounded or of any Ambulance Car will proceed on a journey without written instructions as to his duties, and also a definite statement that the driver has instructions on no account to take orders from any officer other than his own.

8. Acknowledge.

(Sgd) A. MacDougall; Colonel,
A.M.S.
a. D.M.S. 52nd Division.

10/5/18.

Appendix III

A.D.M.S.,
    TETU.

M1037/18.

Reference your Office No. S.R. 42 dated 10/5/18. There is no trace of D.D.M.S. No 2999 nor G.R.O. 3756 in this Office.

With reference to para. 4 & 6 I would point out that after these instructions have been complied with there will be no transport avalable at the M.D.S. of this Ambulance to deal with any casualties in this neighbourhood.

I would suggest that at least one Ambulance Car remain here.

                    (Sgd) James Young Lt. Col.
                           R.A.M.C.(T).
10/5/18.   O.C. 1/3rd Lowland Field Ambulance.

O.C., Appendix III S.R. 42.

   3rd L.F.A.

   Reference reverse.   You may retain one horse Ambulance Wagon at your M.D.S.   All your motor ambulances will be sent to 2nd L.F.A.

                    (Sgd) A. MacDougall, Colonel, A.M.S.,
10/5/18.   A.D.M.S. 52nd Division.

Appendix III

O.C. 1st Low. Fld. Amb.
O.C. 2nd Low. Fld. Amb.
O.C. 3rd Low. Fld. Amb.

SR 44

In the event of hearing Gas Attack the following arrangements will come into force.

(1) Gassed cases will be admitted into 2nd Low. Fld. Amb. Cases of Phosgene and Cloud Gas will be evacuated by M.A.C. if severe. If mild or doubtful will be sent by Divisional Ambulance to 1st Lowland Field Ambulance.

(2) Mustard Gas cases will be treated by methods already described.
If accommodation at 2nd L.F.A. is insufficient the A.D.S. of 3rd L.F.A. will be utilised.
O.C. 3rd L.F.A. will arrange for patients to be sponged with bi-carbonate Soluxtion 4ozs. to the gallon.

(3) Slight cases will be evacuated to 1st Low. Fld. Amb. where the baths will be utilised.

(4) O.C. 3rd L.F.A. will be prepared to send the Nursing Division of 1 Section under an Officer to the Divisional Baths at BERTHONVAL FARM where Divisional Bath Officer has been asked to arrange for Baths for Gassed Cases and to have bi-carbonate of Soda 4ozs to the gallon in tubs.

(5) O.C. Divisional Train has been requested to send FODEN THRESH Disinfector to 1st L.F.A. for steaming Clothes.

(6) Orderlies theating Mustard Gas Cases will wear respirators Gloves, and cover their clothes with water-proof ground sheets.

7. Acknowledge.

(Sgd) A.T.MacDougall Colonel
A.M.S.
A;D.M.S. 52nd Division.

10-5-18

SECRET.   Appendix III   M1070/18
                                                           11-5-18
A.D.M.S.,
   52nd Division.

        Ref. " ADDENDUM TO SUMMARY OF MEDICAL ARRANGEMENTS XVlll CORPS
D.D.M.S. No. 2999 Dated 9/5/18 " - I interviewed Traffic Control
ZIVY today.

        The arrangements for the Railway from ZIVY backwards are not
under the control of Traffic Control ZIVY, but of Railway Control
BOIS de DRAY. I therefore interviewed the officer at this box, who
stated that, on the authority of orders received from XVlll Corps
last night, he posted 6 Trucks at Stuart Siding, in A.8.a. and 6 at
Lindsay Siding A 8.c.   These are to be removed tomorrow morning.
The Railway Traffic Officer, however, informed me that with authority
from the Corps Light Railway Officer, it could be arranged that Trucks
could be at any time available at these two sidings if required at
the Dressing Stations at AUX RIETZ.

        I Reconnoitred the country for a suitable site for the W.W.C.P.
in the forward area.   The most suitable site is on the LENS- ARRAS
Road, between the 2 level crossings in A 5.b.   There are, however,
no huts at this spot and these would have to be supplied.   This
site has the advantage of being suitable for all the roads which
converge to this neighbourhood, while, at the same time, being sited
beside the railway.

        The Traffic Control at ZIVY said that ordinarily no traffic
proceeds in front of ZIVY during the day, but that, in the event of
wounded requiring to be carried, this could be arranged.

                              (Sgd) James Young, Lieut. Colonel,
                                              R.A.M.C., T.F.
                        O.C. 1/3rd Lowland Field Ambulance

Copy.   *Appendix III*   S.R. 45.

Secret.

O.C.,

    3rd L.F.A.

My S.R. 44 of 10th inst is hereby cancelled, and the following arrangements will be adhered to:-

1. In the eent of hearing gas attack the following arrangements will come into force.

    A. All gassed cases will be admitted into 2nd Low. Fld. Amb. Cases of Phosgene and Cloud Gas will be evacuated by M.A.C. if severe. If mixed or doubtful will be sent by Divisional Ambulance to 1st L.F.A.

    B. Mustard gassed cases - Accommodation should be arranged so as to provide (first) for an admission, diagnosing and classification centre. (Second) for unclothing men, washing them with soda solution and reclothing them, and treating them for any special symptoms, i.e. eye and throat. (Third) for detention of cases for (a) evacuation (b) transfer to Divnl. Rest Station.

Mild cases and those only needing change of clothing will be sent to the Gas Centre Berthonville Farm direct from Classification Centre. (No cases will be sent until information is received that this centre is open).

Should the accommodation at M.D.S. of 2nd L.F.A. be insufficient, cases will be diverted to A.D.S. 3rd L.F.A.

O.C. 3rd L.F.A. will make at his A.D.S. all preparations to treat such cases. (c) O.C. 3rd L.F.A. will form a Gas Centre for washing and changing of clothes at the Divisional Baths, Berthonville Farm for which he will detail 1 M.O. a,d 10 Other Ranks.

This party will be specially instructed in methods of treatment of cases suffering from Mustard Gas.

Men will be bathed and washed with bi-carbonate solution, supplied with fresh under-clothing and service dress, or if the latter is unavailable clothing that has been put through the Disinfector.

O.C. Divisional Baths holds 200 sets of vests and drawers. Patients on being treated will be sent to the Divisional Rest Station, or discharged to duty as may be necessary.

O.C. 3rd L.F.A. will have all preparations made beforehand but will not open till he is ordered, and when centre is open will report to this office by wire, and knform the O.C. 2md L.F.A. that the centre is open. (d) The Foden Thresh Disinfector and the supply of bi-carbonate of soda are at the Berthonville Baths. (e) Orderlies treating Mustard Gas cases will wear respirators, gloves and cover their clothes with waterproof ground sheets.

Headquarters,   (Sgd). A. MacDougall, Colonel,
52nd Division,   A.M.S.
11th May, 1918.   A.D.M.S. 52ndDivision.

Appendix III

(1)

O.C.,
  3rd Lowland Field Ambce.   S R 42

   With reference to my S R 42 of 10-5-18 para 2 add ;-
"An orderly will be placed in charge of each Train of Walking
Wounded. He will, on termination of journey, report to M.O. in
command of detraining Party from 1/1st Low. Fld. Amb. at SAVVY,
who will endeavour to return the orderlies by M.A.C. Cars returning
from the C.C.S. at AUBUGNY to 52nd Division".

                            (Sgd) A.T.MacDougall Colonel,
                                                   A.M.S.
11/5/18.   A.D.M.S. 52nd Division

(2)

O.C.,
  3rd Lowland Fld. Amb.   S R 42

   With references to para 5 (e) of D.D.M.S. XVlll Corps No.
2999 of 9th inst and addenda thereto, 1 N.C.O. and 1 Orderly
R.A.M.C. should travel on each Light Railway Train conveying
walking sick and wounded to the detraining centre.
   They will be in charge of the patients and will be
responsible for their comfort and the entraining and detraining of
all patients at the different Stations en route.

                            (Sgd) A. MacDougall, Colonel
                                                   A.M.S.
12/5/18   A.D.MS. 52nd Division

COPY.   *Appendix III*   Copy No. 9.

SECRET.

Reference 52nd Division Order No. 105.

I. INFORMATION. 156th Inf. Bde. will relieve the 155th Inf. Bde. in the Right Section of the Divisional Line on night of 15th/16th inst., and on relief the 155th Inf. Bde. will take over the billets and dispositions of the 156th Inf. Bde.

II. DETAIL.

   1st Lowland Field Ambulance.
      Headquarters: VILLERS AU BOIS: X.19.c.9.9.
      Transport: - do -   - do -
      M.D.S.   - do -   - do -

   2nd Lowland Field Ambulance.
      Headquarters: AUX REITZ: A.8.c.5.5.
      Transport: VILLERS AU BOIS:
      M.D.S.   AUX REITZ: A.8.c.5.5.
      A.D.S.   VIMY: T.25.a.0.4.
             LA CHAUDERIE: S.18.c.9.3.
      Relay Posts. T.13.b.7.6., T.20.b.2.7., T.26.a.5.9.
      R.A.P.   T.8.c.9.5.,   T.16.c.5.9., T.25.a.4.1.,
             B.2.a.9.8.,   B.15.a.0.8.

   3rd Lowland Field Ambulance.
      Headquarters: St. ELOY.   F.8.c.9.4.
      Transport: - do -   - do -
      M.D.S.   - do -   - do -
      A.D.S.   - do -   A.8.c.8.8.

III. MEDICAL ARRANGEMENTS FOR UNITS IN DIVISIONAL LINE.

    All cases of sick and wounded of troops in the trenches will be evacuated through the A.D.Ss. of 2nd Lowland Field Ambulance with the exception of those from the R.A.P. of the right Battalion of the Right Section which are evacuated through the 51st Division to Collecting Post, B.15.c.4.1.

    Sick of Units in neighbourhood of St. ELOY to M.D.S. of 3rd Lowland Field Ambulance.

IV. ACKNOWLEDGE.

                                        (Sgd) A. MacDougall, Colonel, A.M.S.,
13th May, 1918.   A.D.M.S., 52nd (Lowland) Division.

No. S.R.52.   14th May, 1918.

Appendix III

SECRET.   Copy No.6.

MEDICAL ARRANGEMENTS No.3.
52nd (Lowland) Division.

Reference Army Map "D", 1/40,000.   26th May 1918.

1. **LOCATIONS.**

   A.D.M.S. Office :- CHATEAU ACQ. - W.30.b.4.5.
   1st Low. Fld. Amb. - Divisional Rest Station,
                         VILLERS AU BOIS - X.19.c.9.9.
   2nd Low. Fld. Amb. - M.D.S. - ST ELOY - F.8.c.9.4.
                       A.D.S. - A.8.c.8.8.
   3rd Low. Fld. Amb. - M.D.S. - AUX RIETZ - A.8.c.5.5.
                       A.D.S. - VIMY - T.25.a.9.4.
                       A.D.S. - CHAUDIERE - S.18.c.9.3.

Regimental Aid Posts.	Relay Posts.
T.8.c.9.5.	T.13.b.7.8.
T.16.c.6.9.	T.20.b.2.7.
T.28.a.4.1.	T.26.d.8.9.
B.2.a.9.8.	A.11.b.3.9.
B.15.a.0.8.	

2. **WOUNDED.**

   Normally, all wounded will pass through the A.D.S., 3rd Low. Fld. Amb., whence they will be evacuated by Ambulance Motor Cars of the Field Ambulance to the M.D.S. from which they will be evacuated by M.A.C.

   Wounded collected in R.A.P., B.15.a.0.S. will be evacuated through the 51st Division A.D.S.

3. **SICK.**

   Sick of Units in the trenches will be evacuated through A.D.S. to M.D.S. of 3rd Low. Fld. Amb. and thence transferred to A.D.S. of 2nd Low. Fld. Amb.

   Sick of Units in neighbourhood of NEUVILLE ST VAAST will be admitted to A.D.S. of 2nd Low. Fld. Amb. and sent to M.D.S. of 2nd Low. Fld. Amb. at ST. ELOY where they are either evacuated by M.A.C. or transferred to Divisional Rest Station of 1st Low. Fld. Amb.

   Sick of Units in neighbourhood of ST. ELOY will be admitted to 2nd Low. Fld. Amb.

4. **WALKING WOUNDED.**

   During heavy fighting, when there are numbers of walking wounded, the A.D.S. of the 2nd Low. Fld. Amb. will be used as a Walking Wounded Collecting Centre and will be evacuated by Light Railway or Motor Lorry, or other means as directed.

5. **GASSED CASES.**

   Severe cases will be evacuated to C.C.S. from the M.D.S. 3rd Low. Fld. Amb. in the usual manner by M.A.C.

   Slight and doubtful cases will be transferred from 3rd Low. Fld. Amb. to 1st Low. Fld. Amb.

6. **ACKNOWLEDGE.**

                                (Sgd) A.T.MacDougall Colonel A.M.S.
                     A.D.M.S. 52nd (Lowland) DIVISION.

AMENDMENTS TO " MEDICAL ARRANGEMENTS IN THE EVENT OF ACTIVE
     OPERATIONS - 52nd (LOWLAND) DIVISION." (17-5-18)

For "2nd Low. Fld. Amb." read "3rd Low. Fld. Amb." throughout.
For "3rd Low. Fld. Amb." read "2nd Low. Fld. Amb." throughout.

H.Q. 52nd Division.   (Sgd.) A.MacDougall Colonel A.M.S.
   26th May, 1918.   A.D.M.S. 52nd (Lowland) Division.

(copies to all recipients of above Arrangements)

COPY. Appendix III Copy No. 8.
SECRET.

MEDICAL ARRANGEMENTS No. 2

52nd (Lowland) DIVISION.
++++++++++++++++++

Reference:- Map - Army Map "B", 1/40,000. 17th May, 1918.

1. **LOCATIONS.**
   A.D.M.S. Office:- CHATEAU ACQ - W.30.b.4.5.
   1st Lowland Fld. Amb; Divisional Rest Station - VILLERS AU BOIS - X.19.c.9.9.
   2nd Lowland Fld. Amb:- Main Dressing Station - AUX REITZ - A.8.c.5.5.
   Advanced Dressing Stations - VIMY - T.25.a.9.4.
   LA CHAUDERIE - S.18.c.9.3.

3rd Low. Fld. Amb.	Regimental Aid Posts.	Relay Posts.
M.D.S. - St. ELOY	T.8.c.9.5.	T.13.b.7.8.
	T.16.c.6.9.	T.20.b.2.7.
F.8.c.9.4.	T.28.a.4.1.	T.26.a.3.9.
	B.2.a.9.6.	A.11.b.3.9.
A.D.S. - A.8.c.8.8.	B.15.a.0.8.	

2. **WOUNDED.**
   Normally all wounded will pass through the A.D.S. 2nd Lowland Field Amb., whence they will be evacuated by Ambulance Motor Cars of the Field Ambulance to the M.D.S., from which they will be evacuated by M.A.C.
   Wounded collected in R.A.P. - B.15.a.0.8. will be evacuated through the 51st Division A.D.S.

3. **SICK.**
   Sick of units in the trenches will be evacuated through A.D.S. to M.D.S. of 2nd Low. Fld. Amb. and thence transferred to A.D.S. of 3rd Low. Fld. Amb.
   Sick of units in neighbourhood of NEUVILLE St. VAAST will be admitted to A.D.S. of 3rd Low. Fld. Amb., and sent to M.D.S. of 3rd Low. Fld. Amb. at St. ELOY where they are either evacuated by M.A.C. or transferred to Divisional Rest Station of 1st Low. Fld. Amb. Sick in neighbourhood of St. ELOY will be admitted to 3rd Low. Fld. Amb.

4. **WALKING WOUNDED.**
   During heavy fighting when there are numbers of walking wounded, the A.D.S. of the 3rd Low. Fld. Amb. will be used as a Walking Wounded Collecting Centre and will be evacuated by Light Railway or Motor Lorry, or other means as directed.

5. **GASSED CASES.**
   Severe cases will be evacuated to C.C.S. from the M.D.S. 2nd Low. Fld. Amb. in the usual manner by M.A.C.
   Slight and doubtful cases will be transferred from 2nd Low. Fld. Amb. to 1st Low. Fld. Amb.

(Sgd). A. MacDougall, Colonel, A.M.S.,
No. SR 60. A.D.M.S., 52nd (Lowland) Division.

COPY.   Appendix III

SECRET.   Copy No. 8.

MEDICAL ARRANGEMENTS
IN THE EVENT OF ACTIVE OPERATIONS
52nd (Lowland) DIVISION.

17th May, 1918.

1. **EVACUATION.**
   (a) In the event of active operations, stretcher and sitting cases will be evacuated through the A.D.S. to M.D.S. of the 2nd Low. Fld. Amb; walking cases to A.D.S. of 3rd Low. Fld. Amb. (Walking Wounded Collecting Post). Cases will be evacuated by hand carry, wheeled stretchers, Ambulance Cars and wagons, tram trolleys and Light Railway according to circumstances. O;C. 2nd Low. Fld. Amb. is responsible for making arrangements for trains between A.D.S. and M.D.S.
   (b) stretcher and sitting cases will be evacuated from M.D.S. of 2nd Low. Fld. Amb. to C.C.S. by means of M.A.C. Cars.
   (c) walking wounded will be evacuated from A.D.S. of 3rd Low. Fld. Amb. to Detraining Centre at V.29.a.75.65., near MINGOVAL, by means of Light Railway.
   O.C. 3rd Low. Fld. Amb. is responsible for making arrangements for trains on the Light Railway between his A.D.S. and Detraining Station. All applications for trains will be made to "Traffic Control" ZIVY. An N.C.O. and Orderly will accompany each train. A detraining party of the 1st Low. Fld. Amb. is already at the Detraining Station and 4 Motor Lorries will be attached for removing patients from the Detraining Stn. to the C.C.S.
   NO stretcher cases will be evacuated by this train.
   1 Motor Lorry and 1 Motor Ambulance Car will be on duty at the Walking Wounded Collecting Post; the former for evacuation of walking wounded to C.C.S., the latter for cases which may need stretchers.
   (d) SICK.- Serious cases will be sent to M.D.S. 2nd Low. Fld. Amb. and thence on to C.C.S. by M.A.C. Cars. Slight cases will be sent to M.D.S 2nd Low. Fld. Amb. and thence on to Divisional Rest Station by means of Horsed Ambulances of 1st Low. Fld. Amb.

2. **PERSONNEL.**
   O.C., 3rd Low. Fld. Amb. will re-inforce the 2nd Low. Fld. Amb. with his bearers to work under the orders of O.C. 2nd Low. Fld. Amb., who will supply guides and allot the ground that each Section will work over.
   O.C. 3rd Low. Fld. Amb. will detail 2 Officers to assist at the Main Dressing Station of the 2nd Low. Fld. Amb.
   M.O. i/c, Divisional R.E. will also be available for duty at the M.D.S. of 2nd Low. Fld. Amb.
   O.C. 3rd Low. Fld. Amb. will arrange for feeding of walking wounded at his A.D.S.
   O.C. 1st Low. Fld. Amb. will hold his bearer sub-divisions in reserve, ready to re-inforce as necessary.

3. **TRANSPORT.**
   AMBULANCE CARS. - Divisional Ambulance Cars will be used for evacuating in the Divisional Area and will not proceed to C.C.S. without orders from this Office.
   10 M.A.C. Cars (which are under the orders of the O.C., M.A.C.) will evacuate from M.D.S. AUX REITZ to C.C.S.
   O.C. 3rd Low. Fld. Amb. will place his Ambulance Cars, less 2, at the disposal of the O.C. 2nd Low. Fld. Amb. for use in evacuating from A.D.S. 2nd Low. Fld. Amb.
   O.C. 1st Low. Fld. Amb. will hold his cars in reserve.
   2 Horsed Ambulance wagons of 1st Low. Fld. Amb. will be placed at the disposal of O.C. 2nd Low. Fld. Amb. for evacuating cases to the Divisional Rest Station.
   Car Relay Posts between the A.D.S. and M.D.S. of 2nd Low. Fld. Amb. will be arranged by O.C. 2nd Low. Fld. Amb.

4./

Appendix III

(2).

4. MEDICAL.
ANTI-TETANIC Serum will be given at M.D.Ss., except, (a) Walking wounded admitted to A.D.S. 3rd Low. Fld. Amb. (Walking Wounded Collecting Post) where it will be given if not already done so, (b) other cases evacuated direct to a C.C.S. from an A.D.S.
Medical Comforts - Field Ambulances will indent direct o, S.S.O. for food and Medical Comforts for patients.

5. GENERAL.
All changes in A.D.Ss., Relay Posts, R.A.Ps., will be reported to this Office at once.
Applications for bearers, cars etc., will be made to this Office.

(Sgd). A. MacDougall, Colonel, A.M.S.

A.D.M.S. 52nd (Lowland) Division.

No. SR 60/1.

Appendix III

O.C.,
   3rd Low. Fld. Amb.

A.D.M.S 52nd Division.
No. SR 64

The following amendment is made to my SR 64 dated 20/5/18 "Arrangements in the Event of Severe Gac Attack".

Para 2. Clothing is held as follows :-
for 3rd Low. Fld. Amb. ----- Sox -100" read

2nd Low. Fld. Amb. ----- Sox -100".

(Sgd.) A. MacDougall, Colonel, A.M.S.
A.D.M.S. 52nd Division.

H.Q. 52nd Div.
22nd May 1918.

Copy.

SECRET.

O.C.,
   3rd Low. Fld. Amb.

Appendix III

A.D.M.S. No. S.R.64.

Arrangements in the event of a severe Gas Attack.
(Cancelling S.R.45 d/11/5/18.)

All gassed cases, whenever admitted, will be disposed of as follows:-

1. All cases of Phosgene and Cloud gas will be treated at the M.D.S. of 2nd Low. Fld. Amb. and evacuated by M.A.C. O.C. 2nd Low. Fld. Amb. will reserve tents for this purpose.
   O.Cs. 1/1st and 3rd Low. Fld. Amb. will place at the disposal of O.C. 2nd Low. Fld. Amb. their Nitrous Oxide Masks and Oxygen Cylinders as a reserve.

2. All Mustard Gas Cases will be treated at the A.D.S. of 3rd Low. Fld. Amb. where accommodation will be arranged for (a) Admission, (b) un-clothing, washing and re-clothing cases and treating any special symptoms, (c) shelter of patients pending their disposal.
   Cases will be disposed of as follows, according to circulstances. Severe cases evacuated to C.C.S. by M.A.C. cars, (stationed near M.D.S. 2nd Low. Fld. Amb.,) walking cases evacuated by railway or to Divnl. Rest Station.
   Clothing i's held as follows:-

	Service Dress.	Shirts.	Vests and Pants.	Sox.
2nd L.F.A.	100;	100	100	-
3rd L.F.A.	200.	200	200	100
Oi/c Divnl. Baths, Neuville St. Vaast.	200.	200.	200	200.
	500.	500.	500	300.

(Oi/c Divnl. Baths also holds a supply of Soda Carbonate)

Gassed clothing for degassing will be sent to the Divisional Baths, Berthonville Farm, where the Foden Thresh Disinfector is stationed. While being removed it will be covered by a tarpaulin. When clothing for degassing is sent to the Foden the orderly in charge of the Disinfector will be informed that the clothes are infected. All Orderlies dealing with Mustard gassed clothing or patients, will wear respirators, gloves, and waterproof sheets over their clothes.

These arrangements cancel para. Medical Arrangements No. 2 d/17/5/18.

Headquarters,
52nd Division.
20th May, 1918.

(Sgd) A.MacDougall, Colonel, A.M.S.
A.D.M.S. 52nd Division.

SECRET.   Appendix IV   Copy No. 37

52nd DIVISION STANDING ORDER No. 1.
BATTLE.

(All previous Standing Orders are hereby cancelled)

4th May 1918.

1.   Attention is directed to S.S. 135 " Training and the Employment of Divisions".
        These numbers must be rigorously adhered to whenever an action is imminent and may be largely exceeded.
        The very best men are to be ruthlessly withdrawn. They will concentrate at Divisional Wing of Re-inforcement Camp or at the Brigade 1st Line Transport, or as otherwise ordered by the G.O.C.

(a):   The Second in Command of each Command will be left behind.

(b)   Two Company Commanders and two Seconds in Command will be taken out of each Battalion.

(c)   Of the Company Commanders taken out, one will not be moved to the rear but will proceed with Battalion Headquarters to act as Second in Command.

(d)   Sections will go into action 1 N.C.O. and 6 Men. If not possible to go in as 1 N.C.O. and 6 Men, three Sections may be amalgamated into 2, but the L.G. Section will never be amalgamated and must be maintained intact. Before any amalgamation takes place the facts must be laid before the O.C. Company and his sanction obtained.

2.   Officers must always be in possession of x luminous compasses. Before any operations bearings must be taken from the point of departure to their objective. Electric torches should also be carried if possible.

3.   Working or carrying parties, sent up from the rear will carry their rifle and equipment, without pack or haversack, and 40 rounds of ammunition.

4.   Men carrying wire-cutters will have them attached to the shoulder strap by means of a lanyard, and the cutter tucked into the waist-belt.

5.   Troops taking part in the assault are forbidden to carry any copies of Operation Orders. No Map or Sketch carried is to show any more than the bare outline of our front line.

6.   Officers detailed to attend at the synchronisation of watches must bring 2 watches with them. These watches must both have second hands

7.   If the attack is in the nature of a trench to trench attack, Os. C. Battalions are forbidden to take part in the general move forward by their Battalions to the assault unless they consider their presence is necessary to restore the situation or to achieve their objective. The duty of the Os. C. Battalions is to reorganise their Battalions when the objective has been gained and to get the consolidation commenced as soon as possible.
        Their possition should be where messages can reach them from front and rear as quickly as possible, and their reserves should be near them.

8.   Provision must be made to handle the Lewis Gun in case the barrel becomes too hot to hold in the hands.

9.   A system of runners will be maintained between all formations. Runners should carry their messages in the left breast pocket. Verbal communications are NOT to be sent by runners.

10.   It is most important to guard against the waste of rations.

All ranks are to be notified that for one meal, 1 tin of preserved meat will usually suffice for 3 Men ; and that no more tins than necessary should be opened at one time.

11. All Ranks must be warned against wasting their drinking water and against drinking water found in receptacles or wells in captured possitions before it has been examined by a Medical Officer, who will carry labels to mark the wells that have been tested.

12. No man should be allowed to leave the front line without carrying back some salvaged articles to a salvage dump.
Gun sights must not be destroyed unless it is impossible to salve them.

13. The name of a Unit or formation must never be mentioned over the telephone. The code name must be used. If this is unintelligible for any reason, the Commanders name may be used e.g. " Colonel A's. Bn.". Raids or reliefs etc. etc. must similarly never be mentioned.

          (Sgd) G.W. Holditch, Lieut. Colonel,
                     G.S.
                  52nd Division.

Copy

Appendix V.

52nd (LOWLAND) DIVISION.

ADMINISTRATIVE CIRCULAR MEMORANDUM No 1.

7th May 1918

TRANSPORT.

During a recent inspection of Transport on the march the G.O.C. noticed the following points, which require the immediate a attention of all concerned.

1. FITTING OF HARNESS.

Harness, particularly in Unit First Line transport, has been very badly fitted. Breechings in many cases were too loose.

2. SALUTING

Saluting by drivers is very bad. The regulation salute with the whip by the lead Drivers must be done smartly and correctly. Men on the driving seat will salute as follows :-
   (a) If driving on the seat of a G.S. Wagon, etc., the soldier will bring his whip to a perpendicular position, with the right hand resting on the thigh, and turn his head smartly to an officer when passing him. Folding the arms is not part of the Regulation salute.

3. RIDING ON LOADED VEHICLES.

On no account are men, other than the driver (in vehicles with a double driving seat, the driver and one other) to ride on loaded wagons, without the written permission of an officer.

4 BRAKESMEN.

One man to manipulate the brake will invariably march in rear of every vehicle fitted with only a rear brake. Each brakesman must be able to work the brake quickly and intelligently, i.e. at the inspection in question many brakes were too stiff to work properly and vehicles were observed going up a steep hill with the brakes full on

5. COOKERS.

The chimneys of cookers will normally be down on the march. they will only be raised when cooking is actually in progress.

6. WHIPS AND SPURS.

Some Units were deficient of whips and spurs for their drivers, Indents to make good deficiencies will be sent in at once to D.A.D.O.S.

7. TURNOUT OF MEN.

The general turnout of drivers was indifferent. Their association with horses is no excuse for grime. Many men were deficient of cap badges. Great coats when worn will be properly buttoned up, and the collars only turned up during inclement weather. The collar will not be turned half up and half down.

8. VEHICLES.

Vehicles and harness want a great deal of attention. The harness will be carefully dubbined, all metal work will be polished, and vehicles will be kept scrupulously clean.

A new Divisional sign to be painted on all vehicles will shortly be approved, and instructions for painting will be issued to all concerned.

9. SPARE ANIMALS

Spare animals are not to be continuously ridden on the line of march, and never without the sanction of an Officer.

As an exceptional case a man may be permitted to ride a spare animal during a portion of the march, but normally the spare animals will be led in the same way as pack animals.

10. PERSONNEL WITH TRANSPORT.

Any M.G.Cs. or men other than brakesmen, marching with Transport, will do so in a formed body, immediately behind the Transport

of their Unit.   They will not be allowed to straggle up and
down the column.

11; INSPECTION OF TRANSPORT.
    Transport Officers of all Units will invariably inspect
all vehicles before marching off.

    The G;O.C. is determened that the Transport of the 52nd
Division will shortly be the best in France, and as a first step
in this direction he wishes all O.C. Units and Transport Officers
to give the points enumerated above their immediate and careful
attention

                            (Sgd.) G.G.Maude, Lieut. Colonel
                        A.A.& Q.M.G. 52nd (Lowland) Division.

Appendix VII

Headquarters
    52nd Division.   R 212/2

        Owing to recent moves and new conditions the Sanitation of the Division is not as good as it was in Palestine.

        Attention is called to the following points :-

1. SANITARY. Owing to the use of trenches in lieu of buckets for latrines, it is very necessary that great care should be taken to prevent the access of flies to faecal matter.
        This may be done either by the provision of fly-proof seats over trenches(made by Regimental Pioneers or Sanitary Section) or, if an open trench is used, by arranging to cover each deposit with earth and carefully filling in and marking trenches when full.

2. COOK-HOUSE. Great attention should be paid to cook-houses on the lines in practice in the Division.
        Cooks should wear canvas clothing.

3. WATER. No water should be drunk which has not been either boiled or obtained from the water cart. I would suggest that this be a standing order in each Unit/

4 PERSONAL CLEANLINESS. Units should give the men every possible opportunity for personal washing and change of clothing.
        Owing to the large number of men suffering from boils attention should be paid to the cleanliness of nails. Teeth and hair need attention also.
        Full use should be made of the Chiropodist under the supervision of the M.O.
        Every man should be examined once a week by the M.O. when possible.

3/5/18   (Sgd) A.J.MacDougall, Colonel A;M.S
                        A.D.MS. 52nd (Lowland) Division.

- 2 -

    Brigades.

        For information. The strictest attention will be paid to the points brought out in above memo. from A.D.M.S;

                        (Sgd) G. Maude, Lieut.Colonel,
            A.A.& Q.M.G. 52nd (Lowland) Divison.

Appendix VIII

52nd (LOWLAND) DIVISION

ADMINISTRATIVE   CIRCULAR   MEMORANDUM   No. 2

12/5/18

BATHS.

1. Baths are now ready for use at the following places :-

PLACE	SPRAYS	CAPACITY
(a) Neuville St. Vaast	12 Sprays	150 men per hour
(b) Berthonval Farm	17 "	200 -do-
(c) St. Eloi.	14 "	100 -do-

2. Application will be made for their use direct to Officer i/c Baths, 52nd Division, whose headquarters are at Berthonval Farm. Whenever possible 48 hours notice should be given.

3. Bathing Parties of over 20 will be accompanied by an Officer Men will bring their own towel, and for the present, their own soap.

4. Clean clothing is not ready for immediate issue, but it is hoped to remedy this shortly.

12/5/18

(Sgd.) C.G. Maude, Lieut Colonel
A.A. & Q.M.G.   52nd (Lowland) Division.

A.D.M.S. No R 342/4 d/ 12/5/18

Appendix IX

D.G., S.393/37/3.
D.M.S. No. 1498/6.

D/M/S/ First Army.

In the event of U.S. Army Sick and Wounded coming into British Casualty Clearing Stations and Hospitals, the following instructions will be carried out regarding submission of returns -

1. Army Forms A.36 will be rendered from Field Medical Units and Casualty Clearing Stations, and separate Army Forms W.3034 will be rendered from Stationary Hospitals in Army Areas and Hospitals on L. of C. to the American Statistical Section, D.A.G., 3rd Echelon, Rouen.

2. For all cases treated in and discharged to duty from Medical Units within Army Areas, the British Field Medical Card, A.F.W3118 will be completed and forwarded to the American Statistical Section D.A.G., G.H.Q., 3rd Echelon, Base.

Cases transferred to Base Hospitals will be accompanied by the Field Medical Card.

3. (a) On entering the diagnosis on A.F.A36, A.F.W3034, or A.F.W3118 (Field Medical Card), the words "Line of Duty" or "Own Misconduct" will be inserted thereon immediately after the diagnosis. The words "Line of Duty" refer to wounds or sickness not caused through circumstances under the patient's own control. "Own misconduct" represents wounds or sickness contracted under the patient's own control.

(b) In recording the diagnosis, the degree of the severity of the disability will be stated i.e., slight or severe.

4. (a) The Field Medical Cards of all cases treated in and discharged from U.S.A. Base Hospital serving with the British Armies in France will on completion be forwarded to the Chief Surgeon's Office, H.Q., A.E.F., together with Report card (Form 52 M.D.)

(b) The Field Medical Crds of all cases treated in and discharged from British Base Hospitals, will on completion be forwarded to the American Statistical Section, D.A.G., G.H.Q., 3rd Echelon, Base.

5. The Field Medical Card will accompany all cases transferred to Hospitals of the American Expeditionary Forces from U.S.A. Hospitals serving with the British Armies in France and from British Base Hospitals.

The above instructions will take effect forthwith.

11-5-18.
(Sgd) W.G. MacPherson, M.C.
for Director General Medical Services,
British Armies in France.

2

For information and necessary action.

(Sgd) M.P. Davidson, Lieut. Colonel,
for Major General,
British Armies in France.

H.Q. 1st Army
12th May 1918

Appendix X

SECRET.   A.D.M.S. 52nd Div. No. R 105/4

Officer Commanding,
   3rd Lowland Field Ambulance.

        Under instructions from D.D.M.S., XVlll CORPS, send at once
cars :-
        TALBOT, 15230
           "   18410
           "   25835   )Together with additional personnel
           "   29893   )received from 112th Field Ambulance.
        FORD   15700   )
           "   14166   (sent herewith from 1st Low. Fld. Amb.)
all formerly with 112th Field Amb., to NORTHKERQUE, in FENNEL area
(Map HAZEBROUCK, 5A, 1/100,000 - 2.A.3.6.) shewn NORTKERQUE in Map.
These cars should be incharge of an officer, who will, on arrival,
report to 77th American Division.   The Officer, on handing over
cars and obtaining receipts for same will return to 3rd Low. Fld.
Amb. by the most expeditious route.
        Rations for one day following the move will be carried and
sufficient petrol will be taken for the journey.
        All documents relating to the cars and drivers will be taken
and handed over by the officer in charge
        Report departure to this office.

H.Q. 52nd Division.   (Sgd.) A.MacDougall Colonel A.M.S.
16-5-18   A;D.M.S. 52nd Division.
H.7.0.p.m.

(Copy to D.D.M.S., XVlll Corps for information.)

Appendix XI

To:-
   O.C. 3rd Lowland Field Ambulance.
----

1. **Gas Alarm Posts**

   Gas Alarm Posts have been erected for the Unit in the following situations:-
   (a) Outside Orderly Room
   (b) "B" Section Billet
   (c) "C" Section Billet
   (d) Transport (Horse)
   (e) Hospital
   (f) Headquarters and Motor Transport.

   In addition at the base of each post there is a receptacle containing water and washing soda. (strength 2 oz to the gallon and labelled " Soda Solution".)

2. **Scheme suggested for indicating and communicating Gas Alarm.**

   In the event of a Gas Alarm being first received at Orderly Room the Orderly on duty outside the Orderly Room will sound the Alarm at the Orderly Room Alarm Post.
   Any N.C.O. or man rearest the adjoining Alarm Posts will sound the gong and thus spread the alarm.
   The Gas N.C.O. of each Section will see that his Section has been alarmed and after this
   (1) The Gas N.C.O. of "A" Section will proceed to the Horse Transport Lines and Hospital and satisfy himself that they have received the Alarm.
   (2) The Gas N.C.O. of "B" Section will proceed to the Headquarters and the Motor Transport Lines and do likewise.
   (3) The Gas N.C.O. of "C" Section will remain at Section Billets and supervise.

   On a Gas Alarm being given all Respirators will be placed in the "Alert" position
   Respirators will be adjusted either by word of command or when the presence of Gas is actually detected by sense of smell.

17-5-18

(Sgd) R. Stansfeld, Captain
Gas Officer,
1/3rd Lowland Field Ambulance, R.A.M.C., T.F.

SECRET.   S.R. 72. Copy No. 3.

Appendix XII

R.A.M.C. OPERATION ORDER No. 3,
by
A.D.M.S., 52nd (Lowland) Division.

23rd May, 1918.

1. **MOVE.**   The 2nd Low. Fld. Amb. will be relieved by the 3rd Low. Fld. Amb. on the night of 25th/26th inst., and the existing M.D.S., A.D.Ss. and Relay Posts of the 2nd Low. Fld. Amb. occupied by the 3rd Low. Fld. Amb.   The 2nd Low. Fld. Amb. on relief will take over and occupy the M.D.S. and A.D.S. vacated by 3rd Low. Fld. Amb.

2. **TRANSPORT.**   The Transport of the 2nd Low. Fld. Amb. at VILLERS AU BOIS will be used to assist in the move of that unit and will be parked thereafter in the vicinity of the M.D.S. at St. ELOI.
    Transport and heavy stores of the 3rd Low. Fld. Amb. not actually required in the evacuating zone will be parked at VILLERS AU BOIS on site vacated by Transport of 2nd Low. Fld. Amb. previously there.

3. **DETAILS.**   O.C. 2nd Low. Fld. Amb. will furnish in writing to O.C. 3rd Low. Fld. Amb. the information as to positions, trench stores, and strength of personnel at the various posts.

4. **EVACUATION.**   On relief being completed, Medical Arrangements No. 2, Medical Arrangements in the Event of Active Operations (17/5/18) and Arrangements in the Event of Severe Gas Attack (20/5/18) will remain as at present, reading 2nd Low. Fld. Amb. for 3rd Low. Fld. Amb., and 3rd Low. Fld. Amb. for 2nd Low. Fld. Amb.

5. **GENERAL.**   In order to avoid as much as possible unnecessary movement, such stores as wheeled and ordinary stretchers, blankets, Soyers Stoves, spare dressings, drugs etc., will be taken over by the relieving Unit.
    The 115 stretchers taken over from the Canadian Field Amb. will be handed over to O.C. 3rd Low. Fld. Amb.
    As many other stores as possible will not be moved but changed like for like.
    Special clothing and apparatus for use in case of Gas Attacks will be kept in their present locations and handed over.

6. **RELIEFS.**   Reliefs will be notified to this Office.

7. **ACKNOWLEDGE.**

(Sgd) A. MacDougall, Colonel, A.M.S.,
A.D.M.S., 52nd (Lowland) Division.

SECRET.   Copy No. 7.

155th INF. BRIGADE ORDER NO. 96.

Ref. Map MAROEUIL, 1/20,000.   23rd May, 1918.

1. A Projector Gas Attack will take place on the 26th inst., or on the first favourable night afterwards, with the object of surprising and gassing the enemy occupying dug-outs, in the embankment in Square N.34.c.

2. Projectors will be fired from T.9.b.4.8. at targets in N.34.c.&d.

3. "F" Special Coy., R.E will carry out the operation.

4. Copies of 52nd Division Order No. 107 for the operation have been issued to front line battalions.

5. The code word "MYSTERY" will be wired at 1830 on the 26th inst., if favourable, "to indicate Gas will be projected".
   Otherwise the code word "SHIP", meaning GAS will not be projected, will be sent, these words being employed on following days as necessary

6. Zero hour when projectors will be fired will be at 11 p.m;

7. A proportion of the front, as indicated to those concerned, will be cleared of troops before zero hour, and troops in part of T.9.b and T.3. will wear S.B.Rs from Zero until orders for their removal are given by Brigade Gas Officer. These orders will not be given before Zero + 30 minutes at the earliest.

8. Artillery and a proportion of machine guns in the Section will help to disguise the noise and flash of discharge by opening fire at Zero minus 3 minutes.

8. There is a possibility of our barrage bringing down the enemy's barrage on our forward areas. All men in the RED LINE and forward, with the exception of sentries, will therefore withdraw to dugouts at Zero minus 3 minutes, until the retaliation, if any has passed.

9. An Officer from each Unit will report at Brigade H.Q. at 1715 on the 26th inst. and on the following days, if necessary, to synchronise watches.

10. ACKNOWLEDGE.

                                    Sgd. W.M. Burkett.   Capt.
                            Bde. Major, 155th Inf Brigade.

SECRET.   Appendix XIII

Copy No 8.

Amendment to 155 Inf. Bde. Order No. 96.   25th May, 1918.

1. The attack is postponed 48 hours i.e. from 26th to 28th inst.
2. The artillery fire will be a raid barrage from Zero - 2 minutes to Zero + 2 minutes.
3. A machine gun in charge of an Officer will be placed in position close to the point of discharge and it will be ensured that the gun is fired at the moment that the projectiles are discharged.
4. Acknowledge.

                          (Sgd). W. N. Birkett, Capt.
                          Bde. Major, 155 Inf. Bde.

               2?   S.R. 77.

O.C., 3rd Low. Fld. Amb.

    Forwarded for your information.

    Acknowledge.   (Sgd). A. McDougall, Colonel, A.M.S.,
    26/5/18.   A.D.M.S. 52nd Division.

Appendix XIV

SECRET.   A.D.M.S. 52nd Divn. No B.R. 78.

Officer Commanding,
3rd Lowland Field Ambce.

    A reserve of two day's Rations of P.M. and Biscuit for each man in Relay Posts will be kept in the dugouts of each Relay Post. One day's reserve for men in the A.D.S. will be kept at the A.D.S.
    These will not be used except in the case of necessity.
    They will be turned over once a week if possible.

                              Sgd A MacDougall,
                                Colonel, A.M.S.
H.Q. 52ND DIV.   A.D.M.S. 52nd Division.
26th May 1918.

SECRET. Appendix XIV   A.D.M.S. 52nd Div. No SR 82

O.C., 3rd Low. Fld. Amb.
----------------.

      There is a deep dug-out in T 21.b.20.00 allotted to us.

      Please take this over with a view ti its use either as an R.A.P. or a Relay Post and report as to accommodation etc for above purposes.

                            (Sgd) A. MacDougall Colonel,
                                                          A.M.S.
H.Q. 52nd Division.
30th May 1918   A.D.M.S. 52nd Division.

A.D.MS. 52nd Division.

M 1367/18
31/5/18

Ref: your Office No. S R 82 d/ 30-5-18   This Post was manned last night by 4 O.Rs.

It is a deep dug-out with accommodation for 8 Stretcher Cases. The steps leading to it are very steep and it is extremely difficult though possible to carry stretcher cases up and down them.

There is an outlet shaft through the roof which is not Gas proof, and there is only 1 Gas proof curtain at the entrance.

Could you please arrange the required work to be done.

(Sgd) James Young, Lieut.Colonel
R.A.M.C. T.F
O.C. 1/3rd Lowland Field   Ambulance.

Appendix XV

Post with co-ordinates	Personnel Off / O R	Accommodation for Stretcher Cases	Stretchers Held	Blankets Held	Thomas' Splints
M.D.S. AUX RIETZ A 8.c.5.5.	3 / 96	70	46	380	(3 Leg (6 Arm (6 Arm Ang
A.D.S. VIMY T.25.a.9.4.	2 / 35	38	26	42	(14 Leg (6 Arm
A.D.S. CHAUDIERE S.18.c.9.3.	1 / 17	30	44	63	(6 Leg (4 Arm (3 Arm Ang

Relay Posts.

Nos 1. T 13.a.5.5.	(Manned when necessary)				
2. T 13.b.6.3.	4	-	8	12	-
3. T 8.c.4.1.	4	-	6	12	-
4.	(Manned when necessary)				
5. T 20.b.2.6.	10	7	6	24	(2 Leg (2 Arm
6. T 26.a.2.9.	4	4	2	6	-
7. T 21.c.8.7.	-	8	-	-	-
8. T 21.b.2.0.	4	8	2	6	-
9. B.2.a.9.1.	4	38	7	43	(2 Leg
10. B.2.a.9.8.	(Manned when necessary)				
11. T 26.d.9.7.	6	8	6	24	(2 Leg
12. T 27.c.6.3.	(Manned when necessary)				
13. T 27.d.2.6.	- do -				

R.A. Posts.

1. T 8.c.9.5.	4	4	8	12	-(6
2. T 16.c.6.9.	5	8	6	24	(2
3. T 28.a.4.1.	7	19	5	37	-(3
4. B 15.a.0.8.	(Manned when necessary)				

CONFIDENTIAL

War Diary

of

1/3 Lowland Field Ambulance R.A.M.C.(T)

From 1st June to 30th June.

1918.

(Volume 3)

Sheet No. 1

WAR DIARY 1/3² LOWLAND FLD. AMB. R.A.M.C.(T)

INTELLIGENCE SUMMARY

Army Form C. 2118.

Place	Date	Hour	Summary of Events and Information	Remarks and references to Appendices
AUX RIETZ (A.8.c.4.6.)			Ref Map LA TARGETTE 1/20,000	
	1/6/18		Admitted 14 Discharged 1 Evacuated 10 Remaining 2	
			Received ADMS. R676/4 information desired if it was customary to show distinguishing lights to denote the position of Field Ambulance during darkness — Replied :- were only subdued red was light used	
			Strength:- Officers 7	
			R.A.M.C. 182	
			A.S.C.(H.T) 38	
			A.S.C.(M.T) 13	Jm
	2/6/18		Admitted 19 Discharged - Evacuated 18 Remaining 3	
			Advanced Dressing Station at VIMY withdrawn	
			Advanced Dressing Station established in B.2.a.9.4. and called FABUS A.D.S. - 1 Copt and 5 men being left at T.25.a.9.4. to establish Motor Post. - knownfork called VIMY Motor Post.	Jm
	3/6/18		Admitted 21 Discharged 4 Evacuated 19 Remaining 1	
			Reinforcement received	
			Strength A.S.C.(H.T) 1 Oth Rank to hospital	
			" R.A.M.C. 1	Jm
	4/6/18		Admitted 14 Discharged - Evacuated 12 Remaining 3	Jm
	5/6/18		Admitted 9 Discharged 1 Evacuated 8 Remaining 3	Jm

WAR DIARY / INTELLIGENCE SUMMARY

1/3rd LOWLAND FLD. AMB. R.A.M.C.(T) Army Form C. 2118.

Sheet No 2.

Place	Date	Hour	Summary of Events and Information	Remarks and references to Appendices
Aux Rietz	6/6/18		Admitted 9 Discharged – Evacuated 11 Remaining 1. Strength – R.A.M.C. 2 Other Ranks to hospital	JH
	7/6/18		Admitted 9 Discharged – Evacuated 6 Remaining 4. Strength – Officers 7 R.A.M.C. 178 A.S.C.(HT) 39 A.S.C.(MT) 13. Received A.D.M.S. S.R. 91 155th Inf. Bde. to be relieved by 156 & Inf. Bde – No change in Medical Arrangements. 1 Other Rank to hospital. Strength – R.A.M.C.	JH
	8-6-18		Admitted 6 Discharged – Evacuated 8 Remaining 2. Received A.D.M.S. S.R. 94 A/8-6-18. Reserve Battalion H.Q. being consulted – Report required as to suitability for an A.D.S. – Report made. Appendix I	JH
	9-6-18		Admitted 2 Discharged 1 Evacuated 1 Remaining 1. Strength – R.A.M.C. 1 Other Rank to hospital.	JH
	10-6-18		Admitted 9 Discharged – Evacuated 9 Remaining 1. Strength A.S.C.(M.T.) 1 Reinforcement received	JH

Army Form C. 2118.

WAR DIARY

1/3RD LOWLAND FLD. AMB. R.A.M.C.(T)

INTELLIGENCE SUMMARY.

(Erase heading not required.)

Sheet No 3

Instructions regarding War Diaries and Intelligence Summaries are contained in F. S. Regs., Part II. and the Staff Manual respectively. Title pages will be prepared in manuscript.

Place	Date	Hour	Summary of Events and Information	Remarks and references to Appendices
AUX RIETZ	11/6/18		Admitted 13 Discharged 1 Evacuated 11 Remaining 2.	
			Strength – R.A.M.C. 2 Other Ranks to hospital	
	12/6/18		Admitted 4 Discharged – Evacuated 2 Remaining 4	
			Strength – R.A.M.C. 1 Other Rank reinforcement	Appendix 2.
			Received 157 b Inf. Bde. Order No. 106 – Raid on enemy trenches	
	13/6/18		Admitted 3 Discharged 1 Evacuated 6 Remaining set	
			Strength R.A.M.C. 1 Other Rank to hospital	
	14/6/18		Admitted 2 Discharged – Evacuated 3 Remaining set	
			Strength – R.A.M.C. 1 Other Rank to hospital	
			Strength – Officers Lieut L.N. HOST (M.S.R. MRC) attached for temporary duty from 1/1st Lowland Fld. Amb.	
			Strength Officers 7 R.A.M.C. 173 A.S.C.(H.T) 39 A.S.C.(MT) 13	
	15/6/18		Admitted 1 Discharged – Evacuated 1 Remaining Nil	
			Strength R.A.M.C. 10 Other Ranks received from Cyclists Base Depot	

Sheet No. 4

WAR DIARY
or
INTELLIGENCE SUMMARY.

1/3rd LOWLAND FLD AMB R.A.M.C.(T). Army Form C. 2118.

Instructions regarding War Diaries and Intelligence Summaries are contained in F. S. Regs., Part II. and the Staff Manual respectively. Title pages will be prepared in manuscript.

(Erase heading not required.)

Place	Date	Hour	Summary of Events and Information	Remarks and references to Appendices
AUX RIETZ	14/8/18		Admitted 9 Discharged - Evacuated 8 Remaining 1 1 Oth Rank to hospital Strength - R.A.M.C.	Jy
	17/6/18		Admitted 3 Discharged - Evacuated to Remaining Nil Inspection A.D.M.S. 52nd Division inspected Main Dressing Station Received 155th Inf. Bde. Order No 99 - 155th Bde to relieve 157th Inf Bde - No alteration in Medical arrangements	Jy
	18/6/18		Admitted 21 Discharged 1 Evacuated 20 Remaining Nil Officer evacuated is case of Malaria	Appendix 3
	19/6/18		Admitted 14 Discharged 2 Evacuated 10 Remaining 1 1 Died Received "Summary of Medical Arrangements XVIII Corps Received A.D.M.S. R973/7 Precautions against P.U.O. - Moving and wearing Bangles of Oil Permanganate instituted for all ranks (sick or not)	Jy Appendix 4
	20/6/18		Admitted 16 Discharged - Evacuated 16 Remaining 1 Casualty:- 1 Oth Rank R.A.M.C. slightly wounded - remains at duty.	Jy
	21/6/18		Admitted 1 Discharged 1 Evacuated 1 Remaining Nil 1 Oth Rank reinforcement	Jy

Sheet No 5   WAR DIARY   1/3rd LOWLAND FLD AMB R.A.M.C.(T)   Army Form C. 2118.

of

INTELLIGENCE SUMMARY.

(Erase heading not required.)

Place	Date	Hour	Summary of Events and Information	Remarks and references to Appendices
AUX RIETZ	21/6/18	(cont.d)	Strength:- Officers 7 R.A.M.C. 182 A.S.C.(H.T) 39 A.S.C.(M.T) 13	
	22/6/18		Admitted 5 * Discharged 1 Evacuated 3 Remaining Nil * 1 Died R.A.M.C. Bearer Subdivisions to relieve Bearer Subdivisions of 1/1st L.F.A. attacked AIR RAIDS GRO.437 depots not distinguishing lights during darkness by Medical Officers. Admitted 5 Not to be discontinued. Evacuated 3 Remaining 2 Nil	04
	23/6/18		Admitted 3 Discharged - Evacuated 4 Remaining 1 Nil	
	24/6/18		Admitted 1 Discharged - Evacuated 2 Remaining Nil	
	25/6/18		Strength - Officers Lieut L N HOST (U.S.A. M.R.C.) temporarily attached for duty) returned to 1/1st Los. Fld. Ambce 2 Other Ranks attached to Canadian Garrison Artillery Strength R.A.M.C. for temp'y duty.	04

WAR DIARY

Army Form C. 2118.

Sheet No. 6   1/3RD LOWLAND FLD. AMB. R.A.M.C.(T)

INTELLIGENCE SUMMARY.

(Erase heading not required.)

Instructions regarding War Diaries and Intelligence Summaries are contained in F. S. Regs., Part II. and the Staff Manual respectively. Title pages will be prepared in manuscript.

Place	Date	Hour	Summary of Events and Information	Remarks and references to Appendices
AUX RIETZ	26-6-18		Admitted 6. Discharged 1. Evacuated 3. Remaining 2.	
			Exchange of Officers	
			Lieut. P.T.J. O'FARRELL posted to 1/5th K.O.S.B.	
			Captain A.J.G. HUNTER, M.C. joined from 1/5 K.O.S.B.	
	27-6-18		Admitted 2. Discharged 1. Evacuated 3. Remaining Nil.	
			Attachment	
			Revd. A. WATT, C.F. joined from 1/5 K.O.S.B.	
			S.R. 116. 157th Inf. Bde. to relieve 156th Inf. Bde.	
	28-6-18		Admitted 5. Discharged - Evacuated 5. Remaining Nil.	
			Strength	
			Officers 7	
			R.A.M.C. 183	
			A.S.C. (HT) 39	
			A.S.C. (MT) 13	
	29-6-18		Admitted 7. Discharged - Evacuated 7. Remaining Nil.	
			Return of attachment	
			2 Other Ranks rejoined from temporary attachment to Canadian Garrison Artillery.	
			Moves	
			Received A.D.M.S. S.R. 130. - Party to be detailed to proceed to reconnre. Main Dressing Station at MT. ST. ELOI as Advance Party.	Appendix 5.
	30-6-18		Admitted 7. Discharged - Evacuated 7. Remaining Nil.	

WAR DIARY or INTELLIGENCE SUMMARY

Army Form C. 2118.

Sheet No. 7.

1/3rd LOWLAND FLD AMBᶜᵉ R.A.M.C.(T)

Place	Date	Hour	Summary of Events and Information	Remarks and references to Appendices
AUX RIETZ	30-6-18		Note: Received R.A.M.C. Operation Order No 4 - 1/3rd L.F.A. hand over present M.D.S. at AUX RIETZ to 1/2nd L.F.A. and 3rd L.F.A. to move to new M.D.S. at ST. ELOI in F.A.C. Handing over to be completed by noon 2-7-18. Advance Party proceeded to Mt. ST. ELOI 1/7/18	Appendix 4

James Murray Athol
OC 1/3rd Lowland F.Amb

(Appendix 1.)

SECRET.   SR 94

Officer Commanding,
  1/3rd Lowland Field Ambulance.

    C.R.E. informs me that Reserve Battalion Headquarters visited by me today at T.25.b.5.9. is being evacuated. Please report accomodation and suitability for an A.D.S.

8 / 6 / 18.   (Sgd.) A. MacDougall, Colonel,
                                                    A.M.S.
                    A.D.M.S. 52nd (Lowland). Division.

(Appendix 1.)

SECRET.

M1502/18
9-6-18.

A.D.M.S.,
  52nd Division.

Reference your SR 94 dated 8-6-18.
I examined the Reserve Battalion Headquarters in T.25.b.5.9. today and beg to report as follows :—

The accomodation consists of
(1) Tunnel dugouts about 18 feet under ground, fitted with 42 wire netting beds. At each end there is a small free space which could be used for dressings, clerking, etc. Two narrow, very oblique entrances which open direct from the North side of the road. 3 feet ventilating shaft. Gas proof measures complete.
(2) Adjacent superficial splinter proof dugouts made in the bank for cookhouse, latrines and Headquarters staff. The accomodation for the staff consists of 3 dugouts altogether accomodating about 18 men lying.

Suitability for A.D.S.
In my opinion it is unsuitable for this purpose.
(1) It is too far from the Southern line of evacuation.
(2) The entrance to the tunnel dugouts are too narrow and too steep to allow stretchers in.
(3) It is too near VIMY which is persistently shelled to allow of the traffic, incidental to a Dressing Station, being safely carried out.

(Sgd.) James Young Lieut-Colonel,
R.A.M.C., T.F.
1/3rd Lowland Field Ambulance.

Appendix 2

C O P Y.
S E C R E T.

157th Infantry Brigade Order No. 119.

Reference map sheets Artois 51.b. Second Ed. 1/40,000.

1. The 5th A.&S.H. will carry out a raid on the enemy trenches on the night of the 13/14th June, 1916.
The point to be raided will be the enemy trench about square T.23.d.7.2.

2. The object of the raid will be to:-
   (a) Obtain indentifications.
   (b) Inflict casualties.
The raiders are not to stop for (a) when they have once obtained (a).

3. Strength of party not to exceed 4 Platoons. IN 4 Platoons are employed, I will be in support.

4. No artillery will be employed, as a surprise is more likely to be effected by a silent raid. Artillery will be standing by in case help is wanted for the withdrawal.

5. Personnel taking part in the raid will not carry identification marks such as letters, pay books, identity discs, or regimental badges.

6. Live prisoners are required and anything that will establish the identity of the units opposite to us, should be brought away such as enemy shoulder straps, packs etc.

7. The following code will be used between Brigade and Battn. Hqrs.:-

- 2 -

Raid will take place :;; ;;; ;;; BLOOD.
Raid will not take place ;;;......TAY.
Raiding party returned............GLASGOW.
Casualties in raiding party
           (state number)..........HEROES.
Prisoners taken (state number)....
Estimated German casualties
           (State number).....DUDS.

8. Zero hour will be notified later. The reference hour will be 10 p.m. Thus if the raid is to take place at 11 p.m. a wire will be sent as follows:- "BLOOD plus 60". If the raid is to take place at 1-30 a.m. on the 11th the wire will read "BLOOD plus 210".

9. Every effort must be made to bring back any casualties which may be suffered on our side during the raid.

10. An Officer from Brigade Hqrs. will be at the 5th A. & S. H. Hqrs about 6.30 p.m. to synchronise watches.

                              (Sgd.) A. Williams Major,
           Brigade Major, 107th Infantry Brigade.

Originals 3

Captain Smith   1/3rd Lew. Fld. Ambce.
Lieut Host   Midsslles
Captain Greer, M.C.   R.A.M.C., T
Captain Stansfeld,   C   16-6-18
Lieut. O'Farrell.

USE OF MORPHIA

It is understood that cases are not infrequently seen at C.C.Ss and Hospitals on the L. of C. suffering from severe Morphia poisoning. It is found in many of these cases that repeated injections have been given from R.A.P. backwards. After each injection the patient has been sent off without an opportunity being given for the drug to operate. One of the chief objects for which it is given, namely the alleviation of pain and the diminution of shock during transport has thus been defeated and eventually severe morphia poisoning is superadded to severe shock.

(Sd.) Giles Young, Lieut-Colonel,
C.O. 1/3rd Lowland Field Ambulance.

18-6-18

COPY.   D.D.M.S. 2934/23.   SECRET.

Appendix 4

SUMMARY OF MEDICAL ARRANGEMENTS XVIII CORPS

The following is a short summary of/existing medical arrangements for the information of all concerned.

1. Casualty Clearing Stations, Stationary and General Hospitals.

```
1.  C.C.S.............WAVRANS.      33 C.C.S............LIGNY
51. C.C.S.............AIRE.         1. Can.C.C.S........PERNES.
54. C.C.S.............AIRE.         4. Can.C.C.S........PERNES.
22. C.C.S.............PERNES.       6. C.C.S............PERNES.
23. C.C.S.............ANVIN.        7. C.C.S............LIGNY.
42. C.C.S.............AUBIGNY.      8. C.C.S............ELNES
57. C.C.S.............AUBIGNY.      11. C.C.S...........MOULLE.
39. Stat'y Hospl......AIRE.         12. Stat'y Hospl. St. POL.
```

2. Locations Divisional Medical Units (Ref: Maps Sh.36b & 36.c.)

20th Division

```
60 Field Ambulance D.R.S............AIX NOULLETTE R.22.a.8.8.
73 Field Ambualce  M.D.S............FOSSE 10 R.8. central
74 Field Ambualce  D.R.S............GRAND SERVINS Q.34.a.2.5.
Advanced Dressing  Stations.........FORT GLATZ G.35.b.1.7.
```

52nd Division

```
1st Low. Field Ambc. B.R.S..........VILLERS AU BOIS X.1.9.c.9.9.
2nd Low. Field Ambc. ...............LES 4 VENTS W.9. central.
3rd Low. Field Ambc. M.D.S..........AUX RIETZ A.8.c.4.6.
Advanced Dressing Stations..........LE CHAUDERIE S.18.c.9.3.
                                    FARBUS B.2.a.9.1.
```

3. Evacuations.

(a) Mild cases likely to be well within 7 to 10 days to WAVRANS Group of C.C.Ss. Other cases to the PERNES or AUBIGNY-LIGNY Group of C.C.Ss. whichever is more conveniently situated.

(b) Cases of P.U.O. fulfilling the above conditions will be sent to No:1 Casualty Clearing Station (XVIII Corps Rest Station).

(c) Lightly sick, mildly gassed and scabies cases should be treated in Divisional Rest Stations.

(d) All sick and wounded of Corps troops will be sent to the nearest field ambulance.

(e) (1) Dental surgeons visit the following units on the days stated.

20th Division.	24th Division	52nd Division
At H.Q. 60th Fd.AMB.	At H.Q. 74th Fd.AMB.	At H.Q. 1 Low.Fd.AMB
Tuesdays	Mondays	Tuesdays
Thursdays	Wednesdays	Thursdays

-2-

    Saturdays   Fridays   Saturdays

Cases certified by Dental Surgeons to require dentures and and whose mouths are ready for fitting will be sent to ordinary C.C.Ss. from whence they will be transferred, under Army arrangements, to No.12 Stationary Hospital St; POL for treatment at No;3 Mobile Dental Unit.

 (11) <u>Ear, Nose and Throat cases</u>. Allotment of those cases to see the specialist is as follows :- 20th, 24th, and 52nd Divisions 4 places each and 3 places to No.1 C.C.S. A.Ds.M.S. will note that in the event of their requiring more places than the allotted number mutual arrangements will be resorted to rather than the return of cases, above their allotment, to their Unit. The Army centre is at No; 12 Stationary Hospital St Pol, and the days for the attendanc of cases of this Corps are Fridays for Other Ranks and Saturdays for Officers.

3. Evacuations (continued)

 (e) <u>iii Ophthalmic Cases</u> The allotment of cases requiring examination by the Opthalmic Specialist is as follows :-
 20th; 24th, and 52nd Divisions 10 places each and 5 places are allotted to No.1 C.C.S. The same procedure will be followed as in the case of Ear, Nose and Throat cases. The Army Opthalmic Centre is situated at No.22 Casualty Clearing Station PERNES. The days for cases of the XVlll Corps to attend are Fridays for Other Ranks and Saturdays for Officers.

 iv. <u>Infection</u> To No.18 Stationary Hospital except early scarlet fevers, enteric fevers, diptheria and infective jaundice, which should be evacuated to ordinary C.C.S. Cases of suspected dysentery and dysentery should, however be evacuated to Nos 12 or 39 Stationary Hospitals whichever is nearer.

 v. Chinese sick or Chinese labour companies should be sent direct to No 11 Casualty Clearing Station MOULLE.

 vi. <u>Indian Drivers</u>. A section of the Lucknow C.C.S. is attached to No.6 C.C.S. PERNES. All cases of sick and wounded natives, including infectious diseases will be sent to this section.

 vii. <u>Gassed Cases</u>. Cases of gas poisoning will be dealt with as directed in First Army Routine Order No. 2761, dated 8th June.

viii. <u>Self-inflicted wounds</u>. To No:12 Stationary Hospital St. Pol.

 ix. N.Y.D.N. To No.1.C.C.S. WAVRANS.

 x. <u>Portuguese, French, American, Italian</u>. Cases of sick and wounded occurring among these troops will be evacuated in the usual way.

4. <u>MEDICAL STORES</u>.
  No.1..........AIRE No.12........PERNES. No.33....
ST.POL. and SAVY.
  Medical stores will be drawn from the most conveniently situated depot.

5. <u>British Red Cross Stores</u>. The branch for this area is situated at OUVE WIRQUIN (Hazebrouck 5.a.B.5.)

6. <u>Sanitation.</u>
   No.5. Canadian Sanitary Section..........MONT ST.ELOY.
   No.4.   ..   ..FOSSE 10.
   No.3.   ..   ..FRESNICOURT.

7. <u>Mobile Laboratories.</u>
   No.2. ....AUBIGNY. No.6....,THEROUANNE; NO.9 & 20.. .....AVESNES. NO.21.......AIRE. No.3......PERNES

   <u>NOTE</u>. Officer Commanding No.8 Motor Ambulance Convoy collects cases as above except groups E (i), (ii), and (iii) for the whole corps by his ordinary afternoon evacuation convoy.

XVLLL CORPS.
   16th June; 1918.   (Sgd.) M. Burton Capt.
                                              for Colonel,
                              Deputy Director of Medical Services
                                              XVLLL Corps.

Appendix 5

COPY.   S. R. 120.

Officer Commanding,
      3rd Lowland Field Ambulance.

                           S E C R E T.

         Detail a party, strength to be decided by you to get ready the new Main Dressing Station near St.Eloi for occupation.

         Personnel to be accommodated in Huts and Tents till you evacuate your present site.

         Permanent accommodation cannot be provided for personnel till you have evacuated your present site.

         Equipment that you can spare should be sent with the Advance Party and you should be prepared to evacuate your present site on 2/7/18.

                              (Signed) A. McDougall.
                                       Colonel A.D.M.S.
                                       52nd Division.

29/6/18.

SECRET. C O P Y.   Copy No. 3.   S.R. 121

R.A.M.C. OPERATION ORDER NO. 4.
BY
COLONEL A.J. MACDOUGALL, A.M.S.
A.D.M.S., 52nd. (LOWLAND) DIVISION.

29th June 1918

1. MOVE. 1/3rd. Lowland Field Ambulance will hand over the present Main Dressing Station at AUX REITZ and will move to a new site at F.9.c;, opening there.
  1/2nd. Lowland Field Ambulance will take over the present M.D.S. site at AUX REITZ and use it as a walking wounded Collecting Centre in lieu of their present site.
  Handing over will be completed by noon on 2nd. JULY 1918.

2. DUTIES. O.C. 1/3rd. Lowland Field Ambulance will hand over to O.C. 1/2nd. Low. Fld. Amb. agricultural land and water picquet posts on his charge and list of units whose sanitation he is supervising.   O.C. 1/2nd. Low. Fld. Amb. will be responsible for these duties.

3. PATIENTS. Sick and wounded from A.D.S. of 1/3rd. Low. Fld. Amb. will be taken direct to M.D.S. of 3rd. Lowland Fld. Amb. at F.9.c. and either evacuated, retained, or sent to Divisional Rest Station according to the case.
  Sick from Units in NEUVILLE ST VAAST Area will be admitted to Walking Wounded Collecting Centre of 1/2nd. Low. Fld. Amb. and thence to M.D.S. 2nd. Low. Fld. Amb.   O.C. 1/2nd. Low. Fld. Amb. will be responsible for collection of sick needing transport.
  1/1st. Low. Fld. Amb. (vice 1/2nd. Low. Fld. Amb.) commencing noon 2/7/18, will collect sick from the Brigade in Reserve at ST ELOI, one ambulance car will be kept by the former unit at ST. ELOI (near the baths) for emergency cases.

4. COMPLETION OF MOVES. Completion of moves will be reported to this Office.

ACKNOWLEDGE. (Field Ambulances)

(Sgd.) T.W. Burton, Capt. for Colonel A.M.S.
A.D.M.S., 52nd. (Lowland) Division.

Copy No. 3 to 1/3rd. L.F.A.

WAR DIARY
INTELLIGENCE SUMMARY.

Army Form C. 2118.

War Diary

for

1/3rd Lowland Field Ambulance R.A.M.C.(T)

From 1st July to 31st July
1918
(Volume 3)

COMMITTEE FOR THE
MEDICAL HISTORY OF THE WAR
Date 6 SEP. 1918

WAR DIARY

INTELLIGENCE SUMMARY

Sheet No. 1.

1/3rd LOWLAND FLD. AMB.
R.A.M.C. (T.F.)

Army Form C. 2118.

Place	Date	Hour	Summary of Events and Information	Remarks and references to Appendices
AUX RIETZ (A & a 4.6.)	1-7-18		Ref. Map LA TARGETTE 1/20,000	
			Strength R.A.M.C.	
			1 Other Rank rejoined from hospital.	
			Admitted 4. Discharged -. Evacuated 4. Remaining - 94	
	2-7-18		**Move** Headquarters moved from AUX RIETZ to new M.D.S. in F.9.c. at MONT ST. ELOI	
			Admitted 2.x. Discharged -. Evacuated 2. Remaining - 94 x wounded	
			Strength Animals.	
			1 L.D. Horse evacuated to Mobile Veterinary Section.	
Mont St. Eloi. (F.9.c)	3-7-18		Admitted 23. Discharged -. Evacuated 20. Remaining 3. 94	
			Strength Animals.	
			1 L.D. Horse returned from Mobile Veterinary Section	
	4-7-18		Received from A.D.M.S. Summary of Medical Arrangements.	
			Copy of same forwarded to O.C. A.D.S. CHAUDIÈRE and O.C. A.D.S. FARBUS, together with their Medical Arrangements.	Appendix I
			Admitted 15. Discharged 2. Evacuated 15. Remaining 1	

Sheet No. 2

1/3rd LOWLAND FLD. AMB.
R.A.M.C. (T.F.)

Army Form C. 2118.

WAR DIARY

INTELLIGENCE SUMMARY
(Erase heading not required.)

Instructions regarding War Diaries and Intelligence Summaries are contained in F. S. Regs., Part II. and the Staff Manual respectively. Title pages will be prepared in manuscript.

Place	Date	Hour	Summary of Events and Information	Remarks and references to Appendices
MONTST.ELOI	4-7-18.		**Strength Officers** Lieut. WILLIS, J.C., M.R.C., U.S.A., joined for duty from 1/1st Lowland Field Ambulance. — Authority A.D.M.S., 52nd Division 2/4-7-18.	9h
	5-7-18.		**Strength R.A.M.C.** 1 Other Rank rejoined from hospital. Admitted 31½. Discharged —. Evacuated 27. Remaining 4. *Wounded 1. (died)	9h
	6-7-18.		Admitted 21. * Discharged —. Evacuated 18. Remaining 7. *Wounded 3.	9h
	7-7-18.		**Strength** R.A.M.C., Officers 8 Other Ranks, A.S.C. (H.T.) 39 Other Ranks 184 (M.T.) 13 Received A.D.M.S., S.R. 128. Instructions on order being received to "Man Battle Stations".	Appendix II. 9h
	8-7-18.		Admitted 12. Discharged —. Evacuated 9. Remaining 10. Admitted 25.* Discharged 9. Evacuated 21. Remaining 14. *Wounded 9.	9h

1/3rd LOWLAND FLD. AMB.
R.A.M.C. (T.F.)

Army Form C. 2118.

Sheet No 3.

WAR DIARY
INTELLIGENCE SUMMARY
(Erase heading not required.)

Instructions regarding War Diaries and Intelligence Summaries are contained in F.S. Regs., Part II. and the Staff Manual respectively. Title pages will be prepared in manuscript.

Place	Date	Hour	Summary of Events and Information	Remarks and references to Appendices
Mont ST. ELOI.	9-7-18		Admitted 16. Discharged - Evacuated 13. Remaining 17.	JM
			Strength R.A.M.C. 2 Other Ranks to hospital sick.	
	10-7-18		Admitted 29 *. Discharged 1 - Evacuated 30. Remaining 16. * Wounded 14.	JM
	11-7-18		Strength Officers. Captain R. STANSFEILD, M.C. posted to 1/6th H.L.I. for temporary duty. Authority A.D.M.S. R1353/5 d/11-7-18.	
			Strength R.A.M.C. 1 Other Rank to hospital sick.	
			Admitted 19 *. Discharged - Evacuated 16. Remaining 19. * 2 Wounded.	JM
	12-7-18		Strength R.A.M.C. 2 Other Ranks to hospital sick.	
			Admitted 18 *. Discharged - Evacuated 20. Remaining 17. * Wounded 6.	JM

Sheet N° 4.

1/3rd LOWLAND FLD. AMB
R.A.M.C. (T.F.)

Army Form C. 2118.

WAR DIARY

INTELLIGENCE SUMMARY

(Erase heading not required.)

Instructions regarding War Diaries and Intelligence Summaries are contained in F. S. Regs., Part II. and the Staff Manual respectively. Title pages will be prepared in manuscript.

Place	Date	Hour	Summary of Events and Information	Remarks and references to Appendices
MONT ST. ELOI.	13.7.18		Strength R.A.M.C. 1 Other Rank rejoined from hospital. Admitted 24 ※ Discharged 2. Evacuated 17. Remaining 22. ※ Wounded 1.	9a
	14.7.18		Strength R.A.M.C. 35 Bearers temporarily attached from 1/2nd Lowland Field Ambulance, returned to their unit. Received R.A.M.C. Operation Order N° 5 - Relief of 156th Infantry Brigade by 10th Canadian Infantry Brigade. Evacuated 19. Remaining 17. Admitted 16 ※ Discharged 2. ※ Wounded 9.	Appendix 3.
			Strength. R.A.M.C. Officers 8 A.S.C. (H.T.) Other Ranks. 39 Other Ranks. 181 (M.T.) 13	9b
	15.7.18		Transport. One Motor Ambulance Car, while at CHAUDIERE, badly damaged by shell fire.	

Sheet N° 5.

1/3rd LOWLAND FLD. AMB.
R.A.M.C. (T.F.)

Army Form C. 2118.

WAR DIARY
INTELLIGENCE SUMMARY
(Erase heading not required.)

Instructions regarding War Diaries and Intelligence Summaries are contained in F. S. Regs., Part II. and the Staff Manual respectively. Title pages will be prepared in manuscript.

Place	Date	Hour	Summary of Events and Information	Remarks and references to Appendices
Mont St. ELOI	15-7-18		**Strength Officers** Captain G.V.T. McMICHAEL joined for duty from N° 7 General Hospital. Authority A.D.M.S., R1430/5 of 16-7-18.	
			Admitted 13 x. Discharged -. Evacuated 16. Remaining 14. Do.	
			✗ 2 wounded	
	16-7-18		Reinforcements.	
			16 Bearers temporarily attached from 1/1st Lowland Field Ambulance	
			Casualties R.A.M.C.	
			2 Other Ranks wounded (gas) - "Mustard".	
			Casualties A.S.C. (M.T.)	
			1 Other Rank wounded (gas) - "Mustard".	
			Admitted 24 x. Discharged -. Evacuated 21. Remaining 17. Do.	
			✗ 5 wounded	
	17-7-18		155th Infantry Brigade relieved 157th Infantry Brigade in left sector.	
			Admitted 11. Discharged -. Evacuated 13. Remaining 15. Do.	
			✗ 3 wounded	
	18-7-18		Admitted 21. Discharged -. Evacuated 10. Remaining 26. Do.	
			✗ 8 wounded	
	19-7-18		Admitted 22 x. Discharged 3. Evacuated 27. Remaining 18. Do.	
			✗ 6 wounded.	

Sheet No 6.

1/3rd LOWLAND FLD. AMB.
R.A.M.C. (T.F.)

WAR DIARY

INTELLIGENCE SUMMARY
(Erase heading not required.)

Army Form C. 2118.

Place	Date	Hour	Summary of Events and Information	Remarks and references to Appendices
Mont St. Eloi	19-7-18		Received A.D.M.S., S.R. 143/1. - Warning Order reference relief of 52 Division by 8th Division.	Appendix 4.
			Received 155th Infantry Brigade Order O.1- reference relief by a Brigade of 8th Division.	Appendix 4.
			Instructions regarding relief sent to O.C. A.D.S. CHAUDIERE, and O.C. A.D.S. FARBUS.	Appendix 4.
			Strength, A.S.C. (M.T.)	
			1 Other Rank received as reinforcement.	
			Strength Officers.	
			Captain W.E.K. COLES joined for duty from 21st Ambulance.	
20-7-18			Received 155th Infantry Brigade Order No 6. - Move to Billets.	Appendix 4.
			Strength Officers.	
			Captain A.J.G. HUNTER, M.C. left to report to No 4 General Hospital authority D.D.M.S. VIII Corps 3190 of 19/7/18.	
			Captain G.V.T. McMICHAEL posted to 1/7th S.R. in relief of R.M.O.	
			Strength, A.S.C. (M.T.)	
			1 Other Rank to hospital sick.	

Sheet No. 7

1/3rd LOWLAND FLD. AMB.
R.A.M.C. (T.F.)

Army Form C. 2118.

WAR DIARY

INTELLIGENCE SUMMARY

(Erase heading not required.)

Instructions regarding War Diaries and Intelligence Summaries are contained in F. S. Regs. Part II. and the Staff Manual respectively. Title pages will be prepared in manuscript.

Place	Date	Hour	Summary of Events and Information	Remarks and references to Appendices
MONT ST. ELOI	20-7-18		Strength R.A.M.C. 16 Bearers temporarily attached from 1/1st Lowland Field Ambulance returned to their unit. Admitted 7. ℀ Discharged 3. Evacuated 16. Remaining 6. ℀ Wounded 1. Strength. R.A.M.C. Officers 6. Other Ranks 180. A.S.C. (H.T) Other Ranks 39 (M.T.) 13. 9.	
	21-7-18		Strength R.A.M.C. 3 Other Ranks rejoined from Hospital. Received R.A.M.C. Operation Order Nº 6, and 155th Brigade Order Nº 104 — Relief by 8st Division. Received from 155th Infantry Brigade, Amendment to Order Nº 6. Strength Officer Captain J.F. LINDSAY to hospital sick. Admitted 25. ℀ Discharged 1. Evacuated 24. Remaining 6. ℀ Wounded 5.	Appendix A.

WAR DIARY
INTELLIGENCE SUMMARY

113nd LOWLAND FLD. AMB.
March (T.F.)

Sheet No. 8.

Army Form C. 2118.

Place	Date	Hour	Summary of Events and Information	Remarks and references to Appendices
MONT ST. ELOI	21-7-18		Instructions regarding times & method of relief of personnel at Relay Posts and A.D.Ss. sent to O.s.C. respective A.D.Ss.	Appendix 4.
	22-7-18		Moves. A.D.Ss. CHAUDIERE and TARBUS, and M.D.S. MONT ST. ELOI handed over to 26th Field Ambulance. Unit marched to, and took over Billets in FRESNICOURT. Admitted 13. Discharged 1. Evacuated 12. Remaining 6. & wounded 8.	
FRESNICOURT. G.26.a.0.5. Ref. Map Lens 1/20,000	23-7-18		Strength, R.A.M.C. 1 Other Rank to Hospital sick. Received 155th Infantry Brigade O.1/2. — Division in G.H.Q. Reserve. Received 155th Infantry Brigade Order, reference alone — Instructions in the event of a move. Received A.D.M.S. S.R.143/19 — Equipment to be taken with unit in event of move by rail. List of Equipment, suggested to be taken, forwarded to A.D.M.S.	Appendix 5.

WAR DIARY

INTELLIGENCE SUMMARY

Sheet No. 9.

Army Form C. 2118.

1/3rd LOWLAND FLD. AMB.
R.A.M.C. (T.F.)

Place	Date	Hour	Summary of Events and Information	Remarks and references to Appendices
FRESNICOURT	23-7-18		Admitted 11 x. Discharged 4. Evacuated 12. Remaining 1. x Wounded 2.	
	24-7-18		Strength R.A.M.C. 1 Other Rank rejoined from Hospital. Strength A.S.C. (H.T.) 1 Other Rank to hospital, sick.	
	25-7-18		Admitted 10. Discharged —. Evacuated 10. Remaining 1. x Wounded 1. Strength Officers. Lieut. J.C. WILLIS, M.R.C. U.S.A., posted to 1st Army Artillery School in temporary relief of R.M.O. Authority D.D.M.S., XVII Corps., 5/412 of 23-7-18.	
	26-7-18		Admitted 1. Discharged 1. Evacuated 1. Remaining 1. x Wounded 1. Admitted 11. Discharged —. Evacuated 11. Remaining —.	
	27-7-18		Admitted 2. Discharged —. Evacuated 2. Remaining —.	

Sheet No. 10.

WAR DIARY

INTELLIGENCE SUMMARY
(Erase heading not required.)

Army Form C. 2118.

1/3rd LOWLAND FLD. AMB.
R.A.M.C. (T.F.)

Place	Date	Hour	Summary of Events and Information	Remarks and references to Appendices
FRESNICOURT	28.7.18		Admitted 3. Discharged – Evacuated 3. Remaining –	
			Strength. A.S.C. (M.T.) 1 Other Rank reinforcement received.	
	29.7.18		Admitted 3. Discharged – Evacuated 3. Remaining –	
	30.7.18		Received R.A.M.C. Operation Order No. 7. – Unit to relieve 11th Canadian Field Ambulance at M.D.S. MAROEUIL 31.5.8.	
			Received instructions to above – Unit to relieve 2/2nd London Field Ambulance at AUBIGNY and occupy their camp at E.I.C.4.4. as Divisional Rest Station.	Appendix 6.
	30.7.18		Admitted 7. Discharged 5. Evacuated 2. Remaining –	
	31.7.18		Unit moved to AUBIGNY tomorrow and took over Divisional Rest Station.	
			Admitted 23. Discharged – Evacuated 23. Remaining –	
			Strength. R.A.M.C. Officers 6. A.S.C. (H.T.) Other Ranks 38. Other Ranks 182. (M.T.) — 13.	

31-7-18

James Munro Lieut. Colonel
O.C. 1/3rd LOWLAND FLD. AMB, R.A.M.C. (T.F.)

SECRET

Appendix I

MEDICAL ARRANGEMENTS

1/3rd Lowland Field Ambulance.

1/3 LOWLAND FIELD AMBULANCE.

No. O.124/18
Date 7-7-18

O.C. A.D.S. Chaudiere
O.C. A.D.S. Farbus

Forwarded for your information.

Ref. "Summary of Medical Arrangements" para 5, normally all gas cases will be sent to M.D.S. During severe gas attack the Mustard Gas cases will be dealt with as laid down in "Medical Arrangements in the Event of Severe Gas Attack" d/ 31/5/18, i.e., they will be sent direct to Gas Centre at NEUVILLE ST VAAST when information is received that this is open.

Ref. "Medical Arrangements in the Event of Hostile Attack", para 1 (a), information will be sent you later regarding trains from A.D.S. to M.D.S. - Para 2 (a) - Application for additional officers and bearers will be sent by quickest available route to M.D.S., F.9.c. - Para 3 - A car relay post will be established on 8-7-18 at ZIVY Dump consisting normally of 2 cars which will be increased as required.

On its being established the orderly in each car returning from the A.D.S. will report at this relay and a new car will be sent forward. On leaving the M.D.S. the cars will in each case take up their position at ZIVY Dump.

The cars at ZIVY are in addition available for the evacuation of Artillery units in the forward area served by Artillery Post.

Ref. para 4 (a), a reserve of 400 $\frac{AT}{5}$ doses of A.T. Serum will be held at each A.D.S.

James Young
Lieut-Colonel.
R.A.M.C.(T)
O.C. 1/3rd Lowland Field Ambulance.

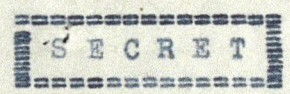 S.R. 125

Copy No 3.

SUMMARY OF
MEDICAL ARRANGEMENTS
52nd (Lowland) Division.

Reference:- Map Army Map "B", 1/40,000   4th July 1918.

1. **LOCATIONS** A.D.M.S. Office:- CHATEAU ACQ - W.30.b.4.5.
   1st Low. Fd. Amb.:- Divisional Rest Station - VILLERS AUX BOIS - X.19.c.9.9.
   2nd Low. Fd. Amb.:- Main Dressing Station - LES 4 VENTS - W.9.d.1.9.
   Walking Wounded Collecting Post - AUX RIETZ - A.8.C.5.5.
   3rd Low. Fd. Amb.:- Main Dressing Station - Mont St ELOI - F.9.c.
   Advanced Dressing Stations -
   LA CHAUDIERE - S.18.c.9.3.
   FARBUS ------- B.2.a.9.4.

Regimental Aid Posts	Relay Posts
T.13.b.5.4.	T.13.a.5.5.
T.21.a.2.0.	T.20.b.2.6.
T.19.c.2.5.	T.26.a.2.9.
T.28.a.4.1.	T.26.d.9.7.
T.26.d.9.7.	T.27.d.2.4.
B.9.a.8.7.	T.19.c.2.5.
	B.2.d.3.3.
	A.11.b.3.9.

   Detraining Centre-------------V.29.a.75.65. (near MINGOVAL)
   Car Relay Posts--------------T.25.a.9.4. and F.8.c.9.4.
   Gas Centre------------------A.9.a.5.5. (Baths-NEUVILLE St VAAST)

2. **WOUNDED** Normally, all wounded will pass through the A.D.Ss whence they will be evacuated by Motor Ambulance Cars of the Field Ambulance to the M.D.S. at F.9.c., from which they will be evacuated by M.A.C. Cars.

3. **SICK** Sick of Units in the trenches will be evacuated through A.D.Ss to M.D.S. F.9.c. and either evacuated, retained, or sent to the Divisional Rest Station according to the case.
Sick of Units in NEUVILLE ST VAAST Area will be admitted to the Walking Wounded Collecting Post and thence transferred to M.D.S and LES 4 Vents. O.C. Field Ambulance at LES 4 VENTS will be responsible for collection of sick requiring transport.
O.C. Divisional Rest Station will collect sick from the Brigade in Reserve at ST ELOI. One Ambulance Car will be kept by this Unit at ST ELOI (near the Baths) for emergency cases.

4. **WALKING WOUNDED** During heavy fighting, when there are numbers of walking wounded, these will be evacuated to Walking Wounded Collecting Post and thence to Detraining Centre by Light Railway or Motor Lorry, or other means as directed.

5. **GASSED CASES** Severe cases will be evacuated to C.C.S. from the M.D.S. at F.9.c.

5. **GASSED CASES** (contd)   Slight and doubtful cases will be ransferred from the M.D.S. at F.9.c. to the Divisional Rest Station.

                                Sgd. A. J. MacDougall, Colonel
                                                                          A.M.S.

ACKNOWLEDGE.   A.D.M.S. 52nd (Lowland) Division

SECRET

ADDENDUM TO MEDICAL ARRANGEMENTS IN THE EVENT OF A HOSTILE ATTACK - 52nd DIVISION.

Insert - Para. 2 (c)
M.O. 1/c Divisional R.E. and M.O. i/c 52nd D.A.C. will report for duty at M.D.S. F.9.c. The M.O. i/c 52nd Bn. M.G.C. will report for duty at the W.W.C.P.

Sgd. A. J. MacDougall, Colonel.
A.M.S.
A.D.M.S. 52nd (Lowland) Division

4/7/18.

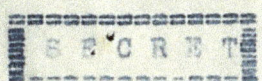

Copy No. 3

MEDICAL ARRANGEMENTS
52nd (Lowland) Division
IN THE EVENT OF A HOSTILE ATTACK

---

1. EVACUATION

(a) In the event of active operations, stretcher and sitting cases will be evacuated from A.D.S. to M.D.S. at F.9.c. and walking cases to Walking Wounded Collecting Post at AUX RIETZ (A.8.c.5.5.). Cases will be collected by hand carry, wheeled stretchers, ambulance cars and wagons, tram trolleys and light railways, according to circumstances.

O.C. M.D.S. at F.9.c. is responsible for making arrangements for trains between A.D.S. and M.D.S.

(b) Stretcher and sitting cases will be evacuated from the M.D.S. at F.9.c. by M.A.C. cars.

(c) Walking wounded will be evacuated from the W.W.C.P. to Detraining Centre at V.29.a.75.65. (near MINGOVAL) by means of the Light Railway. O.C. W.W.C.P. will be responsible for making arrangements for trains on the Light Railway between W.W.C.P. and Detraing.Centre. All aplications for trains will be made to TRAFFIC CONTROL, ZIVY.

An N.C.O. and Orderly will accompany each train to the Detraining Centre. They will be in charge of the patients and will be responsible for their comfort. On detrainment, they will report to the O.C. Detraining Centre who will arrange for their return to the W.W.C.P. in the most expeditious manner, either by returning train or by M.A.C. Cars returning from the C.C.S. Each patient will have a blanket and, in wet weather, a waterproof sheet, which, on detraining, will be collected and returned to W.W.C.P., by the O.C. Detraining Centre in the most expeditious manner as in the case of Orderlies.

A Detraining Party will be detailed (as below) and four motor lorries will be supplied by Corps for removing cases from the Detraining Centre to the C.C.S.

NO stretcher cases will be evacuated by the train from the W.W.C.P.

One motor lorry and one ambulance car will be on duty at the W.W.C.P., and the former for evacuation of cases to the C.C.S. which, on its return, will call at the Detraining Centre and bring back any orderlies or equipment that may be there for return to the W.W.C.P. The ambulance car will be used for any cases requiring removal as stretcher cases.

(d) Sick cases will be sent to the M.D.S. at F.9.c. and thence by M.A.C. to the C.C.S. Slight cases will be sent to the Divisional Rest Station.

2. PERSONNEL

(a) O.C. Field Ambulance at LES 4 VENTS will detail two Officers and all his Bearers to report to O.C. Field Ambulance at M.D.S. F.9.c. who will reinforce his Bearer Sub-divisions as necessary.

(b) O.C. Field Ambulance conducting the Divisional Rest Station will detail an Officer with one N.C.O. and nine privates for duty at the Detraining Centre with equipment already detailed. He will hold his Bearer Sub-divisions in readiness to reinforce as ordered. He will order and Officer to proceed to /

2. contd. / to Forward Battle Stragglers Collecting Station A.11.a.0.8. (Divisional Administrative Instructions No. A.F. 9).

3. TRANSPORT Ambulance cars will be used for evacuation in the Divisional Area and will not proceed to the C.C.S. without orders from this Office.

10 M.A.C. Cars will evacuate from the M.D.S. and F.9.c.

O.C., Divisional Rest Station will place his Ambulance motor cars at the disposal of O.C. M.D.S. F.9.c.

O.C. Field Ambulance at LES 4 VENTS will detail one car for duty at the W.W.C.P. and will hold the remainder in reserve

Two horsed ambulances from the O.C. Divisional Rest Station will be at the disposal of the O.C. M.D.S. F.9.c. to convey cases to the Divisional Rest Station.

Car Relay Posts between the A.D.S. and M.D.S. will be arranged by O.C. M.D.S. F.9.c.

All drivers of cars will have precise orders in writing as to where they are to go and return.

4. MEDICAL (a) Anti-tetanic serum will be given in all cases at the A.D.S. A check will be made at the M.D.S. and any case who has not had A.T.S. will be given it before evacuation.
(b) Dressings may be obtained, if necessary, on urgent indent direct on No. 33 Advanced Depot Medical Stores, SAVY, two copies of the indent being subsequently sent to this Office.
(c) Os.C. Field Ambulances will indent direct on S.S.O. for food and Medical comforts for patients.

5. GENERAL All changes in the positions of A.D.Ss., R.A.Ps. and Relay Posts will be reported to this Office at once.

Applications for bearers, cars etc., will be made to this Office.

Attention is called to D.D.M.S. NO; 2999, Summary of Medical Arrangements, XVIII Corps, in the event of a Hostile Attack.

        Sgd A.J.MacDougall,
        Colonel.
        A.M.S.
    A.D.M.S. 52nd (Lowland) Division.

Copy No. 1 to 1/1st Lowland Field Ambulance
    2   1/2nd Lowland Field Ambulance
    3   1/3rd Lowland Field Ambulance
    4   "G"
    5   "A" and "Q"
    6   D.D.M.S., VIII Corps
    7   A.D.M.S. 20th Division.
    8   A.D.M.S. 24th Division.
    9.   A.D.M.S. 51st Division.
   10;   H.Q. 155th Inf. Bde.
   11.   H.Q. 156th Inf. Bde.
   12.   H.Q. 157th Inf. Bde.
   13.   C.R.A. 52nd Division.
   14.   Diary.
   15.   Diary.
   16.   File.

Appendix 2

SECRET.   A.D.M.S. 52nd Division. No S.R. 18

O.C. 1/3rd Low. Fld. Ambce.

On the Order "Man Battle Stations" the following procedure will immediately be carried out:-

1. O.C. Field Ambulance at Les 4 Vents will detail 2 Officers and all his bearers to report to O.C. Field Ambce at M.D.S. F 9.c; who will reinforce his bearer sub-divisions as necessary.

2. O.C. Field Ambce. conducting the Divisional Rest Station will detail an Officer and 1 N.C.O. and 9 Privates for duty at the detraining centre with equipment already detailed. He will hold his bearer-sub-divisions in readiness to reinforce as ordered. He will order an officer to proceed to Forward Battle Stragglers Collecting Station, A 11. a 0.8. (Divnl Administrative Instructions No A.F. 9.)

3. O.C. Divisional Rest Station will send his Ambulance Motor/Cars at once to O.C. M.D.S. F.9.c.

4. O.C. Field Ambulance at Les 4 Vents will detail one car for duty at the Walking Wounded Collecting post and will hold the remainder in reserve.

5. Two horsed Ambulances from O.C. Divisional Rest Station will be sent to O.C. M.D.S. F.9.c. to convey cases to the Divisional Rest Station.

6. M.O. i/c Divisional R.E. and M.O. i/c 52nd D.A.C. will report for duty at M.D.S. F 9.c   M.O. i/c 52nd Bn M.G.C. will report for duty at the Walking Wounded Collecting Post.

H.Q. 52nd Divn.   Sgd. A.J. MacDougall, Colonel, A.M.S.
7th July 1918.   A.D.M.S. 52nd (Lowland) Division.

SECRET.

S.R.137.

Appendix 3

O.C. 1/3rd Low. Fld. Ambce.

R.A.M.C. OPERATION ORDER No 5.
by
Colonel A.J. Macdougall. A.M.S.
A.D.M.S. 52nd Division.

14th July 1918

Reference:- 52nd Division Order No 111 d/= 13/7/18.
Map:-MAROEUIL.

1. On the 15th and night 15th/16th the 10th Canadian Inf. Bde. will relieve the Troops of the 156th Inf Bde. in the area to be handed over to the 4th Canadian Division, ie Area South of C.P.R. Trench and Mersy Alley.

2. The A.D.S. FARBUS(B.2.a;9.4.) will be retained by the 52nd Division and sick and wounded Canadian Troops from the Area handed over will be evacuated through it for the present.

3. Relay Post B.2.d.3.3. will be handed over.

4. The M.O. in occupation of R.A.P. B.9.a.8/7/ will on evacuating his R.A.P. hand over Trench Stores (blankets, stretchers and Thomas' splints) held as such to O.C. A.D.S. FARBUS.

5. M.Os of Battalions 156th Inf. Bde. relieving Battalions of 157th Inf. Bde. will report their new R.A.P. to O.C. A.D.S. LA CHAUDIERE, and should they give up an R.A.P. without handing it over to a successor will be responsible that trench stores are removed to their new R.A.P. Should the new R.A.P. be already equipped, the surplus will be handed over to O.C. nearest A.D.S.

6. ACKNOWLEDGE.

Sgd. A.J. MACDOUGALL,
Colonel, A.M.S.
A.D.M.S. 52nd Division.

Appendix 4

VERY SECRET. A.D.M.S. 52nd Division No. S.R. 143/1.

O.C. 1/3rd Lowland Field Ambulance.

WARNING ORDER.

52nd Division will be relieved in VIII Corps by 8th Division. On relief, 52nd Division will be transferred to XVII Corps in G.H.Q. reserve, and located in areas adjoining First and Fifth Armies. Relief will probably commence night 19th/20th July.

H.Q. 52nd Division.   Sgd John W. Leitch, Lieut-Colonel,
18th July 1918.   A/A.D.M.S. 52nd (Lowland) Division.

SECRET. *Appendix 4* Copy No 8.

155th Infantry Brigade.

ADMINISTRATIVE INSTRUCTIONS No 6.

Ref. Map Sheet 36 B.
   1/40,000.   20th July 1918.

1.   The 155th Infantry Brigade, 1/3rd Lowland Field Ambulance, 410th Field Coy R.E. 218 Coy A.S.C. and "A" Coy 52nd Bn M.G. Corps will be transferred on the 23rd inst from the 8th Corps to the 17th Corps and will be Billeted as follows:-

Unit	Place	Commandant who will allot Billets.
155th Inf. Bde H.Q.	VERDREL	Area Comdt. VERDREL.
1/4th R.S.F.	VERDREL	- Do -
Trench Mortar Bty.	FRESNICOURT	- Do -
1/3rd Low. Fd Amb.	FRESNICOURT	- Do -
218th Coy A.S.C.	OLHAIN	Town Major, OLHAIN.
410th Fd Coy. R.E.	OLHAIN	- Do -
1/5th R.S.F.	Camblain L'Abbe	Area Comdt. Camblain L'Abbe.
1/4th K/O/S.B.	-Do-	- Do -
"A" Coy. 52nd Bn M.G.C.	GOUY- SERVINS	Area Comdt. GOUY SERVINS.

2.   The above Units will form a Brigade Group, and will proceed to new Billets under orders which will be issued later.

3.   (a) Billeting parties will proceed direct to new Billeting areas in motor lorries on 21st inst. and will be responsible for meeting Units on arrival.

   (b) The following should be the strength of Billeting Parties:-

	OFFICERS	O.R.
Brigade Headquarters	1	-
Per Infantry Battalion	1	3
Per smaller Units	1	1

   1 Bicycle per man should be taken
   (c) 2 lorries for conveyance of this party will start from BERRHONVAL at 2 PM on 21st inst.

4.   (a) Railhead will be at Mont St Eloy till 22nd and at HOUDAIN from 23rd inclusive.
   (b) Rations for the 23rd will be carried in the Supply Wagons of the Train.
   :(c) Refilling Point from the 23rd July inclusive will be at OLHAIN (P24b75 (P 24 b.7.5 Supply Sections will deliver to Units.

5.   Lorries to convey Packs, Quartermaster's Stores etc., to the new area on 22nd July have been allotted as follows:-
      Brigade Headquarters   ---   ---   --- 1 lorry
      Each Battalion   ---   ---xx---   --- 4 lorries
      Trench Morter Bty.   ---   ---   --- 1 lorry.

   Time at which lorries will report will be notified later. Unites requiring lorries to report elsewhere than at BERTHONVAL FARM will wire Brigade Headquarters the number , rendezvous and approximate time

6.   Full establishment of S.B.A. will be taken in Horse Transport.

7.   (a) All Trench and area stores (including Reserve Rations) will be habded over to relieving Units.   Any Soyer's Stoves, Hot food containers, S.D. clothing for Gas cases not returned to D.A.D.O.S. will also be handed over and numbers notified to Brigade Headquarters.

   (b) Yukon Packs, Anti-Gas combination clothing and Meat Safes will be taken with the Units.

(2)

    (c) Paraffin retained in various Camps for a certain period should be handed over to the incoming Unit or the area Commandant.
    (d) Chaff Cutters in the Transport Lines will be handed over to the Area Commandant, BERTHONVAL FARM.

8.   Baggage wagons of the Train will join Units at Transport Lines at 8 am and Supply Wagons at 3pm on 22nd.
    Baggage wagons will remain with Units. Supply wagons will be returned to Train Company as soon as the Supplies have been dumped at the new Quartermaster's Stores.

9.   ACKNOWLEDGE.

                                  MILL
                         L.J.A. Wills, Captain,
                    Staff Captain, 155th Brigade?

SECRET. *Appendix 4* Copy No3.
O.C. 1/3rd Low. Fld Ambce.

R.A.M.C. OPERATION ORDER No6.
by
Lieut-Colonel, J.W. Leitch, D.S.O.
A / A.D.M.S. 52nd (Lowland) Division.

Reference Maps 1/100,000 LENS & HAZEBROUCK; ARMY MAP B.1/40,000.
52nd Division Order No 117 and addenda thereto.

1. **INFORMATION.** The 52nd Division will be relieved by the 8th Division, and on relief will move to G.H.Q. reserve under the Administration of XVII Corps. During the Move Field Ambulances will come under the Administration of G.O.Cs Brigades as follows:-
    1/1st Lowland Field Ambulance - G.O.C. 156 Brigade.
    1/2nd Lowland Field Ambulance - G.O.C. 157 "
    1/3rd Lowland Field Ambulance - G.O.C. 155 "

2. **MOVES.** 1/1st Lowland Field Ambulance will be relieved at VILLERS AU BOIS X19 c. 9.9. on 21st inst. by 25th Field Ambce and will move on 22nd to the neighbourhood of BOIS D'OLBAIN under orders of G.O.C. 156 Brigade.
    Relief to be completed by 2000 on 21st inst;

    1/2nd Lowland Field Ambulance moved on 20th to AUCHEL under orders of G?O.C. 157th Brigade and was relieved by 24th Field Ambulance.

    1/3rd Lowland Field Ambulance will be relieved at Mont St Eloy and Posts in the Forward Area by the 26th Field Ambulance on the 22nd inst.
    All reliefs to be completed by mid-night 22/23rd inst.
    1/3rd Lowland Field Ambulance will on relief move to the neighbourhood of FRESNICOURT under orders of G.O.C. 155th Brigade.

3. **EVACUATION.** Sick or wounded not evacuated will be transferred to relieving Field Ambulance.
    In the new area evacuation will be to the receiving C.C.S. PERNES from 1/1st and 1/2nd Lowland Field Ambces by Motor Ambulances of the Units concerned.
    1/3rd Lowland Field Ambce, will similarly evacuate to the receiving C.C.S. AUBIGNY.
    Until further orders evacuation of cases to the Ear, Eye or Throat Specialist or Dentist will be suspended.
    1/1st L.F.A. will evacuate sick from "B" Coy M.G. Bn. in addition to those of Brigade Group.
    1/2nd L.F.A. will similarly evacuate sick from "D" Coy (not "A" Coy) M.G. Bn. and from Divisional Artillery in accordance with this office S.R. 143/11 dated 20/7/18.
    1/3rd L.F.A. will similarly evacuate sick from "A" Coy M.G. Bn.

4. A.D.M.S. Office will close at CHATEAU D'ACQ at noon on 23rd and will open at PERNES at the same hour.

5. ACKNOWLEDGE.

Sgd John W. Leitch, Lieut-Colonel,
A / A.D.M.S. 52nd (Lowland) Division.

SECRET   Copy No 8.

In continuation of Administration Instruction No 6
dated 20th July 1918:-

1. Cancel para 4(b) and (c) and substitute as follows:-
    4(b) There will be no Refilling point on 23rd July
         Refilling Point for 24th will be notified later.

2. Cancel para 8 and substitute as follows:-
                                    on
    8(a) Rations for consumption for both 23rd July and
24th July will be drawn on 22nd July.

    (b) Rations for consumption on 23rd will be conveyed
to units from Refilling Point in their Baggage wagons arriving
about 8am on the 22nd.
         They will then be transferred to Units First
Line Transport in which they will be conveyed to the new area.
         Baggage wagons will remain with Units until
further notice.

    (c) Rations for consumption 24th will be drawn by
the Supply Sections during the afternoon of 22nd July.
         These wagons will move to the new areas full
and will deliver rations to the new Quartermaster's Stores
under arrangements to be made by O.C. 218th Coy A.S.C.

3. ACKNOWLEDGE.

                              Sgd A. Longmuir, Lieut,
                                        for Captain,
                        Staff Captain, 155th Inf. Bde.

3. Reference para 2(c) above-
    Refilling on 22nd July will be at 7am and 2pm
    Units will ensure that their representatives are at Refilling
Point at both 7am and 2pm.

4. Refilling on 24th July will be at ESTREE CAUCHIE at 10 am.

5. The 218th Company will move to ESTREE CAUCHIE and not OHLAIN.

Secret.

Appendix L

O.C., A.D.S., Chaudiere.   S.R. 58.   21/7/18.

O.C., A.D.S., Farbus.

    The relief of the personnel at the A.D.S. and Relay Posts will commence today. This will start this afternoon and will take place gradually by motor car until by tonight half the personnel will be relieved.

    As the relieving parties report, a corresponding number will be sent from the A.D.Ss. and Relay Posts to the M.D.S.

    One Officer will report today at each A.D.S. to become acquainted with the duties and will remain until the relief is completed tomorrow.

    To facilitate the move tomorrow, more men than are ~~eat~~ mentioned above should be sent back today if that is possible.

    All 1/20,000 and 1/10,000 and Diagram Maps, except those required for records, will be handed over on relief and a receipt obtained. All Diagram Maps in your possession should be handed over.

                                        (Sgd). James Young, Lieut. Colonel
                                                        R.A.M.C.(T),
                              O.C. 1/3rd Lowland Field Ambulance.

Secret. *Appendix 4* S.R. 57.

<u>O.D., A.D.S., Chaudiere.</u>

<u>O.C., A.D.S., Farbus.</u>

    The relief of your personnel will be completed early tomorrow morning.   All the personnel of the 1/3rd Lowland Field Ambulance should be returned to the M.D.S. by mid-day.   The mid-day meal will be eaten at the M.D.S.

                                           Sgd. James Young, Lt. Col.
                                                   R.A.M.C.(T).
21/7/18.   O.C. 1/3rd Lowland Field Ambulance.

SECRET.   Appendix   Copy No 6.

155th Inf. Brigade Order No 104.

Reference Map MAROEUIL 1/20,000
          LENS   1/100,000

1.   155th Inf Bde. will be relieved by 24th Inf Bde. in MERICOURT SECTOR on 22nd inst as already advised.

2.   Details of relief will be arranged by C.Os. concerned, 1/5th R.S.F. withdrawing via HUMBER TRENCH and 1/4th K.O.S.B via BLIGHTY TRENCH.

3.   Defence schemes, Log Books, Maps 1/10,000 and 1/20,000 Photographs, Diagrams, Communications, all trench stores and reserve rations will be handed over and receipts taken.

4.   Completion of relief will be wired Priority to Bde. HQ by Code word "Chop" followed by proposed time of commencing march to new area.

5.   Units will thereafter proceed independently to billet areas in accordance with the attached March Table. Nos 1 to 3 will be clear of LA TARGETTE Cross Roads by the hour indicated, transport marching with unit. Routes should be reconnoitred as necessary.

6.   Details at Divisional Reception Camp will proceed independently on 22nd inst under Command of the Senior Officer present with each Unit to arrive in new areas by noon.

7.   Each Unit will detail a cyclist orderly to report its arrival in billets and to remain temporarily at Brigade H.Q for inter-communication duty.

8/   Brigade H.Q. will close at its present site on completion of the relief and open at VERDREL at the same hour.

9.   Acknowledge.

                              Sgd W.W. Burkett, Capt.

                              Bde Major 155th Inf. Bde.

MARCH TABLE.

Order of March	Unit	Billet Area	Pass LA TARGETTE Cross Roads by	Route
1.	"A" Coy M.G. Bn	GOUY SERVINS	1000	NEUBILLE ST VAAST Branch Road F.10 Central, VILLERS AU BOIS. Mont St Eloy
2.	410th Fld Coy. R.E.	OLHAIN	1100	Mont St Eloy-Estree Cauchie Road.
3.	1/4th R.S.F.	VREDREL	1200	LA TARGETTE- Branch Road F.10 Central- VILLERS AU BOIS - GD SERVINS.
4.	1/3rd L.F. Ambce.	FRESNICOURT	1300	LA TARGETTE- MONT ST ELOY- ESTREE CAUCHIE Road.
5.	218th Coy A.S.C.	OLHAIN.	1500	- Do -
6.	1/4th K.O.S.B.	CAMBLAIN L'ABBEE		Campbell Road- Targette- Mont St ELOY.
7.	1/5th R.S.F.	- Do -		NEUVILLE ST VAAST MONT ST ELOY.
8.	155 L.T.M.Bty.	FRESNICOURT		LA TARGETTE - MONT ST ELOY-ESTREE CAUCHIE ROAD.

Transport of 1/4th K.O.S.B. and 1/5th R.S.F. will proceed to CAMBLAIN L'ABBEE at 1400 under orders of Senior Transport Officer and that of 155th L.T.M.Bty at 1500 with Bde H.Q. Transport.
Probasle time of completion of reliefs will be indicated later.

SECRET. *Appendix S*   O 1/2

23rd July 1918.

Ref. Map LENS. 1/100,000. Sheet 11 a

1. From 12 noon today, the 52nd Division will be in G.H.Q. reserve ready to move by Bus or tactical train at Six hours notice.

2. **MOVE BY TACTICAL TRAIN.**

    Entraining station for 155th Inf. Bde. Group and portion of transport will be ACQ.
    Remaining transport will move by road.

3. **MOVE BY BUS.**
    (a) Embussing Point for 155th Inf. Bde. Group will be on the ESTREE CAUCHIE-GAUCHIN-LEGAL Road (Column may face either way)
    (b) Units moving by Bus will take with them in the busses all their Lewis Guns, Stokes Mortars and Vickers Guns, and 28 filled Lewis gun drums and 10 filled Vickers Guns belts for each gun.
    Signalling Equipment (less buzzer Switch Unit to follow on Transport) will be taken.
    (c) Accommodation. A bus will take 1 Officer 25 O.R. -6
                         A lorry will take 1 Officer 20 O.R. -7
    (d) Troops will rendezvous ready to embuss at the embussing Point a quarter of an hour before the hour detailed for embussing to take place.
    Notice boards will be placed under Brigade arrangements at each end of the embussing point.
    (f) Embussing strengths of Units will be sent in to Brigade Hqrs; immediately on receipt of orders to move by bus.
    (g) Transport will move by road.
    (h) 52nd Division Administrative Circular Memo No 8 of 27/5/18. as to movements by bus or lorry should be studied.

                         Sgd W.M. Burkett, Capt.
                         Bde. Major, 155th Inf. Bde.

SECRET.

Appendix S

Ref. Map.1/40,000 sheet 44b (old 36b)
Ref. O.1/2 dated 23/7/18.

1. In the event of a move by 'Bus:-

(a) Each Unit will detail an embussing and debussing Officer, the former to report to a Brigade Staff Officer at road junction ESTREE CAUCHIE (W 2 a 3.7.) one hour before the first Unit is due to embus. He will be provided with chalk to mark busses.

(b) Units on arrival at the embussing point will approach their busses told off in parties of 1 Officer and 23 O.R/ at 50 yards distance between each party.

(c) The busses will be drawn up on the ESTREE CAUCHIE-LEGAL Road between Q 31 a. 2.7. and Q 32 x c 0.5.

(d) Probable order of embussing:-
  (1) If column proceeds N.W. direction:-
    Brigade Headquarters
    1/4th R.S.F.
    1/3rd R.S.F.
    1/4th K.O.S.B.
    "A" Coy M.G. Bn
    155 L.T.M.Bty
    410th Fd Coy R.E.
    1/3rd Low. Fd Ambce.

  (2) If column proceeds S.E. direction:-
    Brigade Headquarters
    1/5th R.S.F.
    1/4th K/O/S/B/
    "A" Coy M.G. Bn.
    1/4th R.S.F.
    155L.T.M.Bty.
    410th Coy R.E.
    1/3rf Low. Fd Ambce.

(e) Embussing Officers will reconnoitre the embussing point as soon as possible.

2. In the event of a move by Tactical Trains/-

(a) Two Tactical Trains and one omnibus train have been allotted to this Brigade.

(b) Units will travel in the two tactical trains as follows/-

First Train   1/4th K.O.S.B.
               1/5th R.S.F.
Second Train   1/4th R.S.F.
               Bde. H.Q. (less personnel going by
                           omnibus Train)
               410th Fd Coy R.E. (do   do)
               1/3rd Low. Fd Amb. (less Do.)

(c) The "Omnibus Train" will carry:-

	Off.	O.R.	Horses	Limbered Wagons	2 Wheeled carts
Bde Signal Sec.	1	27	2	1	1
Lewis Gun Detachments(4 Limbers per Bn)	-	24	24	12	-
11 Chargers &6 Packs per Bn	-	51	51	-	-
Personnel of M.G. Coy.	16	180	-	-	-
Chargers M.G. Coy		3	3	-	-
Fd Coy. R.E.		1	2	1	-
Field Amb.		2	4	2	(
T.M. Bty.	4	50	-	-	-

In addition there may be room for Battalion Cookers, Field Company Chargers, Transport for all Machine Guns, of the Machine Gun Coy. and Brigade Headquarters.

(2)

3. In addition to the unexpired portion of the day's rations, troops will entrain with one day's complete rations on the man which will be sent to Units on the order to move being received.

4. ACKNOWLEDGE.

23rd July 1918.

Sgd. A.J.A. Mill, Captain,
Staff Captain, 155th Brigade.

Appendix 5

SECRET S.R. 143/17.

O.C. 1/3rd Lowland Field Ambce.

    With reference to attached you will see that each Field Ambulance is allotted space for two Limbered wagons. These should take only the most necessary material e;g; Stretchers, dressings Medical and Surgical Panniers, Medical Comfort Panniers; and material for making hot water, supply of serum, Red Cross Mugs or other similar articles, some cooking Utensils, and such wicker panniers or additional stores as can be carried may be taken to complete the Limber loads.

    The remainder of the Ambulance Transport would probably be moved by Road.

    With a view to uniformity in equipment O.Cs Field Ambulances are invited to forward suggestions to this office in regard to equipment which they would propose should be taken in the two limbered wagons allotted.

    Sgd John W. Leitch, Lieut-Colonel,
23/7/19. A/A.D.M.S. 52nd Division

List of Contents of "B" Section Limber Wagon.

Appendix 5

Description.		Weight (lbs).
Stretchers	6.	186.
Blankets.	30.)	240.
Ground Sheets	30.)	
Pannier "A".	1.	87.
Pannier "E". (1 Primus stove)	1.	76.
Operating Tent.	1.	181.
Dressing Box, (containing):-	1.)	
Bandages, A.T.Serum, Wool, A.T.Syringe, Gauze, Swabs, Jaconet, Lysol.		20.
Pannier, Field Surgical No.1.	1.	90.
Pannier, Medical Comforts	1.	90.
Surgical Haversacks	6.)	
Medical Companion	1.)	55.
Water-bottles	14.)	
Flag Pole.	1.)	61.
Directing Posts.	4.)	
Reserve Dressing Box.	1.	47.
Tables, small.	2.	16.
Stationery		56.

List of Contents of "C" Section Limber Wagon.

Description.		Weight.(lbs).
Stretchers	6	186.
Blankets	30.	200.
Dixies.	6.	51.
Wood.		20.
Coal.		20.
Operating Lamp/	1	65.
Carbide.	tins 12	24.
Entrenching Pannier(containing):-		
Picks 1.)		
Shovels,G.S. 4.)		40.
Pannier "G".	1	63.
Pannier "H".	1	60.
Bread.		20.
Tea.		4.
Sugar.		20.
Milk.	tins 10.	8.
Jam.	" 12.	24.
Candles.		4.
Biscuits(fancy) tin 1,("H" Pannier)		8.
Butcher's Case.	1.	37.

Appendix 5

O.C.
3rd L.F.Ambce.

SECRET.

Ammendment to R.A.M.C. Operation Order No 7.
by
Lieut-Colonel, J.W. Leitch, D.S.O.
A/A.D.M.S. 52nd Division.

Cancel paragraph 2, Moves and substitute:-

2. MOVES. 1/1st Lowland Field Ambulance will take over the Headquarters of 13th Canadian Field Ambulance ECOUIVRES on 31st.

1/2nd Lowland Field Ambulance will move to MAROEUIL on the 31st and will relieve the 11th Canadian Field Ambulance at MDS 3.I.5.8. and posts held by them in the forward area.
Reliefs to be completed by noon on the 1st prox.

1/3rd Lowland Field Ambulance will relieve the 2/2nd London Field Ambulance at AUBIGNY and occupy their Camp E.1 c.4.4. as the Divisional Rest Station.
Relief to be completed on 31st inst.

(sgd) John W. Leitch, Lieut- Colonel,
A / A.D.M.S. 52nd Division.

Secret Copy No 3.

R.A.M.C. OPERATION ORDER No 7
by
Lieut- Colonel, J.W. LEITCH D.S.O.
A/A.D.M.S. 52nd Division.

30th July 1918.

Reference Map- Lens 11, 1/100,000.
" 52nd Division Order No 118 29/7/18.

1. **INFORMATION.** 52nd Division will relieve a portion of 4th Canadian Division in the line from TOWEY ALLEY at H.5a.7.6. inclusive to WESTERN ROAD (Corps Northern Boundary) on July 31st and succeeding days.

2. **MOVES.** 1/1st Lowland Field Ambulance, which moves with 156th Brigade to MAROEUIL on 30th inst, will relieve 13th Canadian Field Ambulance at 3.J.2.6. (ST CATHERINE) and posts occupied by them in th Forward Area.
   Reliefs will be completed by 6p;m; on 31st July.

   1/2nd Lowland Field Ambulance, which moves with 157th Bde., will relieve the 12th Canadian Field Ambulance near AGNEZ LES DUISANS, 3.I.1.8. (road 1 mile North East of Ain AGNEZ) and will form the Divisional Rest Station.
   Relief will be completed by 6p;m; on 1st August.

   1/3rd Lowland Field Ambulance, which moves with 155th Bde. will relieve the 11th Canadian Field Ambulance at M.D.S. at MAROEUIL 31.5.8. and posts held by them in the forward area.
   Reliefs to be completed by 6p;m; on 31st July.

3. **EVACUATION.** Maps of Area and details of present scheme of evacuation will be handed over by Canadian Field Ambulances to relieving Field Ambulances.
   Cases likely to be fit in 7 to 10 days and Cases of Skin Disease and uncomplicated Scabies will be sent to Divisional Rest Station.

4. **REPORTS.** Completion of moves report will be wired to A.D.M.S. 52nd Division .
   A.D.M.S. office will close at PERNES 10 AM on 2nd August and will open at tha same hour at MAROEUIL.

5. **ACKNOWLEDGE.**

(Sgd) John W. Leitch, Lieut Colonel,
A/A.D.M.S. 52nd Division.

War Diary

of

/3rd Lowland Field Ambulance, R.A.M.C.(T.)

From 1st August to 31st August 1918.

(Volume 3.)

Sheet I.

WAR DIARY
or
INTELLIGENCE SUMMARY.

(Erase heading not required.)

Army Form C. 2118.

1/3RD LOWLAND FLD. AMB. R.A.M.C.(T)

Instructions regarding War Diaries and Intelligence Summaries are contained in F. S. Regs., Part II. and the Staff Manual respectively. Title pages will be prepared in manuscript.

Place	Date	Hour	Summary of Events and Information	Remarks and references to Appendices
E.1.c.4.4.	1/8/18		Reference Map - France Sheet 51 c.	
	2/8/18		Admitted 8. Discharged -. Evacuated 4. Remaining 36. Revd. J.A. DUKE reported for duty from Army Chaplain's Department. Admitted 2. Discharged -. Evacuated 1. Remaining 46. Unit Strength:- R.A.M.C. Officers 6. A.S.C.(H.T.) Other Ranks 38. Other Ranks 182. -- (M.T.) -- 13.	
	3/8/18		Strength. Detached for temporary duty with A.D.M.S. 52nd Division - 2 Other Ranks A.S.C.(M.T.) with 1 car and 1 cycle. Detached for temporary duty at 52nd Divisional Baths - 3 Other Ranks R.A.M.C. - Authority A.D.M.S. 52nd Division. Admitted 5. Evacuated 3. Discharged -. Remaining 61. x wounded 1.	
	4/8/18		Admitted 1. Evacuated 4. Discharged -. Remaining 76.	
	5/8/18		Admitted -. Evacuated 4. Discharged -. Remaining 90.	
	6/8/18		Strength - Officers -. Lieut. J.C. WILLIS rejoined for duty from 1st Army Artillery School.	

Sheet 2

Army Form C. 2118.

WAR DIARY
or
INTELLIGENCE SUMMARY.

1/3rd LOWLAND FLD. AMB. R.A.M.C.(T)

(Erase heading not required.)

Instructions regarding War Diaries and Intelligence Summaries are contained in F. S. Regs., Part II. and the Staff Manual respectively. Title pages will be prepared in manuscript.

Place	Date	Hour	Summary of Events and Information	Remarks and references to Appendices
E.1.c.4.4.	6/7/18		Admitted —. Evacuated 5. Discharged —. Remaining 95.	
	7/7/18		Admitted —. Evacuated 9. Discharged 4. Remaining 99.	
	8/7/18		Admitted —. Evacuated 1. Discharged —. Remaining 110.	
	9/7/18		Strength. 1 Other Rank A.S.C. (M.T) rejoined from temporary duty with A.D.M.S. (with cycle.).	
			Admitted 1. Evacuated 2. Discharged 7. Remaining 122.	
	10/7/18		Strength. 2 Other Ranks, R.A.M.C. — applicants for temporary Commissions detailed to Infantry Regiments reported on one months probation. Authority A.D.M.S. 52nd Division.	
			Admitted —. Evacuated 9. Discharged 1. Remaining 134.	
	11/7/18		In accordance with instructions from A.D.M.S. 52nd Division, 2 Officers and 2 N.C.Os. reported to 1st Army R.A.M.C. School of Instruction, to attend 10th Course.	
			Admitted 3. Evacuated 8. Discharged 14. Remaining 128.	

Sheet 3

Army Form C. 2118.

1/3RD LOWLAND FLD. AMB. R.A.M.C.(T)

WAR DIARY
INTELLIGENCE SUMMARY.
(Erase heading not required.)

Instructions regarding War Diaries and Intelligence Summaries are contained in F.S. Regs., Part II. and the Staff Manual respectively. Title pages will be prepared in manuscript.

Place	Date	Hour	Summary of Events and Information	Remarks and references to Appendices
E.l.c.l.d.	12/8/18		Admitted 2. Evacuated 7. Discharged 15. Remaining 123.	
			Unit Strength:–	
			R.A.M.C. Officers 6. A.S.C. (H.T.) Other Ranks 38.	
			Other Ranks 182. " " (M.T.) " 13.	
	13/8/18		Strength – Officers 9	
			Captain K.M. ROSS, R.A.M.C., (T.C.) reported for duty from No. 7 Stationary Hospital, BOULOGNE.	
			Admitted –. Evacuated 6. Discharged 6. Remaining 127.	
	14/8/18		Received A.D.M.S., R.1881/8 dated 14-8-18 – Field Ambulance Medical Equipment to be reduced.	Appendix 1.
			Admitted 1. Evacuated 8. Discharged 8. Remaining 126. 9	
	15/8/18		Strength – Officers 9	
			Captain K.M. ROSS reported to 1/5th H.L.S. for duty as R.M.O. – Authority A.D.M.S. 52nd Division.	
			Admitted 3. Evacuated 3. Discharged 4. Remaining 134.	

Sheet 1.

Army Form C. 2118.

WAR DIARY
1/3RD LOWLAND FLD. AMB. R.A.M.C.(T),

INTELLIGENCE SUMMARY.
(Erase heading not required.)

Instructions regarding War Diaries and Intelligence Summaries are contained in F. S. Regs., Part II. and the Staff Manual respectively. Title pages will be prepared in manuscript.

Place	Date	Hour	Summary of Events and Information	Remarks and references to Appendices
E.1.c.4.4.	15/8/18		Received R.A.M.C. Operation Order No 8 – Unit to remain in present position.	Appendix 2.
	16/8/18		Strength - Officers:- Captain R.A. LENNIE, Lowland Field Ambulance, joined for temporary duty from 1/1st 1st Lieut. FARLOW, U.S.M.R.C. – Authority A.D.M.S., 52nd Division. 1/2nd Lowland Field Ambulance, joined for temporary duty from – Authority as above. Admitted 3. Evacuated 11. Discharged 24. Remaining 111. Main Strength:- R. A. M. C., Officer 6. A.S.C.(H.T.) Other Ranks 38. Other Ranks 182. -.-(M.T.) 13.	
	17/8/18		Strength 1 Other Rank (A.S.C.-H.T.) returned to Base for re-classification. 1 — (R.A.M.C.) reported for duty from R.A.M.C. Base Depot. Admitted 18.x. Evacuated 12. Discharged 15. Remaining 123. x Wounded 8. Received A.D.M.S., S.R. 178 dated 17-8-18 – Unit to be ready to move at 24 hrs notice.	Appendix 3.

Sheet 5.

WAR DIARY
INTELLIGENCE SUMMARY
(Erase heading not required.)

Army Form C. 2118.

1/3rd LOWLAND F.d. AMB. R.A.M.C.(T)

Place	Date	Hour	Summary of Events and Information	Remarks and references to Appendices
E.1.c.1.1.	18/8.		**Strength - Officers** Lieut J.C. WILLIS, U.S.M.R.C. reported to 1/6 L.H. Fd S for duty as R.M.O. - Authority A.D.M.S. 52nd Division. Admitted 4 x. Evacuated 12. Discharged 10. Remaining 140. x wounded 1.	
	19/8.		**Strength** 1 Other Rank R.A.M.C. evacuated to hospital sick. 1 Other Rank R.A.M.C. (Q.M.S.) joined for duty from 1/1st Lowland Field Ambulance. Admitted 16. Evacuated 25. Discharged 5. Remaining 148. **Strength - R.A.M.C.**	
	20/8.		1 Sgt. reported for duty from 2/3rd London Field Ambulance. 1 Sgt. reported for duty from R.A.M.C. Base Depot. 1 Pte. rejoins from hospital. Received A.D.M.S. S.R. 182 dated 20-8-18. - Division to concentrate commencing 20th/21st inst. - Unit to stand fast until further orders. - 3 Horse Ambulance wagons of unit to accompany 156th Infantry Brigade on its march.	Appendix 3

Sheet 6.

WAR DIARY 1/3rd LOWLAND FLD. AMB. R.A.M.C.(T) Army Form C. 2118.

INTELLIGENCE SUMMARY.
(Erase heading not required.)

Place	Date	Hour	Summary of Events and Information	Remarks and references to Appendices
E.1.c.4.4.	20/8		Received A.D.M.S, S.R. 182/1 dated 20-8-18 – Times of moves of Brigades	Appendix 3.
			Received A.D.M.S, S.R. 181 dated 20-8-18 – 2 Sanitary Sub-divisions from unit to be detailed for duty on "Corps skin bath", AUBIGNY, (Honorary Divisional R.n. station.) One Sanitary Sub-division, including 2 Officers and 10 Nursing Orderlies to be held in reserve for duty with C.C.S. XVII Corps. Medical Arrangements No.10 also received.	Appendix 3. Appendix 3.
			Informed Headquarters, 156 Infantry Brigade, of arrangements re Horsed Ambulance wagons. Above arrangements carried out.	Appendix 3.
			Strength – Officers } 2 returned from 1st Army R.A.M.C. School Strength – Other Ranks. } of instruction. 10th Course.	
	21/8		Strength – Officers. 1st Lieut. FARLOW, U.S. M.R.C. returned to 1/2nd Lowland Field Ambulance, from temporary duty.	

Sheet 7.

WAR DIARY of 1/3rd LOWLAND FLD AMB (R.A.M.C.)   Army Form C. 2118.

INTELLIGENCE SUMMARY.
(Erase heading not required.)

Place	Date	Hour	Summary of Events and Information	Remarks and references to Appendices
E.1.c.4.4.	21/8/18		Received instructions from A.D.M.S. 52nd Division, to be prepared to move 2 sections tonight, one section to remain to hand over patients and equipment. Definite orders to follow.	Appendix 3
			Received copy - for information - of D.D.M.S. XVII th Corps 8/36 dated 21-8-18, to H.Q. 57th Division. Arrangements to be made for 1 Sect. Sub-division to take over from unit.	Appendix 3
			Received A.D.M.S., S.R. 181 dated 21-8-18 - Corroboration of above.	
			Move:- One Sect Sub-division from 2/1st West Lancs Field Ambulance arrived and took over Corps Skin Centre.	
			A.D.M.S. informed of above, and that bulk of cases, other than skin, have been evacuated to C.C.S.	
	22/8/18		Strength R.A.M.C. 3 Other Ranks returned from temporary duty with 52nd Divnl Baths. 1 Other Rank to hospital - sick	
			Received R.A.M.C. Operation Order No 9 dated 22-8-18 - 1 N.C.O. and 36 Bearers to report to A.D.M.S. Office tonight.	Appendix 3.

Sheet 8.

WAR DIARY
or
INTELLIGENCE SUMMARY.

1/3RD LOWLAND FLD. AMB. R.A.M.C.(T)

Army Form C. 2118.

(Erase heading not required.)

Place	Date	Hour	Summary of Events and Information	Remarks and references to Appendices
E.1.c.4.4.	22/8/18		In accordance with R.A.M.C. Operation Order No 9 – 1 Sgt. and 36 Bearers reported to A.D.M.S., by whom they were detailed to various Artillery Brigades.	
Ref. Map LENS, 36 A2 1/100,000			Received 155th Inf. Bde. Order No 109 dated 22.4. August – Brigade Group will proceed to FOSSEUX area. Bro. hour 10 p.m.	Appendix 3
	23/8/18	02.30	Received wire from A.D.M.S. – 155th Inf. Bde. Group to move at once to SOMBRIN – BARLY – GOUY.	Appendix 3.
Ref. map Sheet 51c.		04.00	Unit left AUBIGNY and proceeded to BARLY. Arrived at BARLY.	
			Received R. of M.C. Operation Order No 10 dated 23-8-18 Unit to relieve 2/2nd North Midland Field Ambulance at GOUY – in - ARTOIS, and conduct Corps Rest Station.	Appendix 4.
			Received A.D.M.S. S.R. 188/1 dated 23-8-18 – Unit to stand fast at GOUY and await further orders from A.D.M.S. – 3 Horsed Ambulance Wagons to accompany 155th Inf. Bde. on the march.	Appendix 4.
			Received wire from 155th Inf. Bde. – Head of Bde. Column will pass through GOUY about 6 p.m.	
			In accordance with A.D.M.S. instructions, 3 Horsed Ambulance Wagons accompanied 155 Inf Bde to destination, and returned to unit.	

Sheet 9.

Army Form C. 2118.

WAR DIARY
or
INTELLIGENCE SUMMARY.

1/3RD LOWLAND FLD. AMB. R.A.M.C.(T)

(Erase heading not required.)

Instructions regarding War Diaries and Intelligence Summaries are contained in F. S. Regs., Part II. and the Staff Manual respectively. Title pages will be prepared in manuscript.

Place	Date	Hour	Summary of Events and Information	Remarks and references to Appendices
BARLY.	23/8/18	1400	Left for GOUY-en-ARTOIS.	
GOUY-en-ARTOIS.			Arrived, and took over Corps Rest Station, including Collecting Post for Walking Wounded, and Entraining Centre for Walking Wounded, the latter being at AVESNES le COMTE. Patients taken over numbered 850 sick and 150 Walking Wounded, the latter awaiting transport to Entraining Centre.	
			Detachment.	
			1 Officer, 1 N.C.O., and four men sent to take over Entraining Centre.	
			1 Other Rank posted to XVII Corps Main Dressing Station for clerical duties.	
	24/8/18		Received R.A.M.C Operation Order No. 11, dated 24-8-18 – 1 Officer and 1 Section of Bearers to be sent to Combined Ambulance Headquarters for duty with 1/1st Lowland Field Ambulance.	Appendix 5.
			Have complied with.	
			Information received from A.D.M.S. 52nd Division, that 3/2nd West Lancs Field Ambulance will take over Corps Rest Station today. On relief we are to proceed to LE FERMONT.	

Sheet 10.

Army Form C. 2118.

WAR DIARY
of 1/3RD LOWLAND FLD. AMB. R.A.M.C.(T)
INTELLIGENCE SUMMARY.
(Erase heading not required.)

Instructions regarding War Diaries and Intelligence Summaries are contained in F. S. Regs., Part II. and the Staff Manual respectively. Title pages will be prepared in manuscript.

Place	Date	Hour	Summary of Events and Information	Remarks and references to Appendices
GOUY-ent ARTOIS.	24/8/18		3/2nd West Lancs. Field Ambulance arrived and took over Corps Rest Station &c. Unit admitted 175 sick, evacuated, and discharged 150. In addition, between the hours of 1600 – 23/8/18 and 2140 - 24/8/18, 1556 walking wounded (including 60 Prisoners of War) were received and fed; 1,485 were sent to Entraining Centre, from which they were evacuated, and 71 were handed over to relieving Ambulance.	
	25/8/18	2100 0100	Unit, excluding detached parties, proceeded to LE FERMONT. M. which was completed, and A.D.M.S. informed. Strength:- 1 Other Rank, A.S.C.(M.T.) to hospital, sick. 1 Other Rank, R.A.M.C. rejoined from hospital. 1 Other Rank, A.S.C.(H.T.) to hospital, sick. In accordance with instructions received from A.D.M.S. 52nd Div. the following were posted from unit:- 1 Sept. Sub. division, with two Officers, to XVII et Corps Main Dressing Station.	

Sheet 11.

Army Form C. 2118.

WAR DIARY
or
INTELLIGENCE SUMMARY.

1/3RD LOWLAND FLD. AMB. R.A.M.C.(T)

(Erase heading not required.)

Instructions regarding War Diaries and Intelligence Summaries are contained in F. S. Regs., Part II. and the Staff Manual respectively. Title pages will be prepared in manuscript.

Place	Date	Hour	Summary of Events and Information	Remarks and references to Appendices
LE FERMONT.	25/8/18		Four Nursing Orderlies to 2/1st C.C.S. 8 Bearers to XVIIth Corps Main Dressing Station.	
			Received R.A.M.C. Operation Order of 12 dated 25-8-18 – Unit will be prepared to move, at short notice, to M.31.c.2.8.	Appendix 5.
	26/8/18	0955.	Received A.D.M.S. W.616 dated 26-8-18 – Unit to move at once to M.31.c. and to get in touch with 155 Brigade. Above carried out.	Appendix 5.
M.31.c.2.8.			Received instructions from A.D.M.S. to move personnel and transport to MERCATEL, and so to establish A.D.S. Above carried out.	Appendix 5.
	27/8/18	0100.	One Officer and 10 Other Ranks sent out to establish A.D.S. at HENIN.	
			Advanced Dressing Station established, and N.C.O. sent out to establish Relay Posts for evacuation of cases from R.A.Ps.	
			A.D.M.S. informed of above, and that it is proposed to move Headquarters of Ambulance to HENIN, in view of shortage of available Officers, of which only two including O.C. are available for duty.	Appendix 5.

Sheet 12.

Army Form C. 2118.

WAR DIARY
or
INTELLIGENCE SUMMARY.
(Erase heading not required.)

1/3rd LOWLAND FLD. AMB. R.A.M.C.(T)

Place	Date	Hour	Summary of Events and Information	Remarks and references to Appendices
MERCATEL	27/8/18		One Officer and Bearer Section, attached for temporary duty with 1/1st Lowland Field Ambulance; also 1 N.C.O. and 30 Bearers of Sub division attached to Artillery Bearers, rejoined unit.	
HENIN.		1300	Ambulance Headquarters moved to HENIN and joined A.D.S. Captain A.M. ROOME, R.A.M.C. joined for temporary duty from 52nd Division M.G. Bn. Strength R.A.M.C. 1 Other Rank transferred to 1/2nd Lowland Field Ambulance. — Authority, A.D.M.S. 52nd Division. Received A.D.M.S. S.R. 200 dated 27-8-18. — 52nd Division to be relieved forthwith and withdrawn into reserve.	Appendix 6.
	28/8/18	0800.	A.D.S. and Relay Posts handed over to 2/2nd Wessex Field Ambulance. Congratulations on work done, received from C. in C. Wounded dealt with at A.D.S., HENIN, during 24 hours ending 0800 - 28-8-18 numbered 180 including 25 Prisoners of War.	Appendix 6.
		0830	Unit returned to MERCATEL.	
MERCATEL			Captain A.M. ROOME rejoined 52nd M.G. Bn. — Authority A.D.M.S. 52nd Division	

Sheet 13.

WAR DIARY
1/3RD LOWLAND FLD. AMB. R.A.M.S.(T)

INTELLIGENCE SUMMARY.
(Erase heading not required.)

Army Form C. 2118.

Place	Date	Hour	Summary of Events and Information	Remarks and references to Appendices
MERCATEL	28/8		Received XVII th Corps Medical Arrangements No 12, dated 27-8-18.	Appendix 1.
	29/8		Received instructions from A.D.M.S. 52nd Division, to move to district BOIRY-BECQUERELLE and establish XVII th Corps Main Dressing Station.	
			Unit moved to T.1.c.5.5 and cleared ground, preparatory to establishing Corps Main Dressing Station.	
			Corps Main Dressing Station established, and A.D.M.S. informed that it would be ready to receive patients at midnight 29th/30th.	
			Strength	
			1 Other Rank R.A.M.C. reported to Corps Rest Station for General duties - authority A.D.M.S. 52nd Division.	
			Instructions received to open Main Dressing Station at 0630-30th.	
			Strength R.A.M.C.	
			Remaining 6 Bearers, attached for temporary duty to Artillery Brigade, rejoined unit.	
	30/8		Received R.A.M.C. Operation Order No 14, dated 30-8-18 - Division to go into line, tomorrow 31st inst. - Unit to remain in present position :- 1 Officer and 2 Bearer sub-divisions to be detailed for duty with 155 L. Infy. Bde.	

Sheet 14.

WAR DIARY 1/3RD LOWLAND FLD. AMB. R.A.M.C.(T)

INTELLIGENCE SUMMARY.

Army Form C. 2118.

Place	Date	Hour	Summary of Events and Information	Remarks and references to Appendices
T.1.c.5.	30/8/18		Received A.D.M.S., M.O./48. dated 30-8-18. - Reference points which have arisen in recent operations, and steps to be taken to meet defects.	Appendix 8. J.M.
		2145	Enemy Aircraft Raid:- During an enemy air-raid, four bombs fell in vicinity of Main Dressing station causing eleven casualties (including 1 death.) including 3 R.A.M.C. personnel of unit.	
			Strength R.A.M.C. 3 Other Ranks evacuated to hospital - wounded (bomb). 1 Other Rank evacuated to hospital - sick. Received XVII th Corps Medical Arrangements No 13.	J.M.
	31/8/18		A.D.M.S. informed that, when 2 Bearer Sub-divisions are out for duty with 155 Bde., personnel remaining will be insufficient to efficiently man Main Dressing station.	Appendix 9.
			Strength R.A.M.C. 1 Officer and 2 Bearer Sub-divisions sent out for duty with 155 Brigade, in accordance with A.D.M.S. instructions. In accordance with instructions from A.D.M.S., 4 Motor Ambulances with Drivers and 2 Horsed Ambulances with Drivers and teams posted for temporary duty with 1/2nd Lowland Field Ambulance.	

Sheet 15.

Army Form C. 2118.

WAR DIARY 1/3RD LOWLAND FLD. AMB R.A.M.C.(T)
of
INTELLIGENCE SUMMARY.
(Erase heading not required.)

Instructions regarding War Diaries and Intelligence Summaries are contained in F. S. Regs., Part II. and the Staff Manual respectively. Title pages will be prepared in manuscript.

Place	Date	Hour	Summary of Events and Information	Remarks and references to Appendices
T.1.c.5.5.	31/8		Strength R.A.M.C.	

1 Other Rank posted for temporary duty (in connection with testing of water for metallic poisons) to 412 & Stirling Coy. R.E. — Authority — A.D.M.S. 52nd Division.

Unit Strength.
Officers 5. } R.A.M.C.   A.S.C. (H.T.) Other Ranks 36.
Other Ranks 181.   — — (M.T.)   12.

Note:-
Details as to work done at Corps Main Dressing Station will be included in next Diary on date of "closing down" of station.

6/9/18

James Young
Lieut-Colonel.
R.A.M.C. (T.)
O.C. 1/3rd Lowland Field Ambulance

Appendix I.

D.D.M.S.,
XVII Corps.

D.M.S. First Army
No. 770/124.

    It has been decided that the articles of Medical Equipment named below are unnecessary in France and are to be withdrawn.
    Will you therefore please arrange for the Medical Units under your administration to return such articles to Advanced Depot of Medical Stores for transmission to Base Depots of Medical Stores.
    Completion of action to be reported to this office.

<u>Medical Equipment to be withdrawn from Field Ambulances.</u>

    Field Medical Panniers.   Prs. 1
    Field Surgical Panniers.   Prs. 1
    Surgical Haversacks.   12.
    Medical Companions.   2.
    Field Fracture Boxes.   3

(Authority - D.G.M.S., No. 129/1 dated 10/8/19.)

H.Q., First Army.
11/8/18.

    (Sgd.) G.S. Parkinson, Lieut-Colonel,
        for Major General,
    Director of Medical Services.

- 2 -

A.Ds.M.S.,
    Divisions.

    For information, necessary action and report on completion of action This equipment should be handed in to No. 33 A.D.M Stores.

H.Q. XVII Corps.
13th August, 1918

    (Sgd.) G. McSheehy, Major for
        Colonel,   D. .D. M.S.

-3-

O.C. 1/1st Lowland Fld. Amb.
O.C. 1/2nd Lowland Fld. Amb.
O.C. 1/3rd Lowland Fld. Amb.

A.D.M.S. 52nd Division.
No. R 1881/8.

    Forwarded for your information and compliance.
    Completion of action will be reported to this office.

14th August 1918

    (Sgd.) A.J. MACDOUGALL, Colonel,
                      A.M.S.
    A.D.M.S. 52nd Division.

SECRET.   *Appendix 2*   Copy No. 6

R.A.M.C. OPERATION ORDER No. 8.
by
COLONEL A.J. MACDOUGALL, A.M.S.
A.D.M.S. 52nd (LOWLAND) Division.

Reference - Army Map "B".   15th August 1918

1.   1/1st Lowland Field Ambulance will remain in its present location till the 155th Inf. Brigade moves, when it will take over the quarters vacated by the 1/2nd Highland Field Ambulance at CAMBLIGNEUL, W.14, and will collect sick from 155th Inf. Bde. in its new area, CAUCHLIN LEGAL.
    This Unit will evacuate sick of Divisional Artillery in ACQ-FREVIN CAPELLE Area from 16th - 19th inst.
    An Advance Party will be sent today to hold the quarters to be taken over, under arrangements between Os.C. concerned.
    A list of stores taken, and handed over, will be sent to this office.

2.   1/2nd Lowland Field Ambulance will hand over Relay Posts of Left and Centre Brigades and A.D.S. to 26th Fld. Amb. of 8th Division. Relief to be completed by midnight, 16th - 17th inst.
    Relay Posts of Right Bde. will be handed over tonight,(15th) to 1/2nd Highland Fld. Amb. reliefs to be completed by midnight, 15th - 16th inst. Main Dressing Station will be handed over to 1/3rd High. Fld. Amb., relief to be completed by midnight 16th - 17th inst.
    On relief being completed, 1/2nd Lowland Fld. Amb. will proceed to GOUY SERVINS, Q.35.d. and take over quarters vacated by 1/3rd Highland Fld. Amb. On arrival at new area 1/2nd Lowland Fld. Amb. will collect sick from 157th Inf. Bde. in the CTATEAU De La HAIE Area.
    Details of Advanced Parties to be arranged by Os.C. concerned.
    Attached bearers of 1/1st Lowland Fld. Amb. will be returned to their Unit forthwith.
    List of stores handed over will be forwarded to this office, differentiating between those handed over to the 8th and the 51st Divisions.

3.   1/3rd Lowland Fld. Amb. remaining in its present location, will carry on the Divisional Rest Station and will collect sick from the 156 Inf.Bde. when that Bde. moves to the AUBIGNY- SAVY Area on 16th inst.
    This Unit will also arrange to collect sick from 52nd Division Artillery located in ACQ-FREVIN CAPELLE Area from 19th inst. onwards.

4.   A.D.M.S. Office will close at MAROEUIL at 9 a.m. on 16th inst. and re-open at VILLERS CHATEL (2 Kilos W of CAMBLIGNEUL) at the same hour.

5.   ACKNOWLEDGE.

                                              (Sgd.) F.W.C. BROWN, Major,
                                                   for Colonel A.M.S.
52nd D.H.Q.   A.D.M.S. 52nd (Lowland) Division.

Appendix 3.

SECRET.

O.C.
   1/3rd Lowland Field Ambulance.

A.D.M.S. 52nd Division.
No. SR 178 d/ 17/8/18

      Until further orders, your unit will be ready to move at 24 hours notice. All surplus baggage should be collected so that it may be dumped at short notice.

      In future no lorries will be available.

H.Q. 52nd Division.

(Sgd) F.W.C. BROWN, Major,
     for Colonel, A.M.S.
A.D.M.S. 52nd (Lowland) Division.

Appendix 3.

SECRET.
A.D.M.S. SR 182
20th August 1918

O.C., 1/1st Lowland Field Ambulance.
O.C., 1/2nd Lowland Field Ambulance.
O.C., 1/3rd Lowland Field Ambulance.

Division will concentrate commencing tonight 20th - 21st August.

(1) 157th Bde. Group to include 413th Field Coy., 2nd Lowland. Fld. Amb. under G.O.C., 157th Inf. Bde., moves via VILLERS AU BOIS - ACQ - HAUTE AVESNES to "Y" Huts and AGNEZ les DUISANS.

(2) 155th Bde Group to include 410th Fld. Coy., moves via VILLERS CHATEL - AUBIGNY Station to HERMAVILLE - HABARCQ and GOUVES, and MONTESCOURT.

(3) 156th Bde. Group to include 412th Fld. Coy., moves via TILLOY les HERMAVILLE on roads junction West end of HERMAVILLE to LATTRE ST. QUENTIN, WANQUENTIN - WARLUS and BERNAVILLE.

(4) M.G. Bn. to NOYELLETTE.

(5) Pioneers to HERMAVILLE.

(6) 1st Lowland. Fld. Amb. marches in rear of 155th Bde. and passes through 155th Bde. Area to LATTRE ST. QUENTIN, where on arrival it will come under command of 156th Bde.

Following stand fast until further orders :-
R.A.   Div. H.Q.   3rd Low. Fld. Amb.

Restrictions as to times of starting will be wired later.

Billetting parties have already proceeded ahead under "Q" arrangements.

(7) O.C. 1/2nd Lowland Fld. Amb. will arrage to collect sick from 155th and 157th Bdes. on their arrival in their new area.
O.C. 1/1st Lowland Fld. Amb. will arrange to collect sick from 156th Bde.
O.C. 1/3rd Lowland Fld. Amb. will collect sick of Divisional Artillery and D.A.C.
Os. C. 1/1st and 1/3rd will send one Ambulance Car each to 1/2nd Lowland Fld. Amb. to assist in collecting sick of 155th Bde.
Horsed Ambulance Wagons will be used as much as possible in collecting Brigade sick.

(8) Medical Arrangements for Moves of Brigades.

O.C., 1/3rd Lowland Fld. Amb. will send three Horsed Ambulance Wagons to Bde. H.Q. 156th Bde. to accompany Bde. on its march.
O.C., 1/2nd Lowland Fld. Amb. will send three Horsed Ambulances to accompany 157th Bde.
O.C. 1/1st Lowland Fld. Amb. will send three Horsed Ambulance Wagons to Bde. H.Q. 155th Bde. to accompany 155th Bde.
On completion of march, ambulances will rejoin their respective Field Ambulances.

(9) Completion of moves and Map Locations in new area will be notified to this office.

Please acknowledge.

20/8/18.
(Sgd.) A.MACDOUGALL, Colonel,
A. M. S.
A. D. M. S.   52nd Division.

Appendix 3.

Wire to 1/1st, 1/2nd and 1/3rd Lowland Fld. Ambces.

SR 182/1   dated 20/8/18

Ref my SR 182 today AAA H.Qrs. of column will not pass line S. of their Bde. H.Qrs. before following AAA Para. I 2215 para 2 2345 AAA Remainder start as follows AAA para 4 2245 and moves via FREVIN CAPELLE to AGNEZ DUISANS AAA Para 5 2400 para 6 2400 AAA D.H.Q. closes VILLERS CHATEL 0800 21st reopens HERMAVILLE same hour AAA Acknowledge.

From   A.D.M.S. 52nd Division.   (Sgd.) A. MACDOUGALL, Colonel,

SECRET.

Appendix 3.

A.D.M.S. SR 181
20th August 1918

O.C. 1/1st Lowland Fld. Amb.
O.C. 1/2nd Lowland Fld. Amb.
O.C. 1/3rd Lowland Fld. Amb.

Reference XVII Corps Medical Arrangements No. 10, circulated herewith :-

Paras. 3 and 5. O.C. 1/3rd Lowland Fld. Amb. will detail 2 Tent Sub-divisions for duty at the Corps Skin Centre, AUBIGNY.

Para 8. O.C. 1/1st Lowland Fld. Amb. will supply 2 clerks, with necessary A. & D. Books and Stationery, to report at Medical Registration Office of the Corps Main Dressing Station. All sick of the Division will be entered in these books and the clerks will furnish the necessary information to Motor-Cyclist from this office for compiling sick returns.

O.C. 1/2nd Lowland Fld. Amb. will similarly supply 2 clerks with A. & D. Books in which all wounded of this Division (including Divisional Artillery) and other Formations (except extra-Divisional Artillery) will be entered. These clerks will supply the necessary information to make up returns.

Note. Each Division records its own sick and wounded and does not record sick and wounded of Divisions represented at the Registration Bureau. These clerks will be sent off forthwith and a report made to this office.

Para. 13 O.C., 1/3rd Lowland Fld. Amb. will hold in readiness one Tent Subdivision, including 2 Medical Officers and 4 Nursing Orderlies for duty with C.C.S.

You will be notified when Corps Main Dressing Station is ready to receive patients. Till then the present procedure will be carried out.

20/8/18

(Sgd.) A. MACDOUGALL, Colonel,
A.M.S.
A.D.M.S. 52nd Division.

Appendix 3

SECRET.

XVII CORPS MEDICAL ARRANGEMENTS No. 10.

1. Medical Arrangements No. 2 (Provisional) are cancelled.

2. Divisional Rest Stations are abolished; a Corps Rest Station will be opened at LIGNY ST. FLOCHEL :-
   (a) To treat slight cases up to 14 days from Field Ambulances.
   (b) To receive convalescents from Casualty Clearing Stations which might otherwise be evacuated.
   Cases of fever etc., should be sent direct to Casualty Clearing Stations in accordance with para 1. D.M.S. Instruction No. 802/16 dated 10/3/18.

3. 52nd Divisional Rest Station, at present at AUBIGNY, will become for the present the "Corps Skin Centre" for Scabies, its sequelae and complications.

4. Present Divisional Main Dressing Stations will cease to function as such; a Corps Main Dressing Station will be formed at AGNEZ les DUISANS. It is to be subdivided as follows :-
   I. Medical Division (for all Sick, gas, N.Y.D. gas, and N.Y.D.N.).
      (a) Receiving, registration and treatment sections.
      (b) Evacuation section (i. For Corps Rest Station.
                              (ii For Casualty Clearing Stations.
                              (iii For Corps Skin Centre.
      (c) Gas section. (i. For Corps Rest Station.
                        (ii. For Casualty Clearing Stations.
   II. Surgical (Wounded) Division.
      (a) Receiving and Registration sections.
      (b) Lying down cases section, with resuscitation, dressing, operating and evacuating subsections.
      (c) Walking wounded section, with dressing and evacuation subsections (to Corps Rest Station.
                                                                            (to Casualty Clearing Stations.

5. Personnel to be detailed as below :-
   (a) Corps Rest Station.   1 Tent Subdivision.
   (b) Skin Centre.   2 Tent Subdivisions.
   (c) Corps Main Dressing Station.
       Medical Division.   1 Tent Subdivision.
                                     1 Tent Subdivision (for Gas Centre.)
       Surgical Division.   1 Tent Division.
                                     2 Tent Subdivisions.

6. Evacuation to Corps Main Dressing Station will be by Field Ambulance Cars. These can be temporarily supplemented during much pressure by M.A.C. on application to D.D.M.S.
   Lorries. In the event of Active operations, lorries will be detailed to Divisions by the Corps.

7. Disposal of cases from Corps Main Dressing Station
   Wounded, Gas, and sick to Nos. 9 and 33 Casualty Clearing Stations except ;-
   (a) All seriously wounded (which included all fractures of the lower extremities and all cases requiring immediate operation) to No. 57 Casualty Clearing Station, MINGOVAL Road.
   (b) All head wounds, fit to travel, to No. 33 Casualty Clearing Station.
   (c) Self Inflicted wounds to No. 12 Stationary Hospital, ST.POL. except as in (a) and (b) which will be transferred to No. 12 Stationary Hospital ST.POL as soon as fit to travel.
   O.C. No. 8 M.A.C. to be notified by Corps Main Dressing Station and by Casualty Clearing Stations by 9 a.m. daily of the number of S.I. cases for transfer to No. 12 Stationary Hospital, ST.POL.
   (d) Gas cases, slight and N.Y.D. Gas Cases to Corps Rest Station.
   (e) Slight sick cases to Corps Rest Station.
   (f) Scabies and skin to Corps Skin Centre, AUBIGNY.
   (g) N.Y.D.N. (which includes all cases of Nervous disorders) to Corps Rest Station, for subsequent disposal to 30 C.C.S. WAVRANS.

-2-

Corps Rest Station will notify O.C. No. 8 M.A.C. number of cases for transfer daily by 9 a.m.
    (h) Infectious Cases (including Dysentery) to No. 12 Stationary Hospital, ST. POL.
    (i) Urgent eye cases to No. 22 C.C.S. PERNES.
    (j) Chinese to No. 11 C.C.S. MOULLE.
    (k) Indian Drivers to Section, Lucknow C.C.S. attd. No. 6 C.C.S. PERNES.

NOTE. Arrangements for eye, ear nose and throat, and dental cases will be subsequently notified.

8. Registration.
    (a) Two Registration Bureaux will be established, one for the Medical Division, Corps Main Dressing Station and one for the Surgical Division, Corps Main Dressing Station.
    Each Division will supply 2 Clerks to each Bureau with the necessary stationery and A.& D. Books of a selected Field Ambulance of the Division, in which each Division will record its own cases.
    (b) Corps and Army Troops, and other Formations will be recorded as follows :-
Wounded :- 15th Division will record all Artillery, other than Divisional.
        52nd Division will record all Other Formations, except as above.
Sick etc. 56th Division will record all Artillery, other than Divisional.
        57th Divisional will record all Other Formations except as above.
    (c) Field Medical Cards for Walking Wounded will be made out at Corps Main Dressing Station.
    Field Medical Cards for Lying down wounded and for sick will be made out at Advanced Dressing Stations.
    (d) A.F. W.3210 will be made out at Corps Main Dressing Station except for seriously wounded cases which may be sent direct to Casualty Clearing Stations, i, which case the A.F.W 3210 and Field Medical Card will be made out at the Advanced Dressing Station and the A.F. W3210 will be handed in to the Corps Main Dressing Station as the car passes.

9. Anti-Tetanic Serum.
    To be given at Corps Main Dressing Station.

10. Blanket and Stretcher Dump. at Corps Main Dressing Station in charge of O.C. Surgical Division.
    Not to be drwn on by Divisions without D.D.M.S. authority.

11. Exchange blankets, stretchers, forceps, Thomas' Splints, hot water bottles etc.
    Ambulance Car drivers must be given exchanges immediately, both at Casualty Clearing Stations and at Corps Main Dressing Station.
    Divisions should use the chit system as far as possible/
    If any difficulty is experienced, A.Ds.M.S. or Field Ambulances whichever is quickest, will report direct to D.D.M.S.

12. Wires.
    A.Ds. M.S. wil arrange for Motor Cyclists to collect the informatin for the daily wires and states from their own clerks at the two central registries at Corps Main Dressing Station.

13. Each Division will hold in readiness I Tent Subdivision (including) 2 Medical Officers and 4 Nursing Orderlies) for duty with Casualty Clearing Stations.

14 ACKNOWLEDGE.

H.Q. XVII Corps,   (Sgd) H. BRAY, Colonel,
19th August 1918.   D.D.M.S.

APPENDIX No. 1 to XVII CORPS MEDICAL ARRANGEMENTS No.10
dated 19th August 1918
----

1. Divisions will supply forthwith as detailed in XVII Corps Medical arrangements No. 10, para 5, personnel as follows :-

    Corps Rest Station   57th Division.
    Corps Skin Centre.   52nd Division.
    Corps Main Dressing Station :-
        Surgical Division :-
        Tent Division.   56th Division.
        2 Tent Subdivisions   15th Division.
        Medical Division :-
        Tent Division.   51st Division.
        I Tent Subdivision.   15th Division.

2. Tent Subdivisions for Casualty Clearing Stations.
       To 7 Casualty Clearing Station by 15th Division - One.
       To 33 Casualty Clearing Station by 56th Division- One.
   To report forthwith.

3. Corps Rest Station will be ready to receive 100 cases from Divisions on morning of 21st August and daily afterwards from the Divisions and Casualty Clearing Stations.

4. Field Ambulances now acting as Divisional Rest Stations will continue to treat and discharge the sick they are at present holding up.
    Medical Division of Corps Main Dressing Station will normally hold up 200 cases.

H.Q. XVII Corps.   (Sgd) H.BRAY.   Colonel,
19th August 1918.   D. D. M. S.

SECRET.

VI CORPS MEDICAL ARRANGEMENTS. No. XIV.
(OPERATIONS.)

PART "A".
(Present Arrangements.)

1. **CORPS MAIN DRESSING STATION.**

    A Corps Main Dressing Station is established at BAC du SUD (Q.32.a.5.0.) Sheet 51c. on the ARRAS - DOULLENS Road, for clearing all casualties from Divisions of VIth Corps on the line. This is administered by a Field Ambulance supplied by the Centre Division in the line (at present No. 3 Field Ambulance, Guards Division)

    Each of the other Divisions in the line reinforce this Ambulance as follows :-
    (a) One complete Tent Sub-division.
        Personnel to consist of one officer and 19 other ranks (to include four clerks, who will be responsible for all Divisional records - vide para. 2)
    (b) Eight Bearers.

2. **RECORDING OF CASUALTIES.**

    A Central Casualty Office is formed by the O.C., Corps Main Dressing Station for the recording of all casualties arriving there.
    The recording clerks, on the arrival of cases, prepare the Field Medical Cards (A.F. W.3118) and A.F. W.3210, and mark the Division of the case on the top left-hand corner of the A.F. W3210. These forms are passed to the sorting clerks who group them according to Divisions, Corps Troops, etc., A.F. W3210 is passed in to the Central Office and handed to the Divisional Recording Clerks, who compile the A. & D. Books, A.F. A36, and A.F. W3185 (Daily State of Sick and Wounded)
    The Centre Division Field Ambulance Clerks (Guards) will also records casualties of all "other formations". Divisional clerks will be provided with sufficient stationary and A. & D. Books, and the order of Battle of their Division. The A. & D. Book will be that of the Field Ambulance selected by the A.D.M.S. of the Division concerned.
    A.Ds.M.S. will arrage for a Motor Cyclist to collect their detail for wires and dily states from the Central Casualty Office
    No cases will be shown as direct admissions to C.C.S.
    The importance of the correct filling in of the Field Medical Cards should be impressed on all concerned, in order to prevent inquiries, etc., being made later.

3. **CORPS REST STATION.**

    The Corps Rest Station at GOUY is administered by a Field Ambulance of the Division holding the Northern (Left Division) Sector of the VIth Corps, front.
    It is utilised for the treatment of sick of the left Division, Corps Troops, and lightly wounded not requiring evacuation.
    Cases sent here for treatment from other Medical Establishments open in the area will have the Field Medical Crd stamped with the rubber stamp of the Field Ambulance sending them, and will be shown as "transfers". Nominal rolls should be sent with them.
    Cases will be conveyed to the Corps Rest Station under Divisnl arrangements.

4. **EVACUATION OF CASUALTIES.**

    (a) <u>To the Corps M.D.S.</u>
        A.Ds.M.S. will be responsible for the evacuation of wounded to the Corps Main Dressing Station.
    (b) <u>From the Corps M.D.S.</u>

        (i) Walking and Lying cases will be evacuated as faras

as far as possible to Hospitals at FREVENT and LIGNY-SUR-CANCHE (distribution as arranged by A.D.M.S., FREVENT.)

(ii) <u>Serious Cases</u> May be sent to DOULLENS or GEZAINCOURT, if, owing to the shorter and easier journey, this is considered desirable.

Should additional ambulances be required as in (a) ammplication for help from the M.A.C. will be made to this office, stating the reason for which these are required.

Owing to the great distance to be covered in transfering cases to the C.C.S. these applications will not be made except in extreme urgency.

The O.C., 30 M.A.C. is responsible for clearing the Corps Main Dressing Station, and such other Main Dressing Stations and Rest Stations as may be opened in the VIth Corps Area to C.C.Ss.

5. <u>DISPOSAL OF SICK AND WOUNDED.</u>

This will be as laid down in VIth Corps Medical Arrangements No. 13.

6. <u>INSPECTION OF GERMAN PRISONERS OF WAR.</u>

A.Ds.M.S. will arrange for the Medical Inspection of all <u>unwounded</u> prisoners of war in their areas. Any found suffering from Infectious disease will be sent to No. 21 C.C.S.

Wounded Prisoners will be evacuated to C.C.Ss. as soon as possible.

7. <u>ANTI-TETANUS SERUM.</u>

All wounded cases must be given Anti-Tetanus Serum <u>before</u> arriving at the C.C.S. and a note made on the Field Medical Card that this has been administered, and dose given.

8. <u>REPLACEMENT OF SPLINTS AND BLANKETS ON AMBULANCE CARS.</u>

These should be replaced with as little delay as possible.

VIth CORPS MEDICAL ARRANGEMENTS No. XIV. (OPERATIONS)

PART B.
(Additional arrangements in the event of Active Operations.)

1. All Corps and Divisional Rest Stations will clear their sick as far as possible, only retaining such cases as could be returned to their units as fit to march, if the necessity for this arose.

2. On receipt of a wire from this office, parties will at once be detailed as follows :-
    (a) By 2nd Division 1 M.O. for Temp. Duty at 43 C.C.S.
    (b) By Guards Division 1 MO for Temp. Duty at 19 C.C.S.
    (c) By 59th Division 2 M.Os. and 19 O.R. (Tent sub-division to 3rd Canadian C.C.S., LIGNY SUR CAUCHIE.

    The aprties detailed above by (a) and (b) will complete those already doing duty with these C.C.Ss., from the Divisions concerned up to the same strength as thatbdetaildd in (c)

    Names of Officers, and hour of departure of parties, will be wired to this office.

NOTE. M.Os. should be specially selected for their Surgical attainments.
    (d) By 30 M.A.C. 1 Dispatch Rider to A.D.M.S. FREVENT.

3. The O.C., Corps Main Dressing Station is authorised to call, if necessary, upon the A.D.M.S. Division or Divisions concerned in heavy fighting, to supply additional Medical Assistance to complete the parties already provided from each Division at the M.D.S. up to 1 Tent Division.

4. A.Ds.M.S of Divisions, O.C. Corps M.D.S. and No. 30 M.A.C. must keep the D.D.M.S. fully informed of any alteration in the situation, or other important matters. A.Ds.M.S. whose Divisions are actively engaged will send by Despatch Rider a short situation report to this office twice daily. This is required by the D.M.S Third Army, so that early arrangements may be made for re-adjustment of accomodation on C.C.Ss. and for the maintenance of evacuation of casualties.

5. <u>DISPOSAL OF WALKING WOUNDED CASES AT CORPS MAIN DRESSING STATION</u>

    Arrangements have been made with the R.T.O. AVESNES, for the provision of accomodation in trains to convey light (Walking Wounded) Cases from AVESNES le COMTE to C.C.S. at FREVENT.

    All cases must be able to walk a short distance, if necessary.

    All such cases will be sorted out at the Corps Main Dressing Station, and, after treatment and recording there, will besent on at once, either in lorries, if avavilable, or in parties marching under an N.C.O. to the Corps Rest Station, GOUY. Here they will be fed and housed (if necessary for the night), but will not be shewn as passing through the books of the C.R.S. All such cases will be shewn at the Corps Main Dressing Station as being "<u>transferred</u>" direct to the C.C.S.

    Should it be found, after arrival at GOUY, that a case does not require evacuation to C.C.S., he will be taken on the books of the Field Ambulance running the C.R.S. as a transfer, and a notification <u>at once</u> sent to the Corps Main Dressing Station, of the fact, so that the records at the latter place may be amended. It is essential that notification is made within a few hours of transfer more especially during heavy fighting, as otherwise the A.F. A36 may already have been despatched from the Corps Main Dressing Statn.

    The O.C. Corps Rest Station will utilise his own transport, and demand additional transport as required from the Corps Main Dressing Station, to convoy these cases in train parties from GOUY to AVESNES.

    Hour of departure of trains, and available accomodation in each will be arranged direct with the R.T.O. AVESNES, (at least 300 cases daily, and up to, possibly, 1000, if necessary, can be arranged).

    Temporary cover for patients awaiting entrainmentat AVESNES is available opposite point of departure of trains. Should cases be sent to the Station at AVESNES before the dinner hour they should be in possession of one day's rations, or the unexpended portion thereof. The O.C., Corps Rest Station will be responsible for the supervision of entrainment. When large parties are sent, a M.O. will always be detailed for this duty.

The O.C., Rest Station will be careful to notify the A.D.M.S. FREVENT, of numbers and hour of arrival of patients there.

6. ADDITIONAL TRANSPORT.

A certain number of lorries have been placed at the disposal of the O.C., Corps Main Dressing Station for the evacuation of Walking Wounded during operations, either to assist in clearing in front of, or behind, his M.D.S. according to circumstances. All applications from ADs.M.S. Divisions for assistance by the use of these lorries will be made to the O.C., Corps Main Dressing Station. The latter will keep the D.D.M.S. informed as to the number of lorries in use and any change that may occur with regard to them. During heavy fighting, lorries (up to 12 in number) may be asked for by the O.C., Corps Main Dressing Station from the S.M.T.O., VIth Corps direct. Should nay further assistance be required for clearing the Corps Main Dressing Station of stretcher or Walking Wounded Cases beyond the above, nd the available Ambulances of No. 30 M.A.C. application will be made direct to this office direct by telephone or by messenger.

7. Attention is drawn to DG2360/136/18, forwarded under my M3036/1/18, dated 5/4/18 - minute 3 of same is cancelled.

8. ARRANGEMENTS IN THE EVENT OF THE PRESENT C.M.D.S. CLOSING.

Should the present Corps Main Dressing Station at BAC du SUD become untenable as such owing to enemy action,

(i) The Reserve Corps Main Dressing Station at WARLUZEL (at present used as a D.R.S. for the Division in reserve) would at once be opened up. The equipment and personnel at the preset C.M.D.S. (see iv) would be moved back to WARLUZEL, under arrangements made by the O.C., Corps Main Dressing Station with the D.D.M.S.

(ii) Stretcher Cases only would be sent to WARLUZEL in the first instance.

(iii) Walking Wounded Cases would be sent by Divisions direct to the C.R.S. GOUY, which would then be opened up as the Corps Walking Wounded Main Dressing Station - all such cases will then be shewn as admitted there.

(iv) One Tent Sub-division (including o;e officer only) will be transferred at once by the O.C. Corps M.D.S. from each of the Tent Divisional Parties (see para 3) at the Corps M.D.S. to GOUY to assist there.

The clerks of the 59th Divn. Amb. at GOUY will record admission for all "other formations", in addition to those of their own division. A.Ds.M.S. will make arrangements for collecting records from this station.

9. All previous Medical Arrangements (Operations) are cancelled.

H.Q., VI Corps,
13th July, 1918
(Sgd.) R.A. HINGE, Colonel,
D.D.M.S. XI Corps.

Appendix 3.

SECRET.

1/3rd Lowland Fld. Amb.
No. SR 64 d/ 20-8-18

Headquarters,
 156th Brigade.

    In accordance with A.D.M.S. 52nd Division SR 182 dated 20/8/18 herewith :-
    3 Horsed Ambulance Wagons under 1 N.C.O., A.S.C.
    These will accompany the Brigade on the march, thereafter returning to this unit.
    The N.C.O. in charge is ordered to take instructions from the Staff Captain 156th Bde.

(Sgd.) JAMES YOUNG, Lieut-Colonel,
R.A.M.C., T.F.
O.C. 1/3rd Lowland Field Ambulance.

Appendix 3.

SECRET.

O.C.,
   1/3rd Lowland Field Ambulance.

     Be prepared to move Two Sections of your Field Ambulance tonight, one Section remaining to hand over patients and equipment. Definite orders follow later.

21st August 1918   (Sgd.) A.J.MACDOUGALL, Colonel, A.M.S.
   1400   A.D.M.S. 52nd (Lowland) Division.

Appendix 3.

Headquarters,
   57th Division.

D.D.M.S. XVII Corps No. 8/36

In confirmation of telephone message.

     Please arrange to send one Tent Sub-division forthwith to take over from 1/3rd Lowland Field Ambulance at AUBIGNY. All sick there except Scabies should be evacuated to Casualty Clearing Stn.

H.Q. XVII Corps.
21st August 1918

(Sgd) C. McSHEEHY, Major for Colonel,
for D.A. & Q.M.G.

Copies to O.C. 1/3rd Lowland Field Ambulance (for action re
     A.D.M.S. 52nd Division.   evacuation of sick)
     XVII Corps "A"

Appendix 3.

SECRET.
A.D.M.S. SR181

O.C. 1/3rd Lowland Field Ambulance.
----

(1)   In accordance with D.D.M.S. 8/36, A.D.M.S. 57th Division will send a Tent Subdivision to take over from you. Receipts for all articles handed over to be sent to this office.
     You will probably <u>not</u> move tonight.

(2)   On return of M.Os. from 1st Army R.A.M.C. School Lieut. Farlow should be returned to 2nd L.F.A.

21/8/18
(Sgd.) A. MACDOUGALL, Colonel,
A.M.S.
A.D.M.S. 52nd (Lowland) Division.

SECRET.　　　　　　　　　　　　　　　　　　　　　　　　　Copy No. 3

Appendix 3.

R.A.M.C. OPERATION ORDER No. 9
by
COLONEL A.J.MACDOUGALL, A.M.S.
A.D.M.S. 52nd (LOWLAND) DIVISION.

Reference Maps 51b and 51c.　　　　　　　　　　　　　22nd August, 1918.

1. **GENERAL.** Evacuation of wounded will be carried out by means of the existing arrangements of the 2/3rd North Midland Field Ambulances, supplemented by personnel of this Division. All Casualties will be sent to the Corps Main Dressing Station at BAC du SUD (Q.32.a.5.0./51c) through the Advanced Dressing Station at M.31.b;2.8./51b. E. of FICHEUX.
　　Walking Wounded Collecting Post is at R.29.d.2.7./51c. on FICHEUX-WAILLY Road.
　　Location of Regimental Aid Posts.

　　1. Front Line　　(Right) S.4.c.9.0./51b.
　　2. 　"　　　"　　　(Left) M.35.a.2.9./51b. (S.W. of MERCATEL.)
　　　　(By Night only) Car Loading Post - M.29.c.2.2./51b.
　　3. Support.　　　(Right) S.2.b5.0./51b
　　4. 　　　　　　　(Left) M.27.c.1.9./51b.

2. **EVACUATION FROM FRONT LINE.** Cases should be carried to nearest R.A.P., thence evacuated to A.D.S. by wheeled stretcher, or hand carriage during the day, or by Motor Ambulance Cars at M.29.c.2.2. during the night
　　Should the troops advance, the O i/c Bearers will be responsible for ensuring touch between the forward (new) R.A.Ps. and the existing ones located as above.

3. **PERSONNEL AND EQUIPMENT.** O.C., 1/1st Lowland Field Ambulance will send two officers and two Bearer Sub-divisions to 2/3rd North Midland Field Ambulance Main Dressing Station at R.15.b5.3./51c. These will be sent forward in Ambulance Motor Cars. O.C. 1/2nd L.F.A. will send a further 6 Cars to 1/1st L.F.A. to assist in this transportation ; on completion, these 6 cars, less one (which is at present on loan) will return to their unit.
　　O.C., 1/1st L.F.A. will send :-
　(a) Four Clerks, A.& D. Books, stationery (including A.Fs W.3185 to Corps Main Dressing Station.
　(b) 90 Blankets, 5 Wheeled Stretchers, to Main Dressing Station of 2/3rd North Midland Field Ambulance.
　　(O.C., 1/2nd Low. Fld. Amb. will similarly send 5 Wheeled stretchers to M.D.S. of 2/3rd North Midland Fld. Amb. as a temporary loan to 1/1st Lowland Fld. Amb.Party.)
　(c) 5 Motor Ambulance Cars to report to M.D.S. 2/3rd North Midland Fld. Ambulance.
The O i/c, 1/1st Lowland Fld. Amb. Bearer Party will be responsible for this equipment.
　　O.C., 1/3rd Lowland Fld. Amb. will send one N.C.O. and 36 Bearers to report to A.D.M.S. office to-night.

4. **SICK.** Sick of Bdes. in Reserve should be collected by the nearest Field Ambulance and evacuated to the Corps Rest Station in GOUY-EN-ARTOIS at P.18.(51c.) by Horses Ambulance Wagons.

5. **APPLICATION FOR PERSONNEL AND EQUIPMENT.** All applications for Stretchers and Bearers should be made to this office.

　　ACKNOWLEDGE.

H.Q. 52nd Division.　　　　　　　　　　(Sgd.) F.W.C. BROWN, Major,
　　　　　　　　　　　　　　　　　　　　　　for Colonel, A.M.S.
Issued at 8 p.m.　　　　　　　　　　　　A.D.M.S. 52nd Division.

SECRET.
                                Appendix 3.   Copy No. 6

155th INF. BRIGADE ORDER No. 109.

Ref. Map LENS, 1/100,000 Ed. 2.   22nd August, 1918

1.   52nd Division now forms part of VI Corps, Third Army.

2.   155th Inf. Bde. Group will proceed to FOSSEUX Area by march route to-night, in accordance with March Table as over.

       Zero hour will be 10 p.m.

3.   Transport will march with units.

4.   On arrival in the new area, a S.O.S. Orderly from each unit will report to Bde. H.Qrs.

5.   Brigade Headquarters will close at HABARCQ and reopen at BARLY at 11 p.m.

6.   ACKNOWLEDGE.

                                      (Sgd.) W.H. BURKETT, Captain,
                              Bde. Major, 155th Infantry Brigade.

Issued at   p.m. through Signals

SECRET.

MARCH TABLE.

Issued with 155th Infantry Brigade Order No. 109.   Ref map LENS. 1/100,000

Serial No.	Units in order of March.	From	Starting Point Place	Time	xx xxxx to Pass.	Route.	Destination.	Remarks.
1.	1/4th K.O.S.B.	HABARCQ.	Road Junction at Bridge immediately S. of HABARCQ.		Zero	WANQUETIN - Road Junction half a mile N. of X in FOSSEUX.	GOUY-EN-ARTOIS.	Usual distances between units, and halts will be observed.
3.	1/5th R.S.F.	HABARCQ & HERMAVILLE.	As for Serial No.1		Zero plus 30 minutes	As for Serial No.1	BARLY.	
2.	410 Fld. Co. R.E.	HABARCQ.	As for Serial No.1		Zero plus 15 minutes.	As for Serial No. 1	As for Ser.No.1	
4.	1/4th R.S.F.	HERMAVILLE	Cross Roads 50 yds. S. of second E in HERMAVILLE.		Zero	LATTRE ST. QUENTIN-HAUTEVILLE-FOSSEUX.	BARLY	
5.	155 L.T.M. Bty.	LE HAMEAU	Road and Railway crossing S. of LE HAMEAU.		Zero	AVESNES-LE-COMTE.	As for Ser.No.4	
6.	218th Coy. A.S.C.	LE HAMEAU	As for serial No.5		Zero plus 5 minutes.	As for Serial No. 5	As for Ser. No.4	
7.	155th Inf. Bde. Headquarters.	HABARCQ.	As for serial No.1		Zero plus 60 minutes.	As for Serial No.1.	BARLY.	
8.	1/3rd Lowland Fld. Ambulance.	AUBIGNY.	Under own arrangements Not to pass cross Roads before 10.30 p.m.		In C.3. North of NOTELLE-VION		xxxxx of	

(Init.) W.H.R.

Appendix 3.

(Wire)
O.C. 1/3rd Lowland Field Ambulance.

155th Bde. Group moves on receipt this order to SOMBRIN BARLY - GOUY
No road restrictions AAA

For information.

From A.D.M.S. 52nd Division.   (Sgd) A.J.MACDOUGALL, Colonel
                                                  A.M.S.

SECRET. Appendix 4. Copy No. 3

R.A.M.C. OPERATION ORDER No. 10
by
COLONEL A.J. MACDOUGALL, A.M.S.
A.D.M.S. 52nd (LOWLAND) DIVISION.

Reference Maps 51b. and 51c.   23rd August 1918

1.   The Field Ambulances of the 52nd Division will relieve the
Field Ambulances of the 59th Division.
     Reliefs will be completed by 5 p.m. on 23rd August 1918.

2.   Relief will be as follows :-
   (a) 1/1st Lowland Fld. Amb. will relieve the 2/1st North Midland
Fld. Amb. at LE FERMENT - R.21.c.8.2./51c. and will take over the
Divisional Sick Collecting Station.
     O.C. 1/1st Lowland Fld. Amb. will detail one Tent Sub-division,
consisting of one Officer and 19 Other Ranks (including 4 clerks
already sent) for duty at Corps Main Dressing Station.
     All Divisional Cases entered in the Corps Main Dressing Station
will be passed through the A.& D. Books of the 1/1st Lowland Fld. Amb.
at the Corps Main Dressing Station.
     Os.C., 1/2nd and 1/3rd Lowland. Fld. Ambces. will each send
one clerk to the Corps Main Dressing Station to relieve two clerks
of the 1/1st Lowland Fld. Amb. already there, who will on relief,
return to 1/1st Lowland Fld. Amb.
     10 Stretcher Bearers of 1/1st Lowland Fld. Amb. have already
reported to Corps Main Dressing Station.

   (b) 1/2nd Lowland Fld. Amb. will take over from 2/3rd North
Midland Field Amb. at R.15.b. /51.c. -
          A.D.S. at M.31.b.2.8./51b.
          W.W.C.P. at R.29.d.2.8./51c.
and will be responsible for collecting from the Regimental Aid Posts.
     One Officer and the Bearers of the 1/1st Lowland Fld. Amb. at
present working in the forward area will, during the present situation
remain with the 1/2nd L.F.A. and be available for duty with the latter;

   (c) 1/3rd Lowland Fld. Amb. will relieve the 2/2nd North Midland Fld.
Amb. at GOUY en ARTOIS/ and will conduct the Corps Rest Station.
                    and AVESNES le COMTE.
     Divisional Sick will be sent to the Corps Rest Station for
treatment, through other Field Ambulances. Attention is called to
Vlth Corps Medical Arrangements No. XIV Para. 3.

3.   D.M.S. Third Army No. 3073/4/65 of 30/8/18 is published for
information and necessary action :- " From receipt of this letter
until further orders, only serious cases os sickness will be evacuated
to C.C.S. of this Army."

4.   Completion of moves will be reported to this office immediately
after taking over.

CAKNOWLEDGE.

Issued at 2.0 p.m.   (Sgd.) F.W.C. BROWN, Major,
                                         for Colonel, A.M.S.
                              A.D.M.S. 52nd (Lowland) Division.

Appendix 4.

SECRET.

Officer Commanding
    1/3rd Lowland Field Ambulance.

The following has been received from H.Q. 52nd Division and is repeated herewith for your information :-
" 3rd Lowland FieldAmbulance will not march BRETENCOURT but will stand fast GOUY await orders from A.D.M.S. AAA   Addressed 155 repeated A.D.M.S.

Three Horsed Ambulance Wagons will be sent by you to accompany this Brigade on the move. These will return to your unit on completion of move of the Brigade.

23/8/18   (Sgd) A. MACDOUGALL, Colonel,
2.0 p.m.   A.M.S.
                                       A.D.M.S. 52nd   Division.

Appendix 5.

R.A.M.C. OPERATION ORDER No. 11.
by
COLONEL A.J. MACDOUGALL, A.M.S.
A.D.M.S. 52nd (Lowland) DIVISION.

Ref. Maps 51b and 51c.   24th August 1918

1.   The Army will advance and allow the enemy no respite in this retreat.
The VIth Corps has been directed on the line QUEANT-VIS-en-ARTOIS.
     This Division will attack at 7 a.m. to-day; 156th Inf. Bde.
advancing on left of 157th Bde. 155th Inf. Bde. in reserve.
2.   O.C. 1/1st Low. Fld. Amb. will send forward personnel and equipment
to form a A.D.S. at MERCATEL in the vacated R.A.P. at M.35.a.2.9./51b.
which will be pushed forward as the advance proceeds. The Ambulance,
less Tent Sub-division at Corps M.D.S. and Party at A.D.S. will concentrate in the vicinity of the A.D.S. 1/2nd Low. Fld. Amb. at M.31.b.2.8./51b
     1/2nd Low. Fld. Amb. will concentrate at A.D.S., M.31.b.2.8./51b.
and push forward personnel and equipment to form an A.D.S. North of
BOISLIEUX AU MONT in the R.A.P. S.4.c.9.0./51b.   This A.D.S. will
later be pushed forward according to the movements of the troops
keeping N. of River COJAUL as far as HENIN.   The Officer and bearers
at present attached to 1/2nd Lowland Fld. Amb. will at once join their
own unit at the combined Ambulance Headquarters M.31.b.2.8. O.C.
1/2nd Low. Fld. Amb. will return all cars, blankets, wheeled stretchers
etc., belonging to 1/1st Lowland Fld. Amb. to that unit.
     O.C. 1/3rd Lowland Fld. Amb. will at once send up, by means of
Ambulance cars, one officer and one Section of bearers, with two day's
rations to report to the Combined Ambulance Headquarters - M.31.b.2.8.
for duty with 1/1st Lowland Fld. Amb. O.C., 1/3rd Lowland Fld. Amb.
will retain one Ambulance car and send the others for duty with
1/2nd Low. Fld. Amb. at the combined Ambulance Headquarters. A full
supply of petrol and two day's rations for drivers will be necessary.
3.   When new A.D.Ss. are formed, patients will be kept as short a time
as possible at the Combined Ambulance Headquarters.
     The present W.W.C.P. at R.29.d.2.7./51c. will be closed and personnel
withdrawn.
     The O.C. 1/2nd Low. Fld. Amb. will be in control of Dressing
Station M.31.b.2.8. till it is closed. He should apply for assistance
when necessary, to O.C., 1/1st Low. Fld. Amb.
4.   Situation reports, giving position of A.D.S.; numbers evacuated
and awaiting evacuation, and demands for cars and other equipment will
be sent to this office every three hours, commencing 9 a.m. to-day.
5.   A.D.M.S. Office will close at 8 a.m. at present Headquarters and
reopen at the BLAIRVILLE QUARRIES, R.34.d.0.0. at the same hour.

ACKNOWLEDGE.

Issued at 6 a.m.   (Sgd.) F.W.C. BROWN, Major,
                                                  For Colonel, A.M.S.
                                      A.D.M.S. 52nd (Lowland) Division.

SECRET.   Copy No. 3

Appendix 5.

R.A.M.C. OPERATION ORDER No. 12.
by
COLONEL A.J. MACDOUGALL, A.M.S,
A.D.M.S. 52nd (LOWLAND) Division.

Reference Map 51c.   25th August 1918

1.   155th Inf. Bde. will cross the line of the road NEUVILLE VITASSE - HENIN through 156th Inf. Bde.
         155th Bde. H.Q. will be in the sunken road at M.35.d. central.
         The general objective of the Division will be towards FONTAINE CROISELLES.

2.   Casualties may be expected at about N.21.,22.,27.; and HENIN and MARTIN Trenches may be used for evacuation.
         In the latter stages, the neighbourhood of HENIN, as well supplied with roads, may be useful as an A.D.S.

3.   O.C., 3rd Lowland Fld. Amb. will be prepared to move at short notice, to the old A.D.S. at M.31.b.2.8. and await further orders there.
         On arriving there, one officer and bearers of 1/3rd L.F.A. attached to 1/1st L.F.A. will come under orders of their own C.O. who will be prepared to use them independently or to assist the other Ambces. Cars of 1/3rd L.F.A. at present attached 1/2nd L.F.A. will come under command of O.C., 1/3rd L.F.A. when the latter has orders to move forward of M.31.b.
         O.C., 1/2nd L.F.A., if in urgent need of Ambulance Cars, should apply to O.C., 1/3rd L.F.A. who will assist with Cars if the situation on the left flank permits.

4.   Owing to a shortage of lorries, empty returning lorries passing the Corps Main Dressing Station will be used where possible under the following conditions - (a) that an orderly, (returning by empty ambulance cars from C.M.D.S.) accompanies each lorry, and (b) that the lorry is not delayed.
         Ambulance Motor Cars should be reserved, as much as possible, for stretcher cases.

5.   Car orderlies will see that splints, blankets and stretchers are replenished from the C.M.D.S.

6.   Os.C. Field Ambulances will indent direct on O.C., C.M.D.S. for dressings urgently required.

7.   Os.C. Field Ambulances are empowered to indent, on the authority of A.D.M.S., 52nd Division, for ambulance cars from C.M.D.S. but this authority will only be used when absolutely necessary, and the cars sent back as soon as the neseccity for them has ceased.
         No. of cars indented for will be reported to this office.

8.   O.C., 1/2nd L.F.A. will send one lorry to O.C., 1/1st L.F.A. and retain one himself.
         Horsed Ambulances should be used in the early stages of the operations to supplement lorries as far as A.D.S., M.31.b.

9.   Divisional H.Q. will be quarted at BLAIRVILLE.

ACKNOWLEDGE.

Issued at 2345.   (Sgd.) A.J.MACDOUGALL, Colonel,
                                                                    A.M.S.
                                         A.D.M.S. 52nd (Lowland) Division.

Appendix 5.

Wire to SEBO.

W 516   adted 26/8/18

Move at once to M.31.b. AAA Get in touch with SEZU AAA Report situation. AAA

From A.D.M.S.   SENO   (Sgd) A.J.MACDOUGALL, Colonel,
                                                A.M.S.

SECRET.

A.D.M.S.,

    52nd Division.

Appendix 5.

O.673/18.
27/8/18.

    The Headquarters of this Ambulance is situated at M.35.a.2.8. - 51.b.

    I have established an A.D.S. at N.33.c.4.4., which is in communication with the Battalions of the 155 Brigade, the R.A.Ps. of which are situated as follows:-

1/4th K.O.S.B.	-	N.34.a.7.6.
1/5th R.S.F.	-	N.28.d.3.2.
1/4th R.S.F.	-	N.27.a.4.5.

    The route of evacuation is very suitable for stretcher-carriers, and horse ambulance wagons can be taken right up to the Hindenburg Line at night.

    Brigade Headquarters is still at N.21.c.4.4. approximate. I propose, owing to the shortage of Officers, to move the ambulance forward, and to join up with the A.D.S. as soon as a suitable site is obtained.

                                            (Sgd) James Young, Lieut. Colonel,
                                                             R.A.M.C.(T),
                              O.C. 1/3rd Lowland Field Ambulance.

Appendix 5.

O.C.
  1/3rd Lowland Field Ambulance.
----

    (1) Move your transport and personnel to MERCATEL.
    (2) Reconnoitre roads and site for A.D.S. on the line HENIN - FONTAINE CROISELLES and establish an A.D.S..
    Report location.

26.8.18
8 p.m.

                                  (Sgd) A.MACDOUGALL, Colonel,
                                                  A. M. S.
                              A.D.M.S. 52nd Division.

Appendix 6.

Wire to 1/3rd Lowland Field Ambulance.
No.   SR 200   dated 27th Aug. 1918

52nd Division will be relieved forthwith and withdraw to reserve AAA 1/2nd and 1/3rd Low. Fld. Ambs. will be relieved forthwith by the 2/2nd Wessex Fld. Amb. of the 57th Div. and on relief will bivouac, 1/2nd L.F.A. in 157th Bde. Area M.34.d; 1/3rd L.F.A. in 155 Bde. area, M.28.d., AAA Till wounded of Division have been evacuated 1/1st, 1/2nd and 1/3rd L.F.As. will assist 2/3rd Wessex F.A. with bearers and cars but should withdraw transport and unemployed personnel to bivouac in 155 Bde. area M.35.a. AAA It will not be relieved by a F.A. of the 57th Division but will close its dressing Station as soon as clear of wounded AAA (2) As Bde. bivouac areas are limited F.As. will park transport so as not to encrouch on other units areas AAA (3) Strict attention will be paid to sanitation AAA (4) Relief to be reported to this office by wire AAA (5) acknowledge.

From A.D.M.S. SENO   (Sgd.) A.J. MACDOUGALL, Colonel,
                                                    A. M. S.

Appendix 6.

Wire to SEBO

No. W 643   dated 27/8/18

Field Marshall the C. in C. has just visited Div. H.Q. and has asked G.O.C. to convey to Brigadiers, C.Os. and every Officer and Man in the Division his hearty thanks for their great work of the past four days.

From   A.D.M.S. 52nd Division.   (Sgd.) A.J.MacDougall, Colonel,
                                                        A. M. S.
                                          A.D.M.S. 52nd Division.

Appendix 6

A.D.M.S.,
   52nd (Lowland) Division.

    The Corps Commander wishes his congratulations on the splendid work they have done during the last 3 days conveyed to all ranks.

O.C.,
   1/3rd Lowland Field Amb.   A.D.M.S. No. MO/32

    For oyur information and return, please.

SECRET.

Appendix 7.

XVII CORPS MEDICAL ARRANGEMENTS No. 12

1. XVII Corps Medical Arrangements No. II dated 23/8/18 are cancelled.

2. XVII Corps Main Dressing Station at BAC du SUD will close at 12 mid-day 27/8/18 and open at BLAIRVILLE (X.4.a.9.5. approx. Sheet 51c) at the same hour.

PERSONNEL.
   One Tent Division 2/2nd London Field Amb., 56th Division.
Attached :-
   Two Tent Subdivisions now at the 2/1st London Field Ambulance at BAC du SUD, via. One Tent Sub-division from the 52nd Division and one Tent sub-division from 57th Division. Each Tent Sub-division to include 4 clerks.

3. EVACUATION.
   1. WOUNDED.
      (a) All wounded primarly to the Corps Main Dressing Station and recorded by the Central Recording Bureau there, see para 3.
      (b) Walking Wounded through Corps Main Dressing Station to AVESNES le COMTE, via Corps Rest Station, GOUY, see Note below. +
      (c) Other Wounded by No. 15 Motor Ambulance Convoy to FREVENT Group (Nos. 19; 43, and 3 Canadian Casualty Clearing Stations). Distribution arranged by A.D.MS. FREVENT.
         Serious Cases may be sent by the shorter route to the GAZAINCOURT Group (Nos. 3, 29 and 56th Casualty Clearing Stations)
      (d) Gas Cases as for wounded i.e. Serious to Casualty Clearing Stations, very slight and N.Y.D Gas to Corps Rest Station as "transfers" to 2/3rd Wessex Fld. Ambulance.

      (e) Self-Inflicted wounds to No. 6 Stationary Hospital, FILLIEVRE
         Corps Main Dressing Station to notify O.C. MAC (15) by 9 a.m. and 2 p.m. daily of number of cases requiring evacuation.
      (f) N.Y.D.N. and all Nervous Disorders to Corps Rest Station, GOUY as "transfers" for subsequent disposal by Motor Ambulance Convoy to No. 6 Stationary Hospital, FILLIEVRES.
         O.C., Corps Rest Station to notify O.C., M.A.C. by 9a.m. and 2 p.m. daily the number of cases requiring evacuation.
      (g) Urgent eye, ear, nose and throat cases to No. 43 Casualty Clearing Station, FREVENT.
   ll SICK.
      (a) All sick primarly to Corps Main Dressing Station, Sick Section. All sick to be "admitted" by Recording Bureau and "Transferred" as follows :-
         Light cases, including Scabies to Corps Rest Station, GOUY (NOTE. This cancels previous instructions that sick will be "admitted" to books of Corps Rest Station.)
         Seriously ill to Casualty Clearing Stations, as for wounded.
      (b) Infectious cases. Recording as for sick. All other than urgent to Corps Rest Station. Corps Rest Station will arrange to segregate and transfer to No. 21 Casualty Clearing Station, WAVANS.
         O.C. Corps Rest Station to notify O.C.15 M.A.C. daily at 9 a.m. and 2 p.m. number of cases for evacuation, stating number and class of case.
NOTE. Dysenteric diarrhoea and persistent Diarrhoea are to be considered as Infectious.

4. RECORDING.
      Field Medical Cards will be made out at Advanced Dressing Stations. At the Corps Main Dressing Station cases will be admitted to and transferred from the Admission and Discharge Books of the Divisions by the Divisional Clerks, "Other Formations" being apportioned by O.C. Corps Main Dressing Station between the Divisional Clerks.

+ NOTE. :- Walking Wounded from Corps Main Dressing Station are not to be shown as "transfers" to Medical Unit, GOUY, but to the C.C.Ss. at FREVENT. They will only be fed and rested at GOUY.

-2-

A.Ds.M.S. will collect information for Divisional States, etc., direct from their Clerks at the Corps Main Dressing Station.

The 6 a.m. and 6 p.m. Casualty Wires will not be rendered by Divisions as the D.D.MS. office will collect this information direct from the Corps Main Dressing Station.

5. Every Cases arriving at the Corps Main Dressing Station must be in possession of either a tally, a Field Medical Card or a Sick Report legibly signed. The O.C. Corps Main Dressing Station will examine any arriving without an d if found not sick send them under escort to the nearest Straggler's Post. A Nominal Roll of such cases to be kept.

6. Anti-Tetanic Serum can be given at the Corps Main Dressing Station but as the line of evacuation is long as many cases as possible should receive it at the Advanced Dressing Stations.

7. Morphia is to be given hypodermically, not orally.
The importance of noting the dose and the hour on the Field Medical Card must be impressed on all.

8. Corps Stretcher and Blanket Dump is at Corps Main Dressing Station.
A.Ds.M.S. will apply at Corps Main Dressing Station and O.C., Corps Main Dressing station will communicate with the D.D.M.S., except in case of great urgency when up to 50 Stretchers and 100 Blankets may be issued, O.C. Corps Main Dressing station reporting numbers to this office.

9. LOCATIONS OF MEDICAL UNITS.

No. 10 Mobile Laboratory.	FREVENT.
No. 33 Mobile (Hygiene) Laboratory.	FREVENT.
No. 19 Casualty Clearing Station.	FREVENT.
No. 43 Casualty Clearing Station.	FREVENT.
No. 3 Can. Casualty Clear'ng. Stn.	FREVENT.
No. 56 Casualty Clearing Station.	GEZAINCOURT.
No. 6 Stationary Hospital.	FILLIEVRES.
No. 15 Adv. Depot. Med. Stores.	FREVENT.
No. 74 Sanitary Section.	RANSART.
No. 83 Sanitary Section.	SUS ST LEGER.
XVII Corps Rest Station.	GOUY en ARTOIS.

10. Nos. 45 and 46 Casualty Clearing Stations will open at BAC du SUD Time to be notified later.
Advanced Operating Centre is now at BAC du SUD.

11. TRANSPORT.
12 Lorries have been placed at D.D.M.S' disposal by the Corps. They are distributed as follows :-
3 at Corps Rest Station to run to AVESNES le COMTE.
2 running from Corps Main Dressing station to Corps Rest Station.
7 at Corps Main Dressing Station.
2 per Division in the line can be obtained on application to the O.C., 15 M.A.C. at Corps Main Dressing Station.

12. A.Ds.M.S. will send in a short report on the situation twaice a day - at 6 a.m. and 6 p.m.

H.Q. XVII Corps.
26th August 1918
(Sgd.) H. BRAY, Colonel
D. D. M. S.

A.D.M.S. 52nd (Lowland) Division No. SR 197 dated 27/8/18.

Appendix 8.

No. M.C. 48/

O.C.,

1/3rd Lowland Field Ambulance.

The following points have arisen in the recent operations:-

1. Brigadiers have complained that (a) they did not know where the A.D.S. was, (b) Bearers did not get in touch with the R.A.Ps. (c) when an A.D.S. was formed, no information was given to Bde. H.Q.

2. In order to meet these defects:-
(a) Each Field Ambulance will attach to the Bde. H.Q. of its group one runner who will have written instructions to report to Bde. H.Q., and will be the connecting link between the Bde. H.Q. and Fld. Amb. H.Q., and if the Ambulance forms an A.D.S., between that A.D.S. and Bde. H.Q., otherwise between the Bde. H.Q. and the Bearer Officer.
(b) O.C., A.D.S. when established, will communicate location of A.D.S. to nearest Bde. H.Q., and to O.C. Fld. Amb. who will report it immediately to this office, with any subsequent moves.
(c) O.C. Bearers will get into communication, as early as possible, with Bde. H.Q. so as to get in touch with R.A.Ps.
(d) This office will communicate to Os.C. Fld Ambs. location of Bde. H.Q. as early as possible and to Bde. H.Q., locations of A.D.S. and Fld. Amb.

(Sgd).; A. J. MacDougall, Colonel,
A.M.S.,
30th August, 1918.   A.D.M.S. 52nd (Lowland) Division.

SECRET.
Appendix 9

A.D.M.S. 52nd Division.
No. SR 207 d/31.8.18.

XVII CORPS MEDICAL ARRANGEMENTS No. 13.

1. XVII Corps Medical Arrangements No. 12 are cancelled.

2. XVII Corps Main Dressing Station opened at BOIRY-BECQUERELLE. T.1.c.5.5. at 6 a.m. 30.8.18.

PERSONNEL.
One Tent Division of 1/3rd Lowland Field Ambulance, 52nd Division.

Attached.
Two Tent Sub-divisions i.e.
1 Tent-Sub-division from 56th Division.
1 Tent Sub-division from 57th Division.
Each Tent Sub-division to include 4 clerks.

3. EVACUATION.

I. WOUNDED.

(a) All wounded primarily to the Corps Main Dressing Station and recorded by the Central Recording Bureau there, see para.4.

(b) All wounded, other than slight walking wounded, to Casualty Clearing Stations, BAC du SUD. When these Casualty Clearing Stns. are not receiving to FREVENT Group.

(c) Slight Walking Wounded Cases will continue to be sent to Corps Rest Station; GOUY, for evacuation to AVESNES le COMTE, where they entrain for FREVENT. These cases are not to be shown as "transfers" to Medical Unit at GOUY, but to the C.C.Ss. at FREVENT.
They will only be fed and rested at GOUY.
O.C., Corps Rest Station will detail a senior N.C.O. and sufficient personnel to supervise the entrainment at AVESNES and will be responsible for seeing that arrangements are satisfactory there and that due notice by telephone is given to A.D.M.S. FREVENT of arrival of trains.

(d) Gas cases as for wounded, i.e. Serious to Casualty Clearing Stations, very slight and N.Y.D. Gas to Corps Rest Station as "Transfers" to 2/3rd Wessex Field Ambulance.

(e) Self-inflicted wounds to No. 6 Stationary Hospital, FILLIEVRES
Corps Main Dressing Station to notify O.C., 15 M.A.C. at 9 a.m and 2 p.m. daily number of cases requiring evacution.

(f) N.Y.D.N. and all Nervous Disorders to Corps Rest Station, GOUY as "Transfers" for subsequent disposal by Motor Ambulance convoy to No. 6 Stationary Hospital.
O.C., Corps Rest Station to notify O.C., M.A.C. at 9 a.m. and 2 p.m. daily the number of cases requiring evacuation.

(g) Urgent Eye, Ear, Nose and Throat cases to No. 43 C.C.S., FREVENT.

II SICK.

(a) All Sick primarily to Corps Main Dressing Station, Sick Section, except all Sick from Divisions West of ARRAS-ALBERT Railway will be sent as direct admissions to Corps Rest Station, GOUY. Former sick to be "**Admitted**" by Central Recording Bureau, Corps Main Dressing Station, and "transferred" as follows :-
Light cases including "Scabies", to Corps Rest Station, GOUY.
Seriously ill to Casualty Clearing Stations as for wounded.

(b) Infectious cases. Recording as for sick. All other than Urgent to Corps Rest Station. Corps Rest Station will arrange to segregate and transfer to No. 21 Casualty Clearing Station, WAVANS.
O.C., Corps Rest Station to notify O.C., M.A.C. daily at 9. a.m. and 2p.m. number of cases for evacuation, stating number and class of cases.

NOTE.- Dysenteric diarrhoea and persistent diarrhoea are to be considered as infectious.

/ 4. RECORDING.

-2-

4. RECORDING.

Field Medical Crds. will be made out at Advanced Dressing Stations. At the Corps Main Dressing Station cases will be admitted to and transferred from the Admission and Discharge Books of the Divisions by the Divisional Clerks " Other Formations" being apportioned by O.C., Corps Main Dressing Station, between the Divisional Clerks.

A.Ds.M.S. will collect information for Divisional States, etc., direct from their clerks at the Corps Main Dressing Station.

The 6a.m. and 6 p.m. Casualty Wires will not be rendered by Divisions as the D.D.M.S. office will collect this information direct from Corps Main Dressing Station.

5. Every Case arriving at the Corps Main Dressing Station must be in possession of either a Tally, a Field Medical Card or a Sick Report legibly signed. The O.C., Corps Main Dressing Station will examine any arriving without and if found not sick send them under escort to the nearest Stragglers Post. A Nominal Roll of such cases will be kept.

6. Anti-tetanic serum can be given at the Corps Main Dressing Station but as the line of evacuation is long as many cases as possible should receive it at the Advanced Dressing Station.

7. Morphia is to be given hypodermically, not orally.
The importance of noting the dose and the hour on the Field Medical Card must be impressed on all.

8. Corps Stretcher and Blanket Dump is at Corps Main Dressing Station.

A.Ds.M.S. will apply to the Corps Main Dressing Station and O.C. Corps Main Dressing Station will communicate with D.D.M.S. except in case of great urgency when up to 50 Stretchers and 100 Blankets may be issued. O.C. Corps Main Dressing Station reporting numbers to this office.

9. LOCATIONS OF MEDICAL UNITS.

No. 10 Mobile Laboratory.	FREVENT
No. 33 Mobile (Hygiene) Laboratory.	FREVENT
No. 19 Casualty Clearing Station.	FREVENT
No. 43 Casualty Clearing Station.	FREVENT
No. 3 Candn. Casualty Clearing Station.	FREVENT
No. 45 Casualty Clearing Station	BAC DU SUD
No. 46 Casualty Clearing Station.	BAC DU SUD
No. 6 Stationary Hospital.	FILLIEVRES
No. 15 Advanced Depot Med. Stores.	FREVENT
No. 74 Sanitary Section.	RANSART
No. 83 Sanitary Section.	SUS ST LEGER.
No. 15 Motor Ambulance Convoy.	
Advanced H.Q.	BOIRY BECQUERELLE T1.c.5.5.
Rear H.Q.	BEAUMETZ Q.23.d.2.9.
XVII Corps Rest Station.	GOUY en ARTOIS.
XVII Corps Main Dressing Station.	BOIRY BECQUERELLE T.1.c.5.5

10 TRANSPORT.
18 Lorries have been placed at D.D.M.S.' disposal by the Corps.
They are distributed as follows :-
3 at Corps Rest Station to run to AVESNES le COMTE.
15 under orders of O.C., MAC at Corps Main Dressing Station.
2 per Division in the line can be obtained on application to the O.C., 15th M.A.C. at Corps Main Dressing Station.

11. A.Ds.M.S. will send in a short report on the situation twice a day at 6 a.m. and 6 p.m.

12. A.Ds.M.S. will detail (except Division running the Corps Rest Station) 1 clerk for duty at the Corps Rest Station.

H.Q. XVII Corps   (Sgd.) H. BRAY, Colonel,
30th August 1918.   D. D. M. S.

1/3rd Lowland F.A.

COMMITTEE FOR THE WAR
MEDICAL HISTORY 4 DEC 1918

Army Form C. 2118.

WAR DIARY
or
INTELLIGENCE SUMMARY.
(Erase heading not required.)

Vol 3 6
140/3027

WAR DIARY
of
1/3rd Lowland Field Ambulance RAMC (T)

From 1-9-18 To 30-9-18

(Volume 3)

COMMITTEE FOR THE
MEDICAL HISTORY OF THE WAR
4 DEC 1918

Place	Date	Hour	Summary of Events and Information	Remarks and references to Appendices

Army Form C. 2118.

1/3rd LOWLAND FLD. AMB.
R.A.M.C. (T.F.)

WAR DIARY
or
INTELLIGENCE SUMMARY.
(Erase heading not required.)

Sheet 1.

Instructions regarding War Diaries and Intelligence Summaries are contained in F. S. Regs., Part II. and the Staff Manual respectively. Title pages will be prepared in manuscript.

Place	Date	Hour	Summary of Events and Information	Remarks and references to Appendices
T. L. C. 55.			Reference Map - France Sheet 51o.	
	1/98		Strength :- Officers	
			Captain & O.C. C.E.W. COE, R.A.M.C.(T.F.) joined for duty from Base	
			Strength :- R.A.M.C.	
			One Other Rank to hospital - wounded.	
			Detachment.	
			One Other Rank, R.A.M.C. attached to 412 Field Coy R.E. for duty in connection with the testing of water for watering ovens	Appendix 1.
			Authority A.D.M.s. 52nd Division	
			Received Report from O/c. Bearers that Relays have been established	
			and stating locations.	
			Notification of above sent to A.D.M.S.	
	2/98		Received Report from O/c. Bearers as to new route of evacuation	Appendix 1.
			A.D.M.S informed accordingly.	
			Received Commander-in-Chiefs congratulations for work done by 17th	Appendix 2.
			Corps.	

1/3 LOWLAND FIELD AMBULANCE. | Army Form C. 2118.

WAR DIARY
or
INTELLIGENCE SUMMARY.
(Erase heading not required.)

Sheet 2.

Place	Date	Hour	Summary of Events and Information	Remarks and references to Appendices
T.1.c.5.5.	3/8		German Field Medical Companion complete, found at A.D.S. not to Medical warehousemen.	
	4/8		Intimation received from D.D.M.S., XVIIth Corps that new Corps Main Dressing Station at U.25 central (Shell 51.b) controlled by 2/2nd London Field Ambulance will open for walking Wounded Cases at 9 a.m. on 5th inst.	
	5/8		Congratulations of Commander-in-Chief again received for good work done by Division.	Appendix 2.
			Instructions received from D.D.M.S. to take out our Corps Main Dressing Station in relief of 2/2nd London Field Ambulance by 1200 on 6th inst.	
			Intimation of above received from A.D.M.S.	
			Strength:- R.A.M.C.	
			One Other Rank to Hospital - sick.	
			Two Other Ranks received as reinforcements from Base Depot.	
	6/8	1030	Corps Main Dressing Station at T.1.c.5.5 closed down.	

Sheet 3

1/3 LOWLAND FIELD AMBULANCE. Army Form C. 2118.

WAR DIARY
or
INTELLIGENCE SUMMARY.
(Erase heading not required.)

Instructions regarding War Diaries and Intelligence Summaries are contained in F. S. Regs., Part II. and the Staff Manual respectively. Title pages will be prepared in manuscript.

Place	Date	Hour	Summary of Events and Information	Remarks and references to Appendices
T.1.c.5.5.	6/9		During the period 3/st August to 5 Sept. both inclusive the following were dealt with at the Corps Main Dressing Station:-	
			Wounded.- Officers Other Ranks	
			90 1861	
			Sick:-	
			19 905.	
			109 2766	
			109 = 2,875.	
			The station was manned by:-	
			Medical Officers 10 Other Ranks - h. Sect. Sub. Divs. 94	
			9 Lowland Brigade Government Rcd.	
			70 3 XVII Corps Rest Stn.	
			Evacuation was carried out by N° 15 M.A.C.	

(A9175) Wt W2358/P.60 600,000 12/17 D. D. & L. Sch S2a. Form/C2118/5.

1/3 LOWLAND FIELD AMBULANCE.   Army Form C. 2118.

Sheet 1

WAR DIARY
or
INTELLIGENCE SUMMARY.
(Erase heading not required.)

Instructions regarding War Diaries and Intelligence Summaries are contained in F. S. Regs., Part II. and the Staff Manual respectively. Title pages will be prepared in manuscript.

Place	Date	Hour	Summary of Events and Information	Remarks and references to Appendices
AL 25	6/9/18	12.00	Headquarters Section arrived and took over our position Dressing Station in relief of 2/2 London Field Ambulance. Completion of relief notified to D.D.M.S. and A.D.M.S.	
			Received from A.D.M.S. R.A.M.C. Operation Order No. 16 dated 6-9-18.	Appendix A.
			Relief of 52nd Division.	
			O/c. Bearers notified of above, and instructed to return on relief with personnel to site of Corps Main Dressing Station and open Headquarters Section.	Appendix
			Strength – U.K.	
			R.A.M.C. Officers 6 A.S.C. (H.T.) Other Ranks 36.
			Other Ranks 181 —"— (M.T.) —"— 12
			04
	7/9/18		Strength Officers.
			Captain R.A. LENNIE temporarily attached from 4/Cameron Field Ambulance, posted as R.M.O. to 1/4 2 Royal Scots. – authority – A.D.M.S.
			Strength – A.S.C. (M.T.) 1 Other Rank – reinforcement received.

(19175) Wt W3358/P.50 6-0,000 12/7 D. D. & L. Sch 32a. Form/C2118/15

Sheet 5

1/3 LOWLAND FIELD AMBULANCE.

Army Form C. 2118.

WAR DIARY
or
INTELLIGENCE SUMMARY.
(Erase heading not required.)

Instructions regarding War Diaries and Intelligence Summaries are contained in F. S. Regs., Part II. and the Staff Manual respectively. Title pages will be prepared in manuscript.

Place	Date	Hour	Summary of Events and Information	Remarks and references to Appendices
11.2.15	4/2	9	Strength RAMC. 1 Other Rank rejoined from hospital.	
			Bearer Sub division rejoined Headquarter Section.	
	9/2		Strength RAMC. 1 Other Rank to hospital sick	
			Exchange of Duties	
			Captain C.H.K. SMITH posted to 1/1st K.O.S.B. in R.M.O. Authority	
			Lieut. I.N. HOSTMILC, U.S.A. posted from 1/1st K.O.S.B. to 1/3 L.F. Amb S.	
	10/2		Nil.	
	11/2		Memorandum on tactical and site lessons learnt during recent	Appendix 5
			operations called for by A.D.M.S.	
	12/2		Forwarded	
	13/2/15		Strength Med.	
			R A M C Officers 6 A.S.C. (H.T.) Other Ranks 36.	
			Other Ranks 181 — " — 13	
			— " — (M.T.)	

1/3 LOWLAND FIELD AMBULANCE.

Army Form C. 2118.

WAR DIARY
or
INTELLIGENCE SUMMARY.
(Erase heading not required.)

Place	Date	Hour	Summary of Events and Information	Remarks and references to Appendices
AL 2.5	14/9	9	Received A.D.M.S. of S.R. 218/7 dated 14-9-18 – Divisions to	
			note the in relief of 54th Division – 1 Bearer Subdivision	Appendix 6
			of our own Corps to be attached to 155th Infantry Brigade	
			Received A.D.M.S, R.A.M.C. operation Order No. 17 dated 14-9-18 –	
			Details of impending relief	Appendix 6
	15/9		Strengths – Arrival	97
			1 L.D. Horsemen attd.	89
	16/9		One Bearer Subdivision under charge of Major W.W. GREER, M.C. (Beaver)	
			proceeded to 155th Infantry Brigade	99
	17/9		Strength – R.A.M.C.	
			1 Other Rank to hospital – sick	
			Received instructions re/part from O/c Bearers	Appendix 6
			Informed A.D.M.S. accordingly	99
	18/9		Received Report of Reply by O/c Bearer to A.D.M.S regarding	
			necessity of temporary relief of Bearer	
			in reference to above. Bearer Sub division from 1/2 Lowland Field Amb	Appendix 6

WAR DIARY or INTELLIGENCE SUMMARY

1/3 LOWLAND FIELD AMBULANCE.

Army Form C. 2118.

Sheet 7

Instructions regarding War Diaries and Intelligence Summaries are contained in F.S. Regs., Part II. and the Staff Manual respectively. Title pages will be prepared in manuscript.

(Erase heading not required.)

Place	Date	Hour	Summary of Events and Information	Remarks and references to Appendices
AL 25	18/9		Advised Unit Bearer temporary	9y
	19/9		Strength R.A.M.C.	
			1 Other Rank to hospital - wounded	
			Received instructions from A.D.M.S. to parade stretcher bearer Sub Division in relief of that of 1/2nd Lowland Field Amb.	
			doing temporary duty	
			hospital unit	9y
	20/9		Strength R.A.M.C.	
			One Other Rank - evacuated for evacuation - reported from	
			1 month's probation with ? Infantry Regiment	
			Strength Unit	
			R.A.M.C. Officers 6 A.S.C. (H.T.) Other Ranks 36	9y
			Other Ranks 179 ——— 13	
			——— (M.T.)	
	21/9/18		Received A.D.M.S., M.O./361 dated 21-9-18 - Evacuation of Wounded	Appendix
			from R.A.Ps.	
			Received Station Report from Rifle Bearers	9y Appendix 6

1/3 LOWLAND FIELD AMBULANCE.

Army Form C. 2118.

Sheet 8.

WAR DIARY
or
INTELLIGENCE SUMMARY.

(Erase heading not required.)

Instructions regarding War Diaries and Intelligence Summaries are contained in F. S. Regs., Part II. and the Staff Manual respectively. Title pages will be prepared in manuscript.

Place	Date	Hour	Summary of Events and Information	Remarks and references to Appendices
U 25	22/3		Strength:- R.A.M.C.	99
			(a) Other Ranks to hospital – neck	
	23/3		One Other Rank to hospital – sick	
			Strength:- Officers	
			2 v I.N.HOST M.R.C. U.S.A. proceeded as R.M.O. to 1/5th R.S.F. – Authority A.D.M.S.	
			Lieut B.C.BOWIE, R.A.M.C. joined for duty from U.K. Authority A.D.M.S.	
			Report asked for by A.D.M.S. as to advisability of having stretcher-handles fitted with pads for shoulder-carrying	99 Appendix 8
			Report forwarded	
	24/3		Strength:- R.A.M.C.	
			One Other Rank to hospital – sick	
			Revised Situation Report from O/c Bearers	99 Appendix 9
	25/3		Strength:- R.A.M.C.	
			One Other Rank rejoined from hospital	

WAR DIARY
or
INTELLIGENCE SUMMARY.

(Erase heading not required.)

Army Form C. 2118.

1/3 LOWLAND FIELD AMBULANCE.

Sheet 9

Place	Date	Hour	Summary of Events and Information	Remarks and references to Appendices
	25.9.18		Received A.D.M.S. R.M.C. Operation Order No 11 dated 25-9-18	Appendix 9
			Regarding impending operations.	
			Received A.D.M.S. B.R. 230/1 dated 25-9-18 — Resumé of	
			Information contained in 52nd Division Intelligence Summary	
			No AF A/1 dated 24.9.18	Appendix ?
	26/9/18		Copy of R.M. & C. Operation Order No 18 forwarded to O/c Bearers	Appendix ?
			with instructions as to procedure to be adopted by him	
			Notification of "Z" Day and "Zero" hour for operations received from	
			A.D.M.S.	Appendix ?
			Copy sent to O/c Bearers	
			In accordance with R.M. & C. Operation Order No 18 — 3 Horsed	
			Ambulance Wagons with teams and drivers; 3 men per ambulance	
			Motor Ambulance Cars with drivers sent to C.O. 1/2nd Lowland	
	2/7/18		Field Ambulance	
			Strength returns	
			I.O.D. Hose received from Advanced Depôt.	

1/3 LOWLAND FIELD AMBULANCE. Army Form C. 2118.

Sheet 10.

WAR DIARY
INTELLIGENCE SUMMARY.
(Erase heading not required.)

Instructions regarding War Diaries and Intelligence Summaries are contained in F. S. Regs., Part II. and the Staff Manual respectively. Title pages will be prepared in manuscript.

Place	Date	Hour	Summary of Events and Information	Remarks and references to Appendices
U.25.	27/11		Received intimation from D.D.M.S. that new hosp Main Dressing Station is being established at J.3.c. (Sheet 57c) by O.C. 149 (RN) Field Ambulance.	
			On instructions of D.D.M.S. One 3rd Sub divison from unit sent to new Corps Main Dressing Station for duty.	
			Notification received from O.C. 149 Field Ambulance that new Main Dressing Station will be prepared to receive Walking Wounded at 1100 today.	
			Three Horsed Ambulance Wagons with Teams and personnel and 3 riders returned from temporary duty with 1/2 Lowland Field Ambulance.	
			Received instructions from A.D.M.S. to send covering Motor Ambulance to 1/1st Lowland Field Ambulance.	
			Complied with.	
			Strength :– R.A.M.C.(T) Officer 6 A.S.C.(M.T.) O.R. 36	
			Other Ranks 174 ―"― (M.T.) O.R. 13.	

Sheet 11.

[1/3 LOWLAND FIELD AMBULANCE]

Army Form C. 2118.

WAR DIARY
or
INTELLIGENCE SUMMARY.
(Erase heading not required.)

Place	Date	Hour	Summary of Events and Information	Remarks and references to Appendices
U.25.	28/9		Transfer of Corps Main Dressing Station to new site in progress.	
	29/9		Corps Main Dressing Station at U.25 central closed down. Number dealt with at this Station are as follows :-	
			Officers Other Ranks	
			Wounded :- 159 2,378.	
			Sick :- 53 1,752	
			212 4,130	
			212 = 4,342.	
			Station manned by :-	
			Medical Officers 8. Other Ranks 4 Sers Subordinates 9 Bearers.	
			20 % from XVII Corps Field Ams.	
			Evacuation carried out by N° 15 M.A.C.	

1/3 LOWLAND FIELD AMBULANCE.   Army Form C. 2118.

Sheet 1/2.

WAR DIARY
or
INTELLIGENCE SUMMARY.
(Erase heading not required.)

Place	Date	Hour	Summary of Events and Information	Remarks and references to Appendices
M.25.	29/9/18		Two Ambulance Cars returned from temporary duty with 1/2 Lowland Field Ambulance.	
			One Ambulance Car - Do - Do - 1/1st Lowland Field Ambulance.	
			Second Sub-divisions sent to new Corps Main Dressing Station for duty.	
			Instruction received from A.D.M.S. to move with details of unit on completion of "clearing down" to J.5 (sheet 57.c)	
			Received A.D.M.S. S.R./234 dated 29.9.18. To be prepared to open new Corps Main Dressing Station at T.20.c.2.9.	Appendix
			A.D.M.S. informed of position as regards clearing of site and establishing new Corps Main Dressing Station.	Appendix
	30/9/18	0700	Details of Headquarters Section less "clearing up" party - left for Corps Main Dressing Station in J.3.c.	
Reference Map.			Trench Map - Sheet 57.c.	
J.3.c.			Transport left at site in vicinity of Corps Main Dressing Station and advance party proceeded to proposed new site of C.M.D.S.	

Sheet 13.

1/3 LOWLAND FIELD AMBULANCE.

Army Form C. 2118.

WAR DIARY
or
INTELLIGENCE SUMMARY.
(Erase heading not required.)

Instructions regarding War Diaries and Intelligence Summaries are contained in F. S. Regs., Part II. and the Staff Manual respectively. Title pages will be prepared in manuscript.

Place	Date	Hour	Summary of Events and Information	Remarks and references to Appendices
F.20.c.29	30%		New unit selected, and party left to take charge, and form a Dump on top of the ridge.	
J.3.c			Headquarters camp formed in vicinity of XVII Corps Main Dressing Station. Acting on instructions of A.D.M.S. two ambulance cars detailed for temporary duty with No.15 M.A.C. Strength, R.A.M.C. 2 Other Ranks wounded - G.S.W. (Shrapnel) - 1 Dies, and 1 evacuated to hospital.	
	4-9-18.			

James Young
Lieut Colonel
R.A.M.C.(T)
O.C. 1/3rd Lowland Field Ambulance

Appendix I

O.C.,
    1/3rd Lowland Field Ambulance.

    R.A.Ps. have been manned and suitable Relays for evacuation established as follows :-

R.A.Ps.
1/4th R.S.F.   " Magog Pill-box" U.21.a.7.1.
1/4th K.O.S.B. .... U.20.b.2.2.
1/5th R.S.F. .... U.20.a.6.0.

These are connected by chains of relays to my Main Relay Post - where I have taken up my quarters - on the Croiselles - Bullecourt Road at U.19d.8.7.   There is another Relay between this one and Croiselles.

Water.
Will you please send a water cart <u>full</u> to Croiselles - with its supply of empty petrol tins. The water cart should be stationed at Croiselles for the purpose of keeping us supplied with water. L/Cpl. Lamb will be stationed at Croiselles A.D.S. for the purpose of distributing rations and water to us.

Candles.
As we are stationed in a deep dug-out will you please send a supply of candles.

1025.
1/9/18
                            (Sgd.) W.W.Greer,
                                O.C., R.A.M.C. Bearers 155th Bde.

P.S.
    The matter of water is urgent please
    A dozen "Walking Wounded " directing pins would be very useful.

Appendix 7

SECRET.

   O.C.,
      1/3rd Lowland Field Ambulance.

      I am now quartered in the Railway Reserve Trench, just where the Railway Reserve crosses the road in U.27.d.
      The Bde. is operating in C.5. (Map 57c.N.W.) and evacuation will be along the Railway Reserve Trench to this point where a Car Post is being established by O.C., A.D.S.

Time 1230   (Sgd.) W.W.GREER, Major,
2/9/18.   A.C. Bearers, 155th Bde.

(Copy to A.D.M.S., 52nd Division.)

Wire to SEBO.   Appendix II

No. W591   dated 4/9/18

The C-in-C visited D.H.Q. yesterday afternoon and wishes his personal congratulations conveyed a second time to every Officer, N.C.O' and Man in the Division for the splendid work done during the last three days.

From A.D.M.S. 52nd Division.
0830
                                (Sgd.) A.J.MacDougall, Colonel
                                                        A.M.S.

Wire to SEBO   Appendix II

W 540   dated 2/9/18

Following received from Corps begins AAA Commander-in-Chief sends his hearty congratulations to troops of 17th Corps on the success to-day AAA Ends.

From A.D.M.S. SENO

(Sgd.) A.J.MacDougall,
Colonel, A.M.S.

Appendix 4.

SECRET.   Copy No. 3

R.A.M.C. OPERATION ORDER No. 16
by
A.D.M.S., 52nd (LOWLAND) Division.

6th September, 1918

INFORMATION.   52nd Division will be withdrawn to-morrow, 7th inst., and will be concentrated in B.2.,3,5, 7 and 8 and in T.30. in Corps Reserve.   156th Inf. Bde will move via BULLECOURT & CROISELLES (clearing BULLECOURT by 0800) to B.2.,3, and 8.
155 Inf. Bde. will move via NOREUIL to B.5., clearing Hindenburg Line by 0800.
157 Inf. Bde. will move via NOREUIL to T.30., following 155 Bde.

MEDICAL ARRANGEMENTS/

1.   (a) O.C., 1/1st Lowland Fld. Amb. will send to 1/2nd Low. Fld. Amb. for his horsed ambulance wagons and will detail one to report to 155th Bde. H.Q. - located at C.6.b.5.5. - also one to 156 Bde. H.Q. at D.1.a.3.2., before each Bde. is timed to move.

He will move his unit to B.3.a. via CROISELLES, clearing BULLECOURT by 0700.
    (b) O.C., 1/2nd Low. Fld. Amb. willmove his unit to U.25.a., but not prior to the move of 157th Inf. Bde.   He will arrange that his A.D.S. with one Horsed Ambulance Waggon follows the Bde. on the march to the new area.
    (c) O.C., 1/3rd Low. Fld. Amb. will send sufficient horses to O.C., 1/2nd Low. Fld. Amb. on demand, to enable the latter unit to complete its move.   These horses will be returned to their own unit on completion of move.   O.C. 1/3rd Low. Fld. Amb. will continue to carry on the Corps Main Dressing Station as at present.

11.   (a) Commencing noon to-morrow, sick of the Division will be treated and evacuated as laid down in " Ammendments and Additions to Corps Medical Arrangements" forwarded under this office No. S.R.201/1 of to-day.   Field Ambulances will render Daily States to this Office by 2 p.m. daily.
    (b) Daily States will show all sick admitted to Field Ambs. - transferred to C.M.D.S. - remaining in Ambulance - and Discharged to Duty.
    (c) O.C., 1/1st Low. Fld. Amb. willtreat and transfer sick of
                                                        156th Bde.
    O.C., 1/2nd Low. Fld. Amb. will treat and transfer sick of
                                                155th and 157th Bdes.

111   On arrival in new areas, all personnel at present attached to Bdes. will be withdrawn. Likewise all equipment lent to 1/2nd L.F.A. will be returned to the Field Ambulance lending same.

1V   In future March formation will be in column of threes - *not* in fours.
V.   Completion of move and exact locations of 1/1st and 1/2nd L.F.A. will be notified to this office.

V1   Acknowledge (Field Ambulances only)

Issued at 2330   (Sgd.) A.J. MacDougall,   Colonel,
                                                                  A.M.S.
                                              A.D.M.S., 52nd Division.

Appendix 4.

SECRET.

O 800/18
6/9/18

O.C.,
   Bearers,
      155th Brigade.

    Ref my O 798/18 of 6/8/18.   The present location of this Unit Headquarters is U.25.central to which site the 20 bearers referred to should be sent.

    52nd Division will be withdrawn to-morrow, 7th inst, and will be concentrated in B.2.,3,5? 7, and 8 and in T 30. in Corps Reserve.

    156 Bde. will move via BULLECOURT & CROISELLES

    155 "   "   "   " NOREUIL to B 5. (clearing
                                    HINDENBURG Line at 0600)
+ 157 "   "   "   " NOREUIL to T 30. following
                                    155th Brigade.

    On completion of Bde. move you will return with the remainder of your personnel to this Camp (U.25.central)

                            (Sgd.)   JAMES YOUNG, Lieut-Colonel
                                                      R.A.M.C., T.F
                         O.C., 1/3rd Lowland Field Ambulance

P.S.   A.D.S. 1/2nd Low. Fld. Amb. will move with Bde. to new
        Area.

A.D.M.S.,　　　　　　　　　　　　　D.D.M.S., XVII Corps No. 6/100
52nd Division.　　　　　　　　　　A.D.M.S. 52nd Divn. No. MO/192

Appendix 5

   Please forward early a memorandum on the tactical and
other lessons learnt during the recent operations, together with
suggestions, if any, as regards improvements in training, organisation
and equipment/

10th Sept.,1918　　　　　　　(Sgd) S. McSheehy, Major,
　　　　　　　　　　　　　　　　　　for Colonel   D.D.M.S.

O.C.,
1/3rd Lowland Field Ambulance.

   Please forward to this office reports in accordance with above as
early as possible.

11/9/18　　　　　　　　　　　(Sgd.) A.J.MacDougall, Colonel,
　　　　　　　　　　　　　　　　　　　　　　　　　A.M.S.
　　　　　　　　　　　　　　　　　A.D.M.S., 52nd Division.

Appendix 5.

A.D.M.S.,
52nd Division.

O. 838/
12/9/18

Suggested improvements in Organization and Equipment.

Ref. your M.O./192 dated 11/9/18.

1. <u>Blankets at R.A.Ps.</u>   The necessity for having a sufficiency of blankets at R.A.Ps. even when on the move should be brought before R.M.Os.   It frequently happened during recent operations that seriously wounded cases were handed over to the Ambulance bearers from the R.A.Ps. with no blankets at all or with one blanket only. This occurred during cold nights.

2. <u>Transport for Bearer Section</u>.   The Bearer Division should be provided with a limber wagon, to carry camp kettles, rations and blankets.

3. <u>Cycle Orderly for Bearer Division.</u>   This should be attached to the O.C., Bearers to enable him to keep in touch with the changing position of the A.D.S. and the Motor Loading Post.

4. <u>Motor Cycles.</u>   It became evident that the Douglas Cycle is ill adapted to withstand the strain of the rough roads in the forward area.   Breakages were so frequent that the communications were seriously interfered with.   It is strongly recommended that the Triumph be issued instead of the Douglas.

(Sgd.) JAMES YOUNG, Lieut-Colonel,
R.A.M.C.,T.F.
O.C., 1/3rd Lowland Field Ambulance.

Appendix 6

SECRET.   A.D.M.S. 52nd Divn. No. S.R. 218/7

Officer Commanding,
     1/3rd Lowland Field Ambulance.

          155th Inf. Bde. will relieve the Right Sector of 57th Division on night 15th/16th.   The Remainder of Division will relieve 57th Division on night 16th/17th inst.
          Attach 1 Bearer Sub-division under an officer to 155th Brigade, details to be arranged direct with Bde. H.Q.   A second Bearer Sub-division will be held in readiness to proceed, if necessary.
          A.D.S. is conducted by 2/2nd Wessex Field Amb. at D.1.d.5.9. from whom information as to the latest position of R.A.Ps. and collecting posts is to be obtained.
          1/1st Low. Fld. Amb. will relieve 2/2nd Wessex Fld. Amb. on 16th inst.
          Brigade H/Q. will be at D.15.b.5.6.

14/9/18.   (Sgd.) A.J. MacDougall, Colonel,
                                                A.M.S.
                                      A.D.M.S. 52nd Division.

Appendix 6.

SECRET.   Copy No. 3

A.D.M.S., No. S.R. 218/9 dated 14/9/18

R.A.M.C. OPERATION ORDER No. 17
by
A.D.M.S., 52nd (LOWLAND) DIVISION.

14th September, 1918

1. **INFORMATION.** 52nd Division (less Artillery) will relieve 57th Division (less Artillery) in front line of the XVII Corps Sector on nights 15th/16th and 16th/17th September.

   155th Inf. Bde. will take over the right Section on night 15th/16th. During 15th inst 155th Inf. Bde. will concentrate in the HIRONDELLE Valley, S.W. of QUEANT and will not pass Eastwards of a N. and S. line drawn through West edge of QUEANT before 8 p.m.

   156th Inf. Bde. will relieve the Support Bde. of 57th Divn. by daylight on 16th inst.

   157th Inf. Bde. will relieve Left Bde. Section on night of 16th/17th under same arrangements, as regards time, as 155th Bde.

2. **MEDICAL ARRANGEMENTS.**
   (a) Locations of Medical Posts.
   Car Collecting Posts :- D.6.d.6.1. and D.9.d.5.2.
   Trolley Posts   :- D.11.d.5.0.
   Wheeler Posts   ;- D.18.b.4.1. and D.12.b.6.0.
   Advanced Dressing Station :- D.1.d.6.8.
   Corps Main Dressing Station ;- U.25. central.

   (b) O.C., 1/1st Low. Fld. Amb. will take over the A.D.S. and Posts from 2/2nd Wessex Fld. Amb. and will be responsible for the evacuation from the Collecting Posts and to the Corps Main Dressing Station. Relief to be completed by 2.p.m. 16th inst. Details of relief to be arranged between Ambulance Commanders concerned.

   (c) Os.C., 1/2nd and 1/3rd Low. Fld. Ambs. will each attach one Bearer Sub-division, under an officer, to their respective Bdes. All details will be arranged between Bearer Officers and Bde. H.Q. concerned. The remaining Bearers of these Fld. Ambces. will be held in reserve.

   (d) O.C., 1/2nd Low. Fld. Amb. will move to a site at C.11.c.7.6. and hold his Ambulance (less the a/m Bearer Sub-division) in reserve - move to be completed by 5.p.m. on 15th inst.

   (e) O.C., 1/3rd Low. Fld. Amb. will continue to conduct the Corps Main Dressing Station.

3. **GENERAL.** Each Bearer will be in possession of a stretcher sling which should be marked with his name and number and should always be in his possession.

   All ranks will salve abandoned stretchers and return them to the A.D.S. in order to prevent a shortage of stretchers.

   O.C., Bearers will see that stretchers sent from R.A.Ps. are promptly replaced.

   All Field Medical Crds will be signed in full - <u>not</u> merely initialled - by the Medical Officer concerned.

4. Owing to the danger of gas during relief, the greatest care will be taken throughout the relief to conceal any extra movement by daylight, especially on the high ground between NOREUIL and ECOUST, and on that immediately on the W. of QUEANT.

   Sections of Field Ambulances will march at 100 yards intervals. The same distance will be maintained between any four vehicles of any description. Closing up must be specially guarded against.

5.   Locations of Brigade Headquarters, after taking over, will be as follows :-
     155th Inf. Bde.   -   -   -   -   D.15.b.5.6.
     156th Inf. Bde   -   -   -   -   C.6.b.4.8.
     157th Inf. Bde.   -   -   -   -   V.28.d.0.0.W

    Position of Divisional Headquarters will be wired to all concerned as soos as possible.

6   Completion of moves will be reported by Os.C.,1/1st and 1/2nd Low. Fld. Amb. to this office. O.C., 1/1st Low. Fld. Amb. will also include a list of stores taken over.

7.   ACKNOWLEDGE.   (Field Ambulances only)

Issued at 11 p.m.   (Sgd) A.J. MacDougall, Colonel,
                                                          A.M.S.
                        A.D.M.S. 52nd Division.

A.D.M.S.,   Appendix 6.   No. B. 23
   52nd Division.   Ref. Map France, 57cN.E.

      Relays of bearers for the evacuation of 155th Bde. to Motor Loading Post have been established as follows :-
1. near the R.A.P. of 1/4th K.O.S.B. at F.19.d.9.5.
2. at F.19.a.5.7.
3. " D.18.d;6.4.
4. near R.A.P. of 1/4th R.S.F. at D.18.d.1.7.
     This is a wheeled stretcher carrier post and casualties are conveyed thence by the road which crosses D.18.d.- D.18.b. thence to the left through D.18.a. to the Motor Loading Post at D.11.c.5.0.
5. near Motor Loading Post at D.11.c.5.0.
6. near R.A.P. of 1/5th R.S.F. at D.17.d.2.9.
     I am stationed in a dug-out 100 yards West along the trench from D.15.b.5.6.   (Brigade Headquarters)

17/9/18   (Sgd.) W.W. Greer, Major
                                        O.C., Bearers 155th Inf. Brigade.

SECRET. Appendix 6   B 26

O.C.,
   1/3rd Lowland Field Ambulance.

       I to-day inspected all relays and found the men very
exhausted, having been carrying through gassed areas along slippery
trenches during the whole night. Having also been informed by
the B.G.C. 155th Bde. of certain active operations timed for to-
morrow night, I decided these men must have a rest, and as the matter
was one of urgency I saw the A.D.M.S. who has given instructions
that 36 Bearers of 1/2nd Low. Fld. Amb. shall report here to-night.
This will give our men a much needed rest, and I anticipate that all
the bearers will be required to-morrow night., particularly if the
trenches are slippery.

1835.
18/9/18   (Sgd.) W.W. Greer, Major,
                              O.C.,   Bearers   155th Brigade.

O.C., A.D.M.S., No. M.O./361
1/3rd Lowland Fld. Ambulance.

Appendix 1

EVACUATION OF WOUNDED FROM R.A.Ps.

The following procedure will be carried out during mobile and semi-mobile warfare by O.C., A.D.S., O.C., Bearers, and Regimental Officers.

A.1.   O.C., A.D.S. will inform this office and all Bearer Officers locations of, and any changes in Car posts.
2.   He will forward to this office any reports sent through the A.D.S. by Bearer Officers.

B.1.   O.C., Bearers will report at his Brigade Headquarters and arrange to live as close as possible to it and will keep in touch with the Brigade Staff.
    He will post a runner at Bde. H.Q. and will obtain a receipt of his presence from Brigade.
2. (a) He will post at least 4 bearers, and as many more as are necessary with each Regimental M;O. and will post relays between R.A.Ps. and Car Posts or A.D.S. as necessary. He will inform R.M.Os. of position of relay posts and repeat the same information to this office.
    (b) He will arrange for a sufficient supply og blankets and stretchers so that the R.A.Ps. are well supplied and will also ensure that stretchers and blankets are rapidly sent up to replenish those sent down.
3.   If short of blankets etc., he will apply to the nearest A.D.S.

4.   Short reports as to the progress of operations should be sent to this office when possible through the A.D.S. stating any requirements. When evacuation is working normally, these reports are not required, except to report any change in route of evacuation, advance or withdrawal.
5. 1.   R.M.Os. will report to O;C., Bearers the location of their R.A.Ps. and any changes or prospective change in these.
    2. All requests for additional bearers and stretchers etc., will be made to O.C., Bearers through Relay Posts and attached Bearers.
    3. R.M.Os. will ascertain from Bearer Officer positions of Car posts and Relay posts.

                                (Sgd.)   F.W.C. Brown, Major,
                                            for Colonel, A.M.S.
                                    A.D.M.S. 52nd Division.
21st Sept.,1918

Appendix 6.

O.C.,
1/3rd Lowland Field Ambulance.   B.45.

    The situation report for the section is as under :-
    1/5th R.S.F. at D.17 central 1 Cpl. and 4 Men
    1/4th R.S.F. at D.16   1 Sgt. " 6 Men
+ 1/4th K.O.S.B. at D.14.   1 Cpl. " 11 Men

+ One of the men at this post is acting as Bde. runner.
The remainder of the personnel have been collected here
(D.15.b.5.6.)

21/9/18   (Sgd.) W.W.Greer, Major,
                                                     O.C., Bearers, 155 Bde.

Appendix 8.

A.D.M.S.,
  52nd Division.

O 914/
23/9/18

      Reference your No. M.O./367 dated 21/9/18.
      Stretchers are rarely carried on the shoulders in this Ambulance, and no padding is used.
      In some cases this mode of transport is advantageous. A pad for issue to each bearer would be better than fixed pads on the stretcher handles, as this would interfere with the hand grip.

                            (Sgd.) JAMES YOUNG, Lieut-Colonel,
                                                R.A.M.C., T.F.

                    O.C., 1/3rd Lowland Field Ambulance

O.C.,
1/3rd Lowland Field Ambulance.   Appendix 9.   B.34.

    The bearers of 155 Bde. have to-day relieved the bearers
of 156th Bde.   The Relay Posts have been fully manned and equipped
and are located as on A.D.M.S. "Locations of Medical Units " which a
accompanied his W.787 of yesterday, with the addition of one relay Post
which has been established at E.13.c.5.3.
    The R.A.Ps. have been taken over ans are occupied as
under :-
  R.A.Ps.   E.13.d.0.8.   -   -   -   1/4th R.S.F.
            D.18.d.2.6.   -   -   -   1/5th R.S.F.
            E.19.a.8.3.   -   -   -   1/4th K.O.S.B.
            E.19.a.1.9.   -   -   -   1/5th H.L.I.

    A diagram shewing position accompanies.

24/9/18   (Sgd.) W.W.Greer, Major,
                                       O.C., 155th Bde. Bearers.

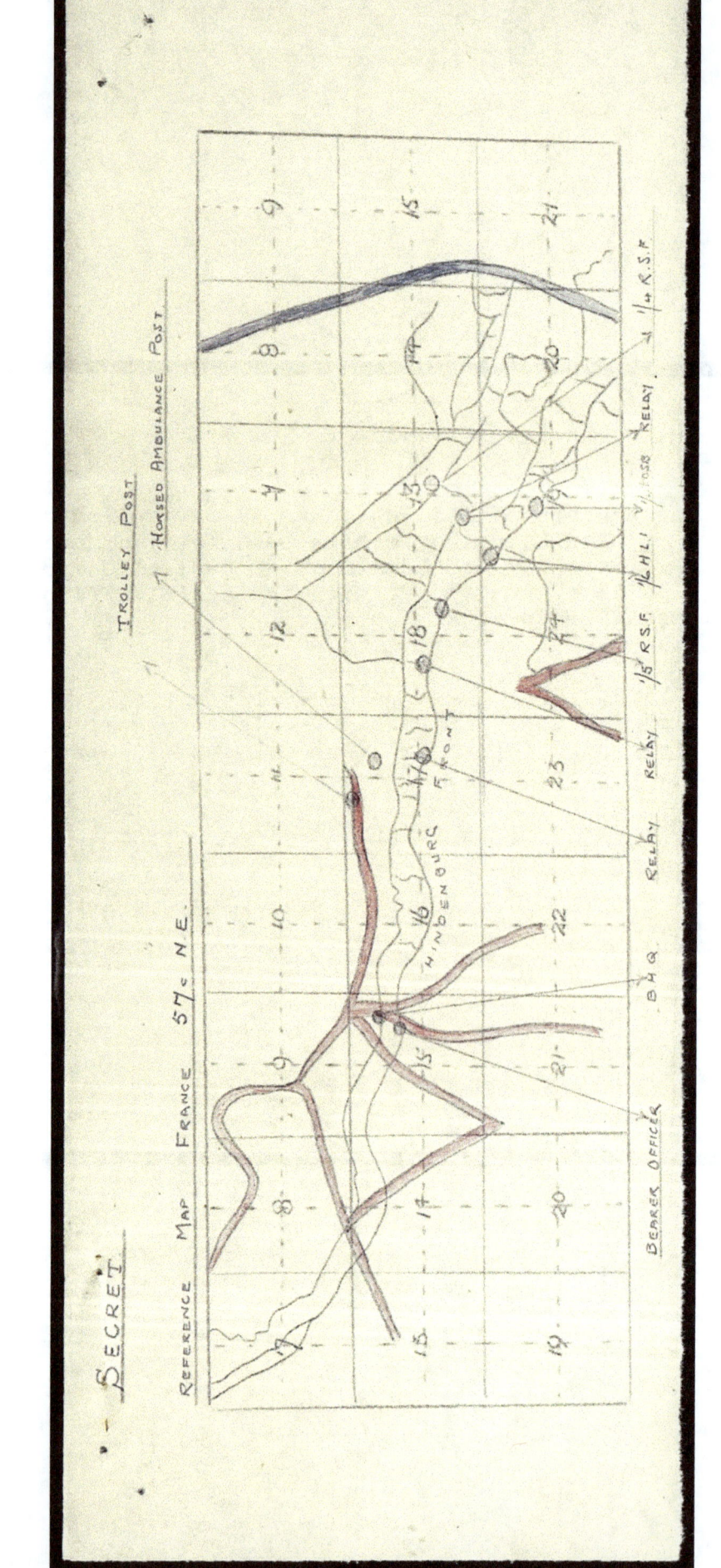

Appendix 9.

Copy No. 3/

SECRET. A.D.M.S. No. SR/230.

R.A.M.C. OPERATION ORDER No. 18
by
A.D.M.S. 52nd (LOWLAND) DIVISION.

25th Sept.1918

Ref. Map 57c.N.E., 1/20,000, and 52nd Div. Order 136.

1. 52nd Division will carry out operations at a date to be notified later.
   The 63rd Division will be on the left, the Guards Division on the right.

II. (a) O.C. 1/1st Low. Fld. Amb. will be in charge of present A.D.S. at D.1.d.5.9. and present Car post.
   He will send one Motor Lorry for Walking Wounded to O.C., 1/2nd L.F.A. on demand.
   He will be responsible for the evacuation of 156th Inf. Bde.

   (b) O.C., 1/2nd L.F.A. will form an A.D.S. at J.9.b.4.1. and a Car Post at J.12.a.2.7. at Zero hour.
   He will hold a Tent Sub-division in readiness to form a further A.D.S. and Car Posts as the Situation demands, reporting sites to this Office and Bearer Officers.
   He will be responsible for evacuation of wounded from 157 Bde. and from 52nd Bn. M.G.C. (R.A.P. - E.25.b;7.3.)

   (c) O.C, 1/3rd Low. Fld. Amb. will conduct the Corps Main Dressing Station and will be responsible, through his Bearer Officer for evacuation of 155th Bde. He will, on demand, place two Ambulance Motor Cars at the disposal of O.C. 1/1st L.F.A., and two at the disposal of O.C., 1/2nd L.F..A. He will also place three Horsed Ambulance Wagons and three Riding Horses at the disposal of O.C., 1/2nd L.F.A.

III Attention is called to my No. M.O./261 of 21/9/18, " Evacuation of Wounded ", forwarded to Field Ambulances, all Medical Officers and Bde. H.Q. These instructions will be strictly complied with.

IV O.C., A.D.S. will be responsible that all Car Posts are marked by a flag or notice board, and O.C., BEARERS that the route for Bearers is indicated by directing posts. When a route is abandoned, these will be withdrawn.

V. (a) Horsed Ambulance Wagons and Wheeled Stretchers will be used wherever possible.
   (b) All ranks will salve abandoned stretchers and blankets and return them to the nearest Relay Post in order to prevent a shortage of stretchers.
   (c) OsC., A.D.S.,Os. i/c Bearers and M.Os. on being relieved by a Unit not belonging to this Division, will obtain a receipt for all blankets, stretchers, etc., handed over as area stores and will send a list of such to this office.
   (d) Field Medical Crds will be signed in full, not merely initialled by the M.O. concerned and will be made out at the A.D.S.
   (e) Morphia will be given Hypodermically - not by the mouth. The dose, and hour at which given, must be entered on the Field Medical Card.
   (f) The advantage of hot drinks with bi-carbonate of soda in haemorrage shock must be remembered.

VI. As directed in my No. MO/361 Os.C. Field Ambs. and A.D.Ss. will forward reports sent by OS.C. Bearers, first reading the report and taking action if necessary, reporting to this office when forwarding the reports what action has been taken.

Os.C., Field Ambulances will render a situation report to this office at 5 a.m. and 5 p.m.

Attention of Field Ambulance Commanders is called to Corps Medical Arrangements already circulated to them.

VII LOCATIONS.

A.D.M.S. Office	D.7.a.5.7.
Left A.D.S. - D.1.d.5.9. closeds at 9 a.m. on 26/9/18	
opens 9 a.m. on 26/9/18 at D.15.b;5.5.	
Car Post	D.15.b.5.5.
Horsed Amb. Post	D.17.b.1.3.
Trolley Post	D.17.a.5.9.
Relay posts	D.17.d.5.8.
	D.18.c.5.8.
	D.18.d.2.6.
	E.19.a.0.9.
	E.19.a.8.3.
Regimental Aid Posts	E.13.d.0.8.
	D.18.d.2.6.
	E.19.a.8.3.
	E.19.a.1.9.
The follow open on ZERO day -	
Right A.D.S.	J.9.b.5.1.
Car Post Right	J.12.a.2.7.
" " Left	D.22.a.9.5.

VIII ACKNOWLEDGE. (Field Ambulances only.)

Issued at 1900   (Sgd.) A.J.MacDougall, Colonel,
                                                          A.M.S.
                                          A.D.M.S. 52nd Division.

SECRET. A.D.M.S., 52nd Divn. No. S.R/230/1.

Appendix 9.

O.C.,

1/3rd Lowland Field Ambulance.

Resume of Information contained in 52nd Division
Administrative Instructions No. A.F. 41 of
24th September, 1918.

---

1. SUPPLIES.

    (a) Refilling Point - - - ECOUST (C;1.d.9.9.)
    (b) Supply situation on morning of Z Day.

        (i) On the man. - Iron Ration and rations for Z Day. Commanding Officers of Units moving forward will ensure that the latter have been distributed to and are carried by individuals prior to the advance.
        (ii) In Train Vehicles ready to deliver to units. 1 Day's rations.
        (iii) In M.T. Company Lorries.- 1 day's rations.

    (c) RUM. An issue of rum will be made to the 72 bearers attached each Brigade.

2. WATER.

    (a) A Mobile Reserve of drinking water is situated at ECOUST in Lorries. Water Lorries may be sent forward to refill water carts as required, on direct application being made to the Water Supply Officer at ECOUST.

    (b) Animal Water Points.

PRONVILLE	D.9.a.2.8.
QUEANT.	D.1.d. central.
NOREUIL	C;10.c.
LONGATTE	C.9.b.
MORCHIES	I.6.c.

3. VETERINARY.

Advanced Collection Station	D.7.a.5.8.
Mobile Veterinary Section	ECOUST.

(Sgd). F. W. C. Brown, Major,
for Colonel, A.M.S.
A.D.M.S., 52nd (Lowland) Division.

25/9/18.

SECRET. 　　　　　　　　Appendix 9.　　　　　　O 935
　　　　　　　　　　　　　　　　　　　　　　　26/9/18

O.C.,
　　Bearers,
　　　　155th Brigade.

　　R.A.M.C. Operation Order No. 18 dated 25/9/18 forwarded for your action where applicable.　As previously arranged you will be directly responsible for the evacuation of the 155th Bde. to Bde. Headquarters and to A.D.M.S. 52nd Division.
　　Duplicates of correspondence will be sent here for recording and for War Diary.

　　　　　　　　　　　　(Sgd.) JAMES YOUNG, Lieut-Colonel,
　　　　　　　　　　　　　　　　　　　　R.A.M.C., T.F.
　　　　　　　　　　　　O.C., 1/3rd Lowland Field Ambulance.

Appendix 9.

SECRET.

Wire to RIPO

No. W 815   dated 26/9/18

"Z" day for the operation will be 27th September AAA   ZERO hour will be 5.20 a.m. on the 27th September AAA   Acknowledge.

Time   (Sgd) F.W.C. Brown, Major
                                       for A.D.M.S. RIKU

Appendix 10.

SECRET.   A.D.M.S., 52nd Divn. No. SR/234

Officer Commanding,
    1/3rd Lowland Field Ambulance.

    You will be prepared to open a new Corps Main Dressing Station (with the two Tent Sub-divisions at present C.M.D.S.) at F.20.c.2.9.   The site should be reconnoitred by you early to-morrow, and arrangements made to have all tentage etc., not now in use at the present C.M.D.S. taken to the new site.
    It is hoped that assistance will be given you to carry out the work of pitching the new Camp.
    It would be advisable for you to move your details to the vicinity of the present C.M.D.S. unless you have by now moved to the vicinity of D.29.d. or J.5.

29/9/18   (Sgd.) A.J. MacDougall, Colonel,
1830   A.M.S.
                                                A.D.M.S., 52nd Division.

SECRET.   Appendix 10.   O 955
                                                   29/9/18

A.D.M.S.,
    52nd Division.

        Ref. your SR/234 dated 29/9/18. I have now 16 other
ranks left and with these I will commence the preparation of the
new C.M.D.S. to-morrow. As a proportion of these consist of
clerks, cooks, sanitary personnel, batmen, etc., I shall be
glad of the help of other personnel to-morrow if this is possible.
        There is still a considerable amount of equipment
to move from this site and this will entail leaving some personnel
behind.

29/9/18   (Sgd.) JAMES YOUNG, Lieut-Colonel,
                                          R.A.M.C., T.F.
                                   O.C., 1/3rd Lowland Field Ambulance.

Army Form C. 2118.

WAR DIARY
or
INTELLIGENCE SUMMARY.
(Erase heading not required.)

Vol 7

40/3400/

Summary of Events and Information

Confidential

War Diary

of

1/3rd Lowland Field Ambulance, R.A.M.C.(T.)

From 1st October 1918.

To 31st October 1918.

Volume III.

Place	Date	Hour		Remarks and references to Appendices
	Oct. 1918			

WAR DIARY
INTELLIGENCE SUMMARY
(Erase heading not required.)

1/3 LOWLAND FIELD AMBULANCE.

Army Form C. 2118.

Sheet 1.

Place	Date	Hour	Summary of Events and Information	Remarks and references to Appendices
			Reference Map Sheet 57c (France).	
T.3.c.	1-10-18		Strength R.A.M.C.	
			One other rank to hospital sick.	
			One other rank admitted to hospital sick, while on U.K. leave, and struck off the strength.	
			Received R.A.M.C. Operation Order No. 19 dated 1-10-18 – Relief of 63rd (R.N.) Division. Unit to remain in present position. Three horsed ambulance wagons and two motor ambulance cars from unit to be placed at disposal of O.C. 1/2nd Lowland Field Ambulance.	
			Copy of above sent to O/C Bearer.	
			In accordance with above, 3 horsed ambulance wagons and 2 motor ambulance cars sent for temporary duty to 1/2nd Lowland Field Ambulance.	
			In accordance with instructions of A.D.M.S. 52nd Division, 2 motor ambulance cars sent to O.C. 15 M. A.C. for temporary duty.	JM
	2-10-18		Nil.	JM

1/3 LOWLAND FIELD AMBULANCE

Army Form C. 2118.

WAR DIARY or INTELLIGENCE SUMMARY

(Erase heading not required.)

Sheet 2.

Instructions regarding War Diaries and Intelligence Summaries are contained in F. S. Regs., Part II. and the Staff Manual respectively. Title pages will be prepared in manuscript.

Place	Date	Hour	Summary of Events and Information	Remarks and references to Appendices
T.3.c.	3-10-18		Nil.	94
	4-10-18		Strength R.A.M.C. One other rank to hospital, wounded.	94
	5-10-18		Strength Officer Captain D.F. BROWN joined for duty. Received A.D.M.S. W. 950. - Warning Order - Unit to be prepared to move at 2 hours' notice. A.D.M.S. requested to arrange for return of detached personnel in order to make above order practicable. Strength - Nil. R.A.M.C. - Officers 6 A.S.C. (H.T.) Other Ranks 36 Other Ranks 173. -"- (M.T.) -"- 13	M.
	6-10-18		Received R.A.M.C. 6 Operation Order No 20 dated 6-10-18 - Division to concentrate today in area W. of NORD CANAL, prior to entrainment at VAUX VRAUCOURT tomorrow. Bearer Section to rejoin unit H.Q. O/C Bearers instructed to inform mounted section on relief.	

(A9173) Wt W2158/P560 60,000 12/17 D. D. & L. Sch 52a. Form/C2118/15

1/3 LOWLAND
FIELD
AMBULANCE

Army Form C. 2118.

Sheet 3.

WAR DIARY
or
INTELLIGENCE SUMMARY
(Erase heading not required.)

Instructions regarding War Diaries and Intelligence Summaries are contained in F. S. Regs., Part II. and the Staff Manual respectively. Title pages will be prepared in manuscript.

Place	Date	Hour	Summary of Events and Information	Remarks and references to Appendices
J.3.c.	6-10-18		Acting on instructions of D.D.M.S. XVIII th Corps, Walking Wounded Gateway Cents closed down and personnel withdrawn.	
			Received A.D.M.S. M.O./542 dated 6-10-18 — Division to move to VIII th Corps area — Unit to entrain at LIGNY.	
			Strength R.A.M.C.	
			Two other ranks evacuated wounded.	
			" " " sick	
			Bearer Sub. division rejoined unit H.Q.	
			A.D.M.S. informed thereof.	
			On instructions of D.D.M.S. XVIII th Corps — "Holding Party" at site of proposed new 6 M.D.S. withdrawn.	
			Two Sergts Sub-division with 3 Officers, reverted from temporary duty at 6 M.D.S.	
			Received 155 Brigade Order No. 125 of 7-10-18 — Time and route of starting.	
	7-10-18	14.00	Unit left for entraining station.	

Sheet 4.

WAR DIARY
or
INTELLIGENCE SUMMARY.
(Erase heading not required.)

Army Form C. 2118.

1/3 LOWLAND FIELD AMBULANCE

Place	Date	Hour	Summary of Events and Information	Remarks and references to Appendices
VAUX VRAU- COURT.	7-10-18	1815.	Entrained for LIGNY.	94
LIGNY.	8-10-18	0100	Detrained, and proceeded by march route for billets in AMBRINES. Reference Map Sheet 11 - F.3.	
AMBRINES.			at 12.30 O.C. informed of completion of move.	
			Special Order of the Day issued to unit by C.O.	Appendix.
			Strength R.A.M.C.	M
	9-10-18		One other rank to hospital, sick.	
			Strength Officers	
			In accordance with A.D.M.S. instructions, Captain W.E.K.COLES. detailed for temporary duty with 242 Army Brigade, R.F.A.	
			Strength R.A.M.C.	
			One Sgt returned from months probation with Infantry Battalion.	
			Strength A.S.E. (H.T.)	
	10-10-18		One other rank admitted to hospital while on U.K. leave.	94
			Strength Officers	
	11-11-18		Lieut W.H.CAINE, M.R.C., U.S.A, joined for duty from 1/2 K.F.D.	94
			Strength R.A.M.C. - One Other Rank rejoined from temporary duty with 412th Bay R.E.	94

Sheet 5.

Army Form C. 2118.

1/3 LOWLAND
FIELD
AMBULANCE.

WAR DIARY
or
INTELLIGENCE SUMMARY
(Erase heading not required.)

Instructions regarding War Diaries and Intelligence Summaries are contained in F. S. Regs., Part II. and the Staff Manual respectively. Title pages will be prepared in manuscript.

Place	Date	Hour	Summary of Events and Information	Remarks and references to Appendices
AMBRINES	12-10-18		Strength R.A.M.C.	
			One other rank to hospital sick.	
			Strength Officers	
			Lieut. W. H. CAINE, M.R.C., U.S.A., detailed for duty with 48th Brigade	
			Army Bells Attery. - Authority A.D.M.S.	
			Received instruction from A.D.M.S. to detail M.O. for temporary duty	
			at 52nd Divisional Reception Camp. Duties to include supervision	
			of graduated physical training of men discharged from hospital.	
			MAJOR R. G. WALKER detailed in accordance with above.	
			Reinforcements - 4 Other Ranks received.	
			Strength - thus.	
			R.A.M.C. Officers 8. — A.S.C. (H.T.) Other Ranks 35.	
			Other Ranks 172. —— (M.T.) 13	
	13-10-18		A.D.M.S. informed that training not being carried out at Reception	
			Camp owing to	
			Major R. G. WALKER, M.C. withdrawn — Authority A.D.M.S.	

Sheet 6.

1/3 LOWLAND
FIELD
AMBULANCE.

Army Form C. 2118.

WAR DIARY
or
INTELLIGENCE SUMMARY.
(Erase heading not required.)

Instructions regarding War Diaries and Intelligence Summaries are contained in F. S. Regs., Part II. and the Staff Manual respectively. Title pages will be prepared in manuscript.

Place	Date	Hour	Summary of Events and Information	Remarks and references to Appendices
AMBRINES	13-10-18		Received instructions from A.D.M.S. to find a Sub-division, with 1 Officer to take over VIII th Corps Skin Centre.	
	14-10-18		Above complied with. Additional 6 personnel, and 1 Sections equipment sent to VIII Ch Corps Skin Centre. Strength, R.A.M.C. Two Other Ranks to hospital, sick.	
	15-10-18		One Other Rank sent for duty at VIII Corps Skin Centre. One Other Rank to hospital sick.	
	16/10/18		One Other Rank returned from abroad duties with XVIII th Corps Rest Station. One Other Rank to hospital, sick. In accordance with A.D.M.S. instructions, 3 other ranks (specialists) sent to VIII Corps Rest Station for temporary duty; also one other rank A.S.C. (M.T.) as motor cyclist. Lieut D.C. BOWIE detailed to take over medical and sanitary supervision	

Sheet 7.

WAR DIARY
or
INTELLIGENCE SUMMARY
(Erase heading not required.)

Army Form C. 2118.

1/3 LOWLAND FIELD AMBULANCE.

Instructions regarding War Diaries and Intelligence Summaries are contained in F. S. Regs., Part II. and the Staff Manual respectively. Title pages will be prepared in manuscript.

Place	Date	Hour	Summary of Events and Information	Remarks and references to Appendices
AMBRINES	18/7/17		of 1/4th & 1/4th Royal Scots. Additional 3 other ranks sent for duty at VIII Corps skin Centre.	9h
	18/7/17		8 trap th R.A.M.C. One other rank rejoined from hospital. In accordance with A.D.M.S. instructions, one other rank (Syk) A.S.C.(H.T.) and one other rank R.A.M.C. (Specialist) sent for duty to VIII Corps Rest Station. Notification of award of Military Medal to the following received R.A.M.C. Other Ranks 6. A.S.C. (M.T.) Other Ranks 1.	Appendix 2.
			Received A.D.M.S. W.39 - Warning Order. - Division placed at disposal of VIII Corps, and will probably move tomorrow to HENIN LIETARD. Received R.A.M.C. Operation Order No. 20. - Unit to proceed with 155 Brigade tomorrow. Received 155 Brigade Order No. 126 - Route and time of starting.	9h
	19/7/17		Strength R.A.M.C. Four other ranks to hospital sick.	

Sheet 8.

WAR DIARY
or
INTELLIGENCE SUMMARY.
(Erase heading not required.)

1/3 LOWLAND FIELD AMBULANCE.

Army Form C. 2118.

Place	Date	Hour	Summary of Events and Information	Remarks and references to Appendices
AMBRINES	19/10/18		Unit left for entraining station – TINCQUES.	9m
	19/10/18	1405	Unit entrained for BULLY GRENAY.	
BULLY GRENAY	Ref. map sheet 44.S.L	2000	Unit detrained, and proceeded by march route to LIEVIN.	
(J.1.) LIEVIN		2200	Arrived and took over billets.	
			Location notified to A.D.M.S.	
			Received A.D.M.S., S.R. 5 of 19-10-18 – Moves to be continued tomorrow. Unit to move under Brigade arrangements to FOUQUIERES.	9m
			Received 153 Brigade Order No. 124 – Details for tomorrow's move	
LIEVIN	20/10/18	1000	Unit moved with 155 Brigade to FOUQUIERES, and took over billets.	9m
			Hospital accommodation arranged for.	
	21/10/18		Arrival strength.	9m
			One H.D. have evacuated sick.	
	22/10/18		One Cpl sub. division, two officers sent for temporary to I.F. 42 C.C.S. DOUAI. – Authority A.D.M.S.	9m
			Received instructions from A.D.M.S. to move to AUBY, under Brigade	

Sheet 9.

1/3 LOWLAND FIELD AMBULANCE.

Army Form C. 2118.

WAR DIARY
or
INTELLIGENCE SUMMARY.
(Erase heading not required.)

Instructions regarding War Diaries and Intelligence Summaries are contained in F. S. Regs., Part II. and the Staff Manual respectively. Title pages will be prepared in manuscript.

Place	Date	Hour	Summary of Events and Information	Remarks and references to Appendices
(R.1) FOUQUERES	22/11/18		Arrangements and take over MAIRIE there as hospital site. Received instructions to time & place of starting from 155 Brigade.	
		1300	Advance party left for AUBY.	
(A.2) AUBY		1500	Arrived and occupied MAIRIE and adjacent billets. Hospital established.	
		2050	Received A.D.M.S. Warning Order – Division will march on 24th inst. and concentrate in FLINES area. Strength RAME. One other rank returned from hospital.	
	23/11/18	0220	Received instructions from A.D.M.S. 52nd Division, to send all motor ambulance cars, less one, with lead sub-division including one Officer to report at L'ECOLE NORMALE INSTITUTEURS, DOUAI, to attend temporarily on French civilian sick & wounded. Necessary clerical steps to be taken.	
		0300	Complied with. Under instructions of A.D.M.S. 2 horsed ambulance wagons sent to report for	

Sheet 10.

1/2 LOWLAND FIELD AMBULANCE.

Army Form C. 2118.

WAR DIARY
or
INTELLIGENCE SUMMARY.
(Erase heading not required.)

Instructions regarding War Diaries and Intelligence Summaries are contained in F. S. Regs., Part II. and the Staff Manual respectively. Title pages will be prepared in manuscript.

Place	Date	Hour	Summary of Events and Information	Remarks and references to Appendices
AUBY	23/7		Temporary duty with 24th Field Ambulance, ST AMAND. Received instructions from A.D.M.S. to move under Brigade arrangements to RACHES, and occupy site to be vacated tomorrow by 1/2nd Lowland Field Ambulance. **Strength Officers** Surgeon Lieut. Commander CAMPBELL ROSS joined for temporary duty. Authority A.D.M.S. Received 155 Bgade Order No 129 - Details for tomorrow move. **Strength R.A.M.C.** Four other ranks (specialists) rejoined from temporary duty with VIII Corps R.I.F. Station.	9y
(B.1) RACHES	24/7		Unit moved to RACHES, and occupied site vacated by 1/2nd Lowland Field Ambulance. 2nd/1st division rejoined from duty at Civilian Hospital DOUAI.	9y 9y
	25/7		Received from A.D.M.S. letter of appreciation from D.D.M.S. VIII Corps of work done by unit sub-division at Civilian Hospital DOUAI. Appendix 9y 3	

Sheet 11.

WAR DIARY
or
INTELLIGENCE SUMMARY.
(Erase heading not required.)

Army Form C. 2118.

1/3 LOWLAND FIELD AMBULANCE.

Place	Date	Hour	Summary of Events and Information	Remarks and references to Appendices
RACHES.	26/10		Under instructions of A.D.M.S, 1 ambulance car, with driver, sent to No. 32 Labour group for temporary duty.	
			Received Warning Order from A.D.M.S – Division will relieve 12th Division in line on night 28th–29th inst.	9ч
	27/10		Received R. & M. 6 Operation Order No 21 – Unit to move with 155 Brigade tomorrow to LANDAS.	9ч
			Received 155 Brigade Order No 130 – Details of move tomorrow.	
	28/10		3 x N.C.O.s. drivers reported from temporary duty with 427 C.C.S.	
			Unit moved to LANDAS.	
(D.I.) LANDAS			Received instructions from A.D.M.S. to reconnoitre sites in Brigade area where largest possible number of cases could be held under medical treatment, in view of possible epidemic of influenza.	
			Complied with, and A.D.M.S. notified that the School LANDAS will accommodate 130 cases.	
			Under instructions of A.D.M.S, heliograph party sent to BEUVRY to test ambulance site there.	

1/2 LOWLAND FIELD AMBULANCE.

Army Form C. 2118.

WAR DIARY or INTELLIGENCE SUMMARY
(Erase heading not required.)

Sheet 12.

Instructions regarding War Diaries and Intelligence Summaries are contained in F. S. Regs., Part II. and the Staff Manual respectively. Title pages will be prepared in manuscript.

Place	Date	Hour	Summary of Events and Information	Remarks and references to Appendices
LANDAS	28/12		As instructed by A.D.M.S., Captain D.F.BROWN attd to 1/1st Lowland Field Ambulance for temporary duty.	
			Strength R.A.M.C.	94
	29/12		Four other ranks to hospital sick.	
			Received instructions from A.D.M.S. to establish Divisional Rest Station.	
			Complied with.	
	30/12		Strength R.A.M.C.	94
			Two other ranks rejoined from hospital.	
			Strength Animals	
			One H.D. horse evacuated.	
			Strength Officers.	
			Captain W.E.K. COLES rejoined from temporary duty with 242 Army Brigade R.F.A.	
			Strength Officers.	94
	31/12		Captain W.E.K. COLES posted for temporary duty at 52nd Divnl. Reception Camp. - Authority A.D.M.S.	

Sheet 13

1/8 LOWLAND FIELD AMBULANCE.

WAR DIARY
INTELLIGENCE SUMMARY
(Erase heading not required.)

Army Form C. 2118.

Place	Date	Hour	Summary of Events and Information	Remarks and references to Appendices
LANDAS	31/1?		Strength Animals	
			Coy. H.D. horse evacuated sick.	
			Strength - Unit.	
			R.A.M.C. Officers 8. A.S.C.(H.T.) Other Ranks 35. 9y	
			Other Ranks 170. —"(M.T.) — 13.	
			James Murray	
			Lieut Colonel	
			R.A.M.C.(T.)	
			O.C. 1/3rd Lowland Field Ambulance	
	2-11-18.			

Copy.

Appendix I.

SPECIAL ORDER OF THE DAY

by

Lieut-Colonel J. Young,
Commanding 1/3rd Lowland Field Ambulance, R.A.M.C., T

8th October, 1918

Now that the unit is allowed a period of rest afetr the recent operations, the Commanding Officer wishes to place on record his high appreciation of the services given by all officers and other ranks.

The greatest trials of work and danger fell to the party working with the 155th Inf. Brigade under the command of Major Greer, M.C. The Commanding Officer, although he himself was unable to witness the work done by this party, knows that the spirit which has at all times marked the work of the Ambulance, was shewn on this occasion. At no period in our Active Service has there been a greater demand on the devotion and endurance of all ranks. It will be a gratification to all ranks to know that the G.O.C. 155th Inf. Bde. has testified to the constant success with which the attendance on the Brigade was carried out. The Commanding Officer congratulates Major Greer, M.C. and his N.C.Os. and men on the manner in which they availed themselves of a great opportunity.

The work done by the Tent Sub-divisions at the Corps Main Dressing Stations it is impossible to praise too highly. That the 1/3rd Lowland Field Ambulance was selected for this responsible duty, from all the Ambulances of the Corps, is a signal tribute to the efficiency of the unit.

Every Officer, N.C.O., and man recognised the responsibility and acted up to it. The Commanding Officer thanks all ranks, R.A.M.C., A.S.C.,(H.T.) & A.S.C.,(M.T.)

On several occasions the work done at the Corps Main Dressing Stations was the object of praise by officers of high authority including the Director of Medical Services, Third Army

Before the Unit left the Corps Area, the D.D.M.S., XVIIth Corps, wrote thanking the Commanding Officer for the valuable services rendered by the whole unit at the Corps Main Dressing Stations.

It will interest all to know that the D.D.M.S. decided to adopt the scheme elaborated by this unit for all future Corps Main Dressing Stations.

(Sgd.) W.W. Greer, Major,

1/3rd Lowland Field Ambulance, R.A.M.C.,T.F.

Appendix 2

R O U T I N E   O R D E R
by
Major General F.J. MARSHALL, C.M.G., D.S.O., Commanding
52nd (Lowland) Division.

18th October, 1918

271 <u>IMMEDIATE AWARDS.</u>

The Army Corps Commander has awarded the Military Medal to the following N.C.O. and men.
The congratulations of both the Corps and Divisional Commanders should be conveyed to the recipients.

<u>MILITARY MEDAL</u>

320167	Cpl.	J.A. McMurtrie, J.A.	1/3rd Lowland Fld. Ambulance.
328071	Pte.	C.P. Lyle	-do-
320223	"	G. Angus,	-do-
320108	"	R.L. Watt	-do-
320041	"	P.A. Pullen	-do-
320063	"	L. Horsburgh	-do-
M1/09026	"	G.E. Nutbrown	A.S.C., M.T. attached 1/3rd Lowland Field Ambulance.

Appendix 8.

COPY.   25 th October 1918

Dear Mc Dougall,

I want to put on record my appreciation of the excellent work done by Captain Brown & and the personnel of your Division sent to the ECOLE NORMALE, DOUAI.

It was largely due to the energy and initiative of this party that the building was prepared for patients in so short a time.

I should like all ranks to know how much I appreciate their work on this occasion.

Yours Sincerely,

(Sgd.) H.V. Prynne,

Dear Young,
I forward the D.D.M.S. letter which please return.
Please let all ranks know how much Col. Prynne appreciates their work.

Your Sincerely,
(Sgd.) A.J. MacDougall.

… /34 01

Confidential

War Diary
of
1/3rd Lowland Field Ambulance R.A.M.C. (T.F.)

From 1st November 1918.
To 30th November 1918.

Volume III.

Sheet 1.

Army Form C. 2118.

1/3rd LOWLAND FLD. AMB.
R.A.M.C. (T.F.)

WAR DIARY
or
INTELLIGENCE SUMMARY.
(Erase heading not required.)

Instructions regarding War Diaries and Intelligence Summaries are contained in F. S. Regs., Part II. and the Staff Manual respectively. Title pages will be prepared in manuscript.

Place	Date	Hour	Summary of Events and Information	Remarks and references to Appendices
H.28.a.8.4. (LANDAS)			Reference Map, France Sheet 44.	
	1/4/18		Nil.	
	2/4/18		In accordance with instruction of A.D.M.S., M.O. detailed to attend daily sick of 52nd Divl. Train H.Q.	
			Strength.	
			Captain D.F. BROWN returned from temporary duty with 1/1st Lowland Field Ambulance.	
	3/4/18		Move.	
			Received word from 155 Brigade H.Q. that Brigade will probably move up on 5th inst in support of 157 Bde.	
	4/4/18		Move.	
			Received from A.D.M.S. Warning Order that sub-divisions will probably take over from 2/1st Field Ambulance in F.8.a on night of 4th-5th; an Officer to reconnoitre and get into touch with 2/1st Field Ambulance; Bearer sub-division Bearer Officer will move out with Brigade on 5th inst.	Appendix 1.
			Captain D.F. BROWN sent out for reconnoitring purpose.	

/ 1/3rd LOWLAND FLD. AMB.
R.A.M.C. (T.F.)

Army Form C. 2118.

Sheet 2.

WAR DIARY
or
INTELLIGENCE SUMMARY
(Erase heading not required.)

Instructions regarding War Diaries and Intelligence Summaries are contained in F. S. Regs., Part II. and the Staff Manual respectively. Title pages will be prepared in manuscript.

Place	Date	Hour	Summary of Events and Information	Remarks and references to Appendices
H.28.a.8.4.	4/11/18		<u>Move</u>. Received A.D.M.S. No. S.R./18 of 3-11-18 - Procedure to be adopted on withdrawal of the enemy	Appendix 2.
			Received 155 Brigade Order No 131 of 4-11-18 - Division to relieve 8th Division. 155 Brigade to move on 5th inst.	
			Received R.A.M.C. Operation Order No 202 - Reference above move. Unit to take over A.D.S. at P.9.c.9.8. and Car Post at P.9.c.9.8. and Car Post at Opononvia 1. Relief to be completed by 0600, 5th inst.	Appendix 1.
			<u>Strength</u>:- R.A.M.C. 1 Other Rank to Hospital-sick.	
	5/11/18		<u>Move</u>. Captain D.F.BROWN and party moved out and took over A.D.S. at P.9.c.9.8. from 2/4th Field Ambulance. Bearer Section moved until 155 Brigade to RUMEGIES. Headquarters Section moved to LA VALLEE, the site vacated by 2/4th Field Ambulance H.Q.	94 94

… Sheet 3.

1/3rd LOWLAND FLD. AMB.
R.A.M.C. (T.F.)

Army Form C. 2118.

WAR DIARY
or
INTELLIGENCE SUMMARY.
(Erase heading not required.)

Instructions regarding War Diaries and Intelligence Summaries are contained in F.S. Regs., Part II. and the Staff Manual respectively. Title pages will be prepared in manuscript.

Place	Date	Hour	Summary of Events and Information	Remarks and references to Appendices
O.16.c.9.9. (LA VALLEE)	6/7/18		Strength:- R.A.M.C. 1 Other Rank rejoined from Hospital. 4 Other Ranks (Nursing Orderlies) returned from temporary duty with No. 21 C.C.S. Strength:- Officers Captain W.A. TODD joined for duty - Authority A.D.M.S. Move Received R.A.M.C. Operation Order No. 23 - Procedure to be adopted on receipt of the word "Hunt" when the Division will advance	Appendix 3
	7/7/18		Strength:- R.A.M.C. 1 Other Rank rejoined from Hospital. Received wire from A.D.M.S. "Hunt".	
	8/7/18		Headquarters' Section moved to ST. AMAND - F.9.c.9.8. - and joined A.D.S. party.	Appendix 3.
	9/7/18		Received R.A.M.C. Operation Order No. 24. - Headquarters' Section to move to site of present A.D.S.	Appendix 3.

WAR DIARY
INTELLIGENCE SUMMARY

Sheet 4.

1/8th LOWLAND FLD. AMB.
R.A.M.C. (T.F.)

Army Form C. 2118.

Place	Date	Hour	Summary of Events and Information	Remarks and references to Appendices
P.q.c.q.8. (ST. AMAND)	9/11		Strength:- M.S.M. R.A.M.C. Officers 7. A.S.C. (H.T.) 3.S. Other Ranks 171. A.S.C. (M.T.) 13. Strength:- R.A.M.C. 1 Other Rank returned to Base Depot for re-classification. Received A.D.M.S. No. S.R.118/3 - Headquarters Station and A.D.S. Party to move at once to neighbourhood of RIEUX DE CONDÉ; A.D.S. to be pushed forward to clear 157 Bgde.	Appendix 4.
		1400	6 one horse carried out. A.D.S. established at POMMEROEUIL.	
		2200	Received A.D.M.S. wire No. W.283 - Advance to be continued - Unit to move to HARCHIES.	
	10/11	0100	Headquarters Station moved to HARCHIES. Strength:- R.A.M.C. 1 Other Rank struck off the strength on being admitted to Hospital while on route to U.K. and transferred to Home establishment.	Appendix 5.
HARCHIES (G.29. Sheet 4.5.)		1130	Received A.D.M.S. wire W.288 - Advance to be continued - Unit to move to HARCHIES.	Appendix 5.

WAR DIARY

INTELLIGENCE SUMMARY

Sheet 5.
1/3rd LOWLAND FLD. AMB.
R.A.M.C. (T.F.)
Army Form C. 2118.

Place	Date	Hour	Summary of Events and Information	Remarks and references to Appendices
HARCHIES	10th	1130	Received A.D.M.S. wire W. 289. - Cancelling previous wire - 155 Brigade moving to SIRAULT. - MDS to move up and keep in touch with Brigade. A.D.S. moved to SIRAULT. Bearer Section moved with Brigade. Headquarters Section moved to HAUTRAGE. Received A.D.M.S. Warning Order. - 155 Brigade to advance in direction of JURBISE and pass through 156 Brigade. Unit to get in touch with 155 Brigade.	Appendix 6. Appendix 7.
	11th	0600	Headquarters Section moved to SIRAULT and joined up with A.D.S. Move continued to HERCHIES.	
		1040	Received A.D.M.S. wire W. 309 - Mobilibrion will come at 1100 today. Troops to stand fast or move westward as other times. A.D.S. moved to JURBISE with Brigade. Received 155 Bde. wire G.H.5 - Headquarters Section to billet in ERBAUT under own arrangements. Headquarters Section moved to Chateau Dascamps near ERBAUT. Strength: A.S.C.(M.T.)	Appendix 8. Appendix 9.
D. 26 a 6 9 12th (Sheet 45.)			1 Other Rank rejoined from Hospital.	

Army Form C. 2118.

Sheet 6.

WAR DIARY
INTELLIGENCE SUMMARY
(Erase heading not required.)

Instructions regarding War Diaries and Intelligence Summaries are contained in F. S. Regs., Part II. and the Staff Manual respectively. Title pages will be prepared in manuscript.

Place	Date	Hour	Summary of Events and Information	Remarks and references to Appendices
D.26.a.6.9.	12/2		Received A.D.M.S. wire No 338 - Division will be transferred to 22nd Corps by 15th inst. and then move forward to RHINE.	Appendix 9
	13/2		Nil.	
	14/2		Strength A.S.C. (H.T.)	JM
			1 Other Rank rejoined from Hospital.	
			Lt. Col. Quinan rejoined from DOUAI.	JM
	15/2		Received A.D.M.S. No R.467/1 - 6 gunners to be relieved.	Appendix 9
			Received instructions further to above. - Whole Stretcher Bearers not to be taken.	Appendix 9
	16/2		Strength: Officers	
			Surgeon Lieut. Commander C. ROSS, R.N. posted to 1/1 Lowland Field Amb. in accordance with A.D.M.S. instructions.	
			Strength: - Animals.	
			1 Rider and 2 H.D. Horses received from 1/2nd Lowland Field Ambulance.	
			Strength: - R. and M.	
			1 Other Rank rejoined from Hospital.	
			Received A.D.M.S. R.465/5 - Field Ambulances going forward to be made up to 6 Medical Officers.	Appendix 9
	17/2		Nil	JM

Army Form C. 2118.

Sheet 7

1/3rd LOWLAND FLD. AMB.
R.A.M.C. (T.F.)

WAR DIARY
INTELLIGENCE SUMMARY
(Erase heading not required.)

Instructions regarding War Diaries and Intelligence Summaries are contained in F. S. Regs., Part II. and the Staff Manual respectively. Title pages will be prepared in manuscript.

Place	Date	Hour	Summary of Events and Information	Remarks and references to Appendices
D.26.a.6.9.	18/7/18		Received A.D.M.S. R.497/1 – Surplus stores and equipment to be sent in.	Appendix 9.
	19/7/18		C.O. visited LENS with a view to obtaining a site suitable for all the Ambulance personnel, with the exception of a small party to act as A.D.S., in order that arrangements for education and recreation may be facilitated. Suitable accommodation obtained. Surplus stores and equipment returned.	9/7 9/7
	20/7/18		A.D.M.S. requested to grant approval of move of Ambulance to LENS.	9/7
	21/7/18		Strengths R.A.M.C. 3 Other Ranks to Hospital sick.	9/7
	22/7/18		Approval of proposed move to LENS received from A.D.M.S. O.C. A.D.S. have been informed of impending move, and instructed as to carrying out move of personnel less small party to control A.D.S.	9/7
	23/7/18		Headquarters Section moved to LENS.	

Sheet 8.

Army Form C. 2118.

1/3rd LOWLAND FLD. AMB.
R.A.M.C. (T.F.)

WAR DIARY
INTELLIGENCE SUMMARY.
(Erase heading not required.)

Instructions regarding War Diaries and Intelligence Summaries are contained in F. S. Regs., Part II. and the Staff Manual respectively. Title pages will be prepared in manuscript.

Place	Date	Hour	Summary of Events and Information	Remarks and references to Appendices
V.28.a.3.4.-23½ (LENS) Sheet 38.	21/2/18		Bearer Section and party from A.D.S. personnel arrival and rejoined Headquarters.	M
	22/2/18		Strength: R.A.M.C. Offrs. 7. Other Ranks. 171. M.T., A.S.C. (Other Ranks) 13. H.T., — "— (— ". —) 36.	
	25/2/18		Strength: R.A.M.C. 1 Other Rank to Hospital - sick. 2 Other Ranks rejoined from Hospital.	M
	26/2/18		2 " " " " "	M
	27/2/18		Nil	
	28/2/18		Strength: R.A.M.C. 1 Other Rank rejoined from Hospital.	M
	29/2/18		1 " " " " "	M
	30/2/18		Nil	M
			Strength: R.A.M.C. Offrs 7. A.S.C. (H.T.) O.R. 36. Other Ranks. 143. —"— (M.T.) —"— 13.	
			O.C. 1/3rd Lowland Field Ambulance	
			James Murray Lieut Colonel R.A.M.C.(T.)	
			2nd December 1918.	

Appendix 1.

SECRET.   Wire to O.C., 1/3rd Low. Fld. Amb.

No' W 216   dated 4th Nov. 1916.

WARNING ORDER AAA One Tent Sub-division 3rd L.F.A. will probably take over from the 24th Field Amb. P.8.a. on night of 4th /5th AAA Send an officer to reconnoitre and get into touch with 24th Field Amb. pending receipt of orders AAA Bearers under Bearer Officer will join 155 Bde. when they move on 5th.

From A.D.M.S., 52nd Division.   (Sgd.) A.J. MacDougall,
                                                        Colonel, A.M.S.

Appendix 1.

SECRET.   Copy No. 3

R. A. M. C.
OPERATION ORDER No. 22
by
A.D.M.S., 52nd (Lowland) DIVISION.

4th November, 1918

Reference Map - 1/40,000 - Sheet 44

INFORMATION.
        157th Inf. Bde. relieves 23rd Inf. Bde. (8th Divn.) in the line tonight.
        155th Inf. Bde. will move to LECELLES Area on 5th inst. and will be in Divisional Support.

MEDICAL ARRANGEMENTS.
        O.C., 1/3rd Lowland Fld. Amb. will take over A.D.S. 24th Field Ambulance at P.9.c.9.8. and Car Post at O.14.a.7.5. to-night, relief to be completed by 0600 on 5th inst. He will also send a holding party to 24th Field Amb. (O.15.c.9.9.) to-night, preparatory to moving his Headquarters to that site tomorrow.

        He will, before moving his Headquarters, evacuate all Rest Station Cases to Headquarters, 1/1st L.F.A. at O.2.a.4.1. and will arrange to collect sick from 155th Inf. Bde. before that Brigade moves from LANDAS Area.

        On arrival in new area, he will be responsible for evacuating all 157th Inf. Bde. cases to his A.D.S.

        O.C., 1/2nd Low. Fld. Amb. will not move his Ambulance at present and will be responsible for evacuation of sick of 155th Inf. Bde. on its arrival in LECELLES Area. Any cases evacuated will be sent to 1/1st Low. Fld. Amb.

        O.C., 1/1st Low. Fld. Amb. will not move his Field Ambulance at present, but will open his Headquarters as the Divisional Rest Station, from tomorrow.

        Any sick cases evacuated from 8th Division Artillery will be sent to 26th Field Ambulance, BOUVIGNIES.

        Lists of stores taken over will be sent to this office.

        Completion of moves and exact Map locations will be reported to this office.

ACKNOWLEDGE.

                              (sgd.) F.W.C. Brown, Major,
                                    for Colonel, A.M.S.
S.R. 19   A.D.M.S. 52nd (Lowland) Division.
4/11/18.

Appendix 2.

SECRET.   A.D.M.S., 52nd Divn. No. S.R./18.

O.C., 1/1st Low. Fld. Amb.
O.C., 1/2nd Low. Fld. Amb.
O.C., 1/3rd Low. Fld. Amb.

Reference 52nd Divisional Order No. 143 dated 3/11/18.

On the withdrawal of the enemy, the Brigade in line will cross the ESCAUT and JARD Canal by foot-bridge etc.

The following bridges for H.T. will be erected at the earliest opportunity :-

Bridges A and B, near COUPURE, K.27.d.3.1.
X and Y, near PONT DE LA VERNETTE.

When bridges A and B are open for traffic, a red flag will be hoisted at K.31.b.8.3. and a blue flag will be hoisted at K.25.a.4.5. when X and Y bridges are open.

Bearers of 1/1st Lowland Fld. Amb. will accompany 156th Inf. Brigade under orders of Bearer Officer.
Bearers of 1/2nd Lowland Fld. Amb. will accompany 157th Inf. Bde.
Bearers of 1/3rd Lowland Fld. Amb. will accompany 155th Inf. Bde.

O.C., 1/2nd Lowland Fld. Amb. will form an A.D.S. and Car Post, reporting location to this office and repeating same to his Brigade and to 156th Inf. Bde., and to 155th Inf. Bde.

Cases will be evacuated to M.D.S. of 1/1st Lowland Fld. Amb.

Headquarters of Field Ambulances will not move until ordered by this office.

3rd November, 1918.   (Sgd.) A.J. MacDougall, Colonel,
Issued 0800 4/11/18.   A. M. S.
                                                     52nd Division.

Appendix 3.

Wire to O.C., 1/3rd Low. Fld. Amb;
No. W 256   dated 8th Nov. 1918
Ref. my S.R. 18 AAA   HUNT.

From A.D.M.S., 52nd Division.   (Sgd) F.W.C. Brown, Major
                                              for A.D.M.S.

Appendix 3.

SECRET.   Copy No. 3

R.A.M.C. OPERATION ORDER No. 23
by
A.D.M.S., 52nd (LOWLAND) DIVISION.

Reference my S.R./18 of 3/11/18.   6th November, 1918

On the receipt of the word "HUNT", the 52nd Division will advance.

1.   The following procedure will then, but not till then, come into operation :-
   1/1st Low. Fld. Amb. will evacuate all cases in the Divisional Rest Station except Scabies cases, and will close down (except for the reception of wounded and serious sick) and will be ready to move on orders to do so being received.
   Bearer Division, under Bearer Officer, will at once join the Brigade.
   (See also para. 2 +)

2.   O.C., 1/2nd Low. Fld. Amb. will at once open an A.D.S. at HAUTE RIVE - J.36.a.0.9. and form Car Posts as necessary informing all concerned of their location.
+   As soon as this A.D.S. is opened, the A.D.S. of 1/1st Low. Fld. Amb. will close, except as a Car Relay Post., and the personnel will rejoin their unit.
+   O.C., 1/1st Low. Fld. Amb. will station 2 Cars at I.36.a. (his present A.D.S.), the cars going up to the new A.D.S., J.36.a. as cars come down.
   The new A.D.S. will evacuate to 1/1st Low. Fld. Amb. at O.2.a.4.1.
   O.C., 1/2nd Low. Fld. Amb. will be prepared to open a further A.D.S. when necessary, but he will not cross the Canal DU JARD till the Artillery have crossed.
   Bearers are with 157th Inf. Bde. and will accompany it when it moves.

3.   O.C., 1/3rd Low. Fld. Amb. will send all his M.A.C. Cars to 1/1st Low. Fld. Amb. and by means of his own cars will send patients for evacuation to 1/1st Low. Fld. Amb.   He will be prepared to move on receipt of orders.

ACKNOWLEDGE.

                              (Sgd.) A.J. MacDougall, Colonel,
                                                    A.M.S.
                              A.D.M.S., 52nd Division.

Issued at 1800
S.R. /18
6/11/18.

± Scabies cases will move with the Ambulance.

Appendix 3.

SECRET.   Copy No. 3

R.A.M.C. OPERATION ORDER No. 24
by
A.D.M.S. 52nd (LOWLAND) Division.
----

1.   Headquarters of 1/2nd Low. Fld. Amb. will move to
 UBRAY - P.4.c.
        O.C. will report when his A.D.S. at HAUTE RIVE - J.36.
a.0.9. and Headquarters at P.4.c. are open giving exact
locations.

2.   Headquarters 1/3rd Low. Fld. Amb. will move to present
A.D.S. at P.9.c.9.8.   O.C. will report completion.

3.   As soon as all patients at present in the Divisional
Rest Station (except Scabies) are evacuated, O.C., 1/1st
Low. Fld. Amb. will send all M.A.C. Cars, less 2, to A.D.S. in
P.9.c.9.8.   He will at the same time inform O.C., A.D.S. of
1/2nd Low. Fld. Amb. at J.36.a.0.9. that he has done so. the
roite of evacuation will then be to P.9.a.9.8. and not to
O.2.a.4.
        When O.C., 1/1st Low. Fld. Amb. is satisfied that the
new route of evacuation is open, he will withdraw his present
Car Posts.
        O.C., 1/1st Low. Fld. Amb. will be responsible for the
evacuation of sick of 155th Inf. Bde.
        O.C., 1/1st Low. Fld. Amb. will report when the D.R.S.
is clear.

4.   O.C., 1/3rd Low. Fld. Amb. will assist O.C., 1/2nd Low.
Fld. Amb. with cars if necessary on application.

Issued at 1145
9/11/18   (Sgd.) A.J. MacDougall, Colonel,
S.R./18/1.   A. M. S.
                                        A.D.M.S., 52nd Division.

Appendix 4.

SECRET'   URGENT.   A.D.M.S., 52nd Divn. No. S.R. 118/3

    Move at once to neighbourhood of RIEUX DE CONDE and push
A.D.S. forward to clear 157th Inf. Bde.
    Cross the Canal by Bridge at K.27.d.3.1.
    Road in K.30.c.4.5. stated to be blown up.
    Headquarters of 157th Inf. Bde. is moving.
    1/2nd Low. Fld. Amb. H.Q. are now at K.23.c.3.3.
    Send 4 M.A.C. Cars to O.C., 1/2nd L.F.A. at K.23.c.3.3. and
retain 4 yourself.
    Report exact location on completion of move.

9/11/18.   (Sgd.) A.J. MacDougall. Colonel,
                                                                  A.M.S.
                                              A.D.M.S., 52nd Division.

Appendix 5

Wire to O.C., 1/3rd Low. Fld. Amb.

No. W 283   dated 9th Nov. 1918

Move to HARCHIES - G. 29 Sheet 45   AAA 157th B.H.Q. are at
VILLE POMMEROEUIL H.26.   AAA Get in touch with and evacuate cases
of 157th Bde.   AAA   The ~~Brigade~~ BRIDGE in G.22.c.7.0. is said to be fit
for traffic.

From   A.D.M.S., 52nd Division.   (Sgd) A.J. MacDougall,
                                                  Colonel, A.M.S.

Appendix 5.

O.C., 1/3rd Low. Fld. Amb.

Wire No. W 288   dated   9th Nov.,1918

Advance will be continued tomorrow the 10th up to line
Rly. O.4., E.34. and I 27. Road to NEUF MAISON AAA After
relief by 8th Division 157th Bde. close up on VILLEROT AAA
156 Bde. close up on SIRAULT AAA Cyclists and Sqdrn. 4th
Hussars to les BACHELL FRIES, T.13.c. CH LA PREVOTE C.25.d.
AAA   155 Bde. move to HAPPART, not to cross ANTOING CANAL
before 1000 no road restrictions AAA 9th Bde. R.F.A. must be
prepared to cover front held by 8th Divn. until relieved AAA
R.E. Pnrs. move as ordered by C.R.E. AAA 3rd L.F.A. moves
HARCHIES, 2nd L.F.A. Bruyere , 1st L.F.A. BONSECOURS.

From A.D.M.S., 52nd Divn.   (Sgd.) A.J. MacDougall, Colonel,
                                                    A.M.S.
                                        A.D.M.S., 52nd Division

Wire to O.C., 1/3rd Low. Fld. Amb.   Appendix 6.

No. W 289   dated 10th November, 1918

My W 288 of 9th is cancelled AAA   Canadian Corps moving high ground
E. and N.E. of MONS AAA   Cav. 5th Army moving up on our left AAA
Enemy in full retreat and 52nd Division will pursue AAA 8th Corps.
Cyclists will make good MONS - JURBISE road K.19., D.10. by 1300 AAA
157 Bde. move to D.27. ERBISOEUL and will cover ground with infantry
as far S. as 8th Corps boundary to protect batteries adequately
till 8th Division arrives AAA   156 Bde. to ERBAUT D.14. AAA
155 Bde. move to SIRAULT   AAA Bde. H.Q. 157, 156 will be established
VACRESSE C.20.c. AAA   Field Ambces will move up and keep in touch
with the Bdes. they are now administering AAA   Economy should be
exercised in rations owing possible scarcity 11th AAA D.H.Q. closes
MT. PERUWELZ opens SIRAULT 1300.

Time   From A.D.M.S. 52nd Division.

Appendix 7

Wire to 1/3rd Lowland Fld. Amb.

No. W 299   dated 10th Nov., 1918

WARNING ORDER AAA 155th Bde pass through 156th Bde. early tomorrow AAA Direction of advance roughly through ,JURBISE, D 16 and 17 AAA 1/1st L.F.A. will move to SIRAULT I. 1.c. AAA 1/2nd L.F.A. will get in touch and evacuate cases from 157th Bde. AAA 1/3rd L.F.A. will get in touch with and evacuate cases from 155th Bde. AAA 1/2nd L.F.A. in addition to evacuating 157th Bde. evacuate 156th Bde. till 155th Bde. have passed through 156th Bde. and all cases are cleared AAA On the arrival of 1/1st L.F.A. at SIRAULT, O.C., will get in touch with 156th Bde. and evacuate sick and wounded.
H.Q. 155 Bde. at SIRAULT move to VACRESSE tomorrow.
H.Q. 156 Bde. at VACRESSE C. 30.
H.Q. 157 Bde. at SIRAULT move VACRESSE tomorrow.

Time 2000   From A.D.M.S.   (Sgd.) A.J. MacDougall,
                      52nd Division.   Colonel.

Appendix 8.

O.C., 1/3rd Low. Fld. Amb.

Wire   No. W 309   dated 11th Nov., 1918

Following received from G.H.Q. begins AAA   Hostilities will cease at 1100 on Nov. 11th AAA   Troops will stand fast on line reached at that hour which will be reported to this office AAA   Defensive precautions will be maintained   AAA   There will be intercourse of any description with the enemy AAA acknowledge.

                                           (Sgd.) F.W.C. Brown, Major
Issued at 0800   D.A.D.M.S.
From A.D.M.S., 52nd Division.

Appendix 9.

Wire to O.C., 1/3rd Low. Fld. Amb.
--- --------------------

No. G.45   Dated 11th Nov., 1918

You will billet in ERBAUT under your own arrangements.
Bde. H.Q. JURBISE.

From 155 Inf. Brigade.   (Sgd.) S. Hutton, Major.

Wire to O.C., 1/3rd Low. Fld. Amb.   Appendix 9.

No. W 338   dated 12th Nov.,1918

52nd Divn. will be transferred to 22nd Corps by 15th inst. and then move forward to the RHINE.

From A.D.M.S. 52nd Division.   (Sgd.) A.J. MagDougall,
                                           Colonel, A.M.S.

Appendix 9.

SECRET. A.D.M.S., 52nd Divn. No. R 467/1

O.C., 1/1st Low. Fld. Amb.
O.C., 1/2nd Low. Fld. Amb.
O.C., 1/3rd Low. Fld. Amb.

     Under instructions of D.D.M.S., Field Ambulances of this Division will only carry equipment as authorised in G.1098 and G.R.O's Nos. 419 and 248 (Wheeled Stretchers.)

     Any equipment surplus to that authorised above will be reported to this office at once so that arrangements may be made for its disposal.

18/11/18.

(Sgd.) A.J. MacDougall, Colonel,
A.M.S.
A.D.M.S., 52nd Division.

O.C., 1/3rd Lowland Fld. Amb.   Appendix 9.   R.467/1

    Further to my R 467/1 of yesterday's date, please note that only the extra Blankets mentioned in G.R.O. 419 will be taken, Pyjamas, Bed socks, and Slippers will be added to the stores to be collected.
    Wheeled Stretcher Carriers will not be taken;

16/11/18   (Sgd.) A.J. MacDougall, Colonel,
A.M.S.
A.D.M.S. 52nd Division.

O.C., 1/1st Low. Fld. Amb.   A.D.M.S., 52nd Div. R 465/5
O.C., 1/2nd Low. Fld. Amb.
O.C., 1/3rd Low. Fld. Amb.

Appendix 9.

      Thefollowing D.M.S. First Army wire is forwarded for your information :-

" British Field Ambulances going forward to be completed up to 6 Medical Officers including O.C., from Field Ambulances remaining behind AAA No British Field Ambulances to go forward with more than 6 Medical Officers AAA Action to be completed by noon 16th inst.

      These adjustments will be made from this office and further orders will be issued to you if necessary.

16/11/18   (Sgd.) A.J. MacDougall, Colonel,
                                                      A. M.S.
                                         A.D.M.S. 52nd Division.

Appendix 9.

<u>A.D.M.S., 52nd Div., No. R 497/1</u>

O.C., 1/1st Low. Fld. Amb.
O.C., 1/2nd Low. Fld. Amb.
O.C., 1/3rd Low. Fld. Amb.
----

1.   Hand in all Red Cross Stores on charge to an Army Dump for-med at No. 57 C.C.S., ST SAULVE.

2.   Hand in all Stretchers and Blankets (+) surplus to Mobilization Store Tables. (+ See para. 3)

3.   Hand in such part of the extra equipment authorised under G.R.Os. 419 and 1676, as is not considered necessary to be taken.

   Copies of receipts obtained for the above will be forwarded to this office.

18/11/18.   (Sgd.) A.J. MacDougall, Colonel,
                                             A.M.S.
                              A.D.M.S.   52nd Division.

WAR DIARY
or
INTELLIGENCE SUMMARY.
(Erase heading not required.)

Army Form C. 2118.

1/3 LOWLAND FIELD AMBULANCE

War Diary
of
1/3rd Lowland Field Ambulance, R.A.M.C.(T)

From 1st December, 1918.

Volume IV.

Sheet 1.

WAR DIARY
or
INTELLIGENCE SUMMARY.
(Erase heading not required.)

Army Form C. 2118.

1/3 LOWLAND FIELD AMBULANCE

Place	Date	Hour	Summary of Events and Information	Remarks and references to Appendices
Y 28 a 34 (Sheet 38)	1/12/18		**Strength. Officers.**	
			In accordance with instructions of A.D.M.S., Captain W.A. TODD, R.A.M.C. detailed for duty with 1/5th K.S.L.I. in relief of Lieut. I.N. HOST, M.O.R.C., U/S.A. who reported this am for duty.	
			Received from A.D.M.S. instructions to detail 2 M.Os & bearer sub to report to O.C. 1/2nd Lowland Field Ambulance for duty at the station. MONS.	M
	2/12/18		Complied with.	
	3/12/18		In accordance with instructions of A.D.M.S. 1/2nd and 2 A.D.Ks, 1/2nd Lowland Field Ambulance for temporary duty attached to 1/2nd Lowland Field Ambulance at MONS.	
	4/12/18	1430.	In accordance with instructions of A.D.M.S. Captain D.T. BROWN detailed for temporary duty with 1/2nd Lowland Field Ambulance. Received instructions from A.D.M.S. – 2 sections to proceed to MONS, to establish hospital in URSULINE CONVENT, and any wounded C.C.S cases, Officers and party temporarily attached to 1/2nd Lowland Field Ambulance to return to unit.	

Sheet 2.

WAR DIARY
INTELLIGENCE SUMMARY.
(Erase heading not required.)

Army Form C. 2118.

1/3 LOWLAND
FIELD
AMBULANCE

Place	Date	Hour	Summary of Events and Information	Remarks and references to Appendices
MONS	4/11/18	16.30	Two Sections proceeded to Mons, and established hospital in URSULINE CONVENT. — Admitted from 2000-24hrs & 0300-5hrs — 402 patients. In accordance with instructions of A.D.M.S., all O. details to visit daily sick of 1/4th Scottish Rifles, and supervise sanitation. Strength:- R.A.M.C. 1 Other Rank rejoined from hospital. One officer and 25 O.Rs. temporarily attached to 1/2nd Lowland Field Ambulance rejoined unit. Strength:- R.A.M.C. 1 Other Rank rejoined from hospital.	M M
	5/11/18		Strength:- Officers Lieut. I. N. HOST, M.O.R.C. U.S.A., detailed to report to A.D.M.S. 66th Divn for duty. Authority - A.D.M.S. 525. Divn. Strength:- Arrival.	
	6/11/18		3 horses taken from horse lines, night of 5-6/11/18. Move:- Ursuline Convent, MONS, handed over to No. 4 Canadian C.C.S.	

Sheet 3.

Army Form C. 2118.

1/3 LOWLAND FIELD [AMBULANCE]

WAR DIARY

INTELLIGENCE SUMMARY.

(Erase heading not required.)

Instructions regarding War Diaries and Intelligence Summaries are contained in F. S. Regs., Part II. and the Staff Manual respectively. Title pages will be prepared in manuscript.

Place	Date	Hour	Summary of Events and Information	Remarks and references to Appendices
V.28.a.2.1.	6/12/18	2200	Move:- Two Sections returned to LENS from MONS.	M
			Strength:- R.A.M.C.	
			1 Other Rank to hospital sick.	
			Strength:- A.S.C. (M.T.)	
			1 Other Rank to hospital sick.	
	7/12/18		Strength:- Unit	
			R.A.M.C. Officers 36. 9h	
			Other Ranks 13.	
	8/12/18		Strength:-	
			6. A.S.C. (H.T.) Other Ranks 175. 9h	
			— (M.T.) —	
	9/12/18		Strength:- R.A.M.C.	
			2 Other Ranks to Hospital sick	9h
	10/12/18		Nil.	9h
	11/12/18		Nil.	9h
			Move.	
			Received instructions from A.D.M.S. — 2 Sections to proceed to MONS	
			tomorrow and open up ECOLE NORMALE as overflow O.C.S.	9h

Sheet 4.

Army Form C. 2118.

1/3 LOWLAND FIELD
AMBULANCE

WAR DIARY
or
INTELLIGENCE SUMMARY.
(Erase heading not required.)

Instructions regarding War Diaries and Intelligence Summaries are contained in F. S. Regs., Part II. and the Staff Manual respectively. Title pages will be prepared in manuscript.

Place	Date	Hour	Summary of Events and Information	Remarks and references to Appendices
MONS.	12/9/18		Move:- In accordance with previous instructions – 2 Sections moved to ECOLE NORMALE, and established Hospital there.	
	13/9/18		Nil.	XY
	14/9/18		Unit Strength:-	XY
			R.A.M.C. Officers. – 6 A.S.C.(HT) Other Ranks 36	
			Other Ranks 192. (MT) – – 12.	XY
	15/9/18		Nil.	XY
	16/9/18		Nil.	XY
	17/9/18		Strength R.A.M.C.	
			One Other Rank to Hospital sick.	XY
	18/9/18		Received instructions from DDMS 22nd Corps to send Relieving Party to the ECOLE MOYENNE and the ECOLE PROFESSIONELLE, to prepare site for Corps Troops Rest Station.	XY
			Move completed.	
			Strength Officers - Major J BROWNE, R.A.M.C.(T) attached for temporary duty from 1/1st Lowland Field Ambulance - Authority A.D.M.S.	XY
	19/9/18			XY

Sheet 5.

1/3 LOWLAND
FIELD
AMBULANCE.

Army Form C. 2118.

WAR DIARY
INTELLIGENCE SUMMARY
(Erase heading not required.)

Instructions regarding War Diaries and Intelligence Summaries are contained in F. S. Regs., Part II. and the Staff Manual respectively. Title pages will be prepared in manuscript.

Place	Date	Hour	Summary of Events and Information	Remarks and references to Appendices
MONS.	20/12/15		In accordance with instructions of A.D.M.S. Baptou D.M BROWN detailed to visit daily sick and arrange evacuation at 52nd Divisional Reception Camp, MONS.	94
	21/12/15		Unit Strength. R.A.M.C. Officers 6. A.S.C. (H.T.) Other Ranks 36. 94 Other Ranks 171. --- (M.T.) 12. 94	
	22/12/15		Strength, R.A.M.C. One Other Rank transferred to R.T. 52nd Divl. Signal degut dating Anthony Cie. R.A.M.C. Section Two Other Ranks rejoined from hospital Notification sent to D.D.M.S. 22nd Corps and A.D.M.S. 52nd Div. that 16th Corps Rest Station will be the Camamar for reception of patients.	94
	23/12/15		Move:- Two Sections moved from ECOLE NORMALE & ECOLES MOYENNE and PROFESSIONELLE to extablish Corps Rest Station	94

Sheet 6.

Army Form C. 2118.

1/3 LOW LAND
FIELD
AMBULANCE.

WAR DIARY
or
INTELLIGENCE SUMMARY.
(Erase heading not required.)

Instructions regarding War Diaries and Intelligence Summaries are contained in F. S. Regs., Part II. and the Staff Manual respectively. Title pages will be prepared in manuscript.

Place	Date	Hour	Summary of Events and Information	Remarks and references to Appendices
MONS.	24/12		Nil.	
	25/12		Nil.	
	26/12		Strength R.A.M.C.	
			O/Rs Other Rank to hospital sick.	93
			One Other Rank transferred to Home Establishment from sick in hospital whilst on leave to U.K.	93
			In accordance with instructions of D.D.M.S. 227 C.of.S. nursing	93
	27/12		April	93
	28/12		April	94
	29/12		April	94
	30/12		April	97
			Orderly detailed for temporary duty at C.of.S. H.Q.	
			Strength Officers.	
			Captain W.E.K. COLES rejoined from temporary duty with 52 D.	
			Divl. Train.	
			Exchange of Duties.	
			Capt.n W.E.K.COLES posted to 1/1st H.L.I. in relief of Lieut TARLOW	
			M.O.R.C. U.S.A. who joined unit in relief.	95

Sheet 1.

Army Form C. 2118.

1/3 LOWLAND FIELD AMBULANCE

WAR DIARY
INTELLIGENCE SUMMARY

(Erase heading not required.)

Instructions regarding War Diaries and Intelligence Summaries are contained in F. S. Regs., Part II. and the Staff Manual respectively. Title pages will be prepared in manuscript.

Place	Date	Hour	Summary of Events and Information	Remarks and references to Appendices
MONS	3/1/19		Nil.	94
	3-1-19		James Brown Lieut Colonel R.A.M.C. (T) O.C. 1/3rd Lowland Field Ambulance	

WAR DIARY
INTELLIGENCE SUMMARY

Army Form C. 2118.

52 DIN

War Diary

of

1/3rd Lowland Field Ambulance, R.A.M.C.

from 1st January 1919 to 31st January 1919.

Volume 4.

Confidential

Army Form C. 2118.

1/3 LOWLAND
FIELD
AMBULANCE

Sheet 7.

WAR DIARY
INTELLIGENCE SUMMARY.
(Erase heading not required.)

Instructions regarding War Diaries and Intelligence Summaries are contained in F. S. Regs., Part II. and the Staff Manual respectively. Title pages will be prepared in manuscript.

Place	Date	Hour	Summary of Events and Information	Remarks and references to Appendices
MONS	1/1/19	Strength		
			1 Other Rank posted to Collecting Centre, Preston, for accounting work.	
			Authority — O.C. London District Labour Centre, of 3-12-18.	94
	2/1/19	Nil.		94
	3/1/19	Nil.		94
	4/1/19	Strength Animals		
			1 A.D. Horse sent to Mobile Veterinary Section — sick.	
		Strength – Nil.		
			R.A.M.C. — Officers 6. A.S.C. (H.T.) Other Ranks 36.	
			Other Ranks 170. " — (M.T.) " " 12.	
	5/1/19	Nil.		94
	6/1/19	Nil.		94
	7/1/19	Nil.		94
	8/1/19	Nil.		94
	9/1/19		One Ambulance Car with driver and orderly, attached to 52nd Divl. Artillery.	
			Auth — Authority A.D.M.S. 52nd Division.	94

Army Form C. 2118.

1/3 LOWLAND FIELD AMBULANCE

Sheet 21

WAR DIARY
INTELLIGENCE SUMMARY.
(Erase heading not required.)

Instructions regarding War Diaries and Intelligence Summaries are contained in F. S. Regs., Part II. and the Staff Manual respectively. Title pages will be prepared in manuscript.

Place	Date	Hour	Summary of Events and Information	Remarks and references to Appendices
MONS	10/9		Strength - R.A.M.C.	
			2 Other Ranks despatched to Dispersal Station for demobilisation	
	11/9		Strength - Nil	
			R.A.M.C. Officers 6 A.S.C. (HT) Other Ranks 36	
			Other Ranks 169 --- (M.T.) --- 12	
			Strength - R.A.M.C.	
			5 Other Ranks despatched to Dispersal Station for demobilisation	
			Strength - A.S.C. (HT)	
			1 Other Rank despatched to Dispersal Station for demobilisation	
	12/9		Strength - R.A.M.C.	
			4 Other Ranks despatched to Dispersal Station for demobilisation	
	13/9		Nil	
	14/9		Strength - R.A.M.C.	
			2 Other Ranks despatched to Dispersal Station for demobilisation	
			1 Other Rank transferred to 52nd D.H.Q. for duty with A.D.M.S. - Authority	
			A.D.M.S. 52nd Division	

Army Form C. 2118.

1/3 LOWLAND FIELD AMBULANCE.

WAR DIARY
INTELLIGENCE SUMMARY.
(Erase heading not required.)

Sheet 3

Instructions regarding War Diaries and Intelligence Summaries are contained in F. S. Regs., Part II. and the Staff Manual respectively. Title pages will be prepared in manuscript.

Place	Date	Hour	Summary of Events and Information	Remarks and references to Appendices
Mons	15/9		Strength R.A.M.C.	
			1 Other Rank dispatched to Dispersal Station for demobilization	94
	16/9		Nil	94
	17/9		Strength R.A.M.C.	
			1 Other Rank died — G.S.W. Head S.I. wilful	
			Received instructions from A.D.M.S. 52nd Division — D.R.S. Lonnelle to be handed over to 1/1st Lowland Field Ambulance — 2 Ambulance Cars to be attached to this Station from unit	
			In accordance with above 2 Cars and the 1/1st Lowland Field Ambulance 94	
	18/9		Strength Unit	
			R.A.M.C. Officers 6 A.S.C. (H.T.) 35	
			Other Ranks 154 -:- (M.T.) 12	94
	19/9		In accordance with instructions of A.D.M.S. 52nd Division, 2 Other Ranks proceeded for temporary duty with No. 22 Sanitary Section.	
			Received instructions from A.D.M.S. 52nd Division to close down XXII Corps Troops Rest Station — Patients to be transferred to No. 1 C.C.S.	

Army Form C. 2118.

1/9 LOWLAND FIELD AMBULANCE

WAR DIARY
INTELLIGENCE SUMMARY.
(Erase heading not required.)

Instructions regarding War Diaries and Intelligence Summaries are contained in F. S. Regs., Part II. and the Staff Manual respectively. Title pages will be prepared in manuscript.

Place	Date	Hour	Summary of Events and Information	Remarks and references to Appendices
MONS	10/9		Rct. & G. Personnel has made strength, to be transferred temporarily	
			to No 1 L.G.S.	99
	20/9		Detachment	
			20 Other Ranks R.A.M.C. transferred temporarily to No 1 L.G.S.	
			In accordance with foregoing instructions, patients transferred to No 1	
			L.G.S.	
			M.V. returned to "base" strength	
			Detachment	
			2 Officers and 74 Other Ranks, R.A.M.C. transferred to No 1 L.G.S.	
			Move	
			Hailes MOYENNE and PROFESSIONELLE vacated and have of unit	
			moved to 36 Rue de la POTERIE.	99
	21/9		Strength :- R.A.M.C.	
			2 Other Ranks despatched to Disposal Station for demobilisation	99
	22/9		2 Ambulance Cars and Drivers posted to 1/2nd Lowland Field Ambulance	
			for temporary duty.	

Army Form C. 2118.

1/3 LOWLAND
FIELD
AMBULANCE.

Sheet 5.

WAR DIARY
or
INTELLIGENCE SUMMARY.
(Erase heading not required.)

Instructions regarding War Diaries and Intelligence
Summaries are contained in F. S. Regs., Part II.
and the Staff Manual respectively. Title pages
will be prepared in manuscript.

Place	Date	Hour	Summary of Events and Information	Remarks and references to Appendices
MONS	22/19		Received instructions from A.D.M.S. to attach 2 hand stretcher wagons for temporary duty with 155 Brigade.	93
	23/19		Above carried out with R.A.M.C.	93
	24/19		Strength, R.A.M.C. One other rank admitted to U.K. lines, as from 9-1-19	93
	25/19		Strength:- M.T. Ratio 6 officers. 5 A.S.C (H.T.) Other Ranks 35 Other Ranks 150 -- 12. -- (M.T.)	93 93
	26/19		Nil	93
	27/19		Nil	93
	28/19		Strength:- Officers Major W.W.GREER, M.C. released from military Service whilst on U.K. leave, as from 10-1-19	93
	29/19		Strength:- R.A.M.C. One Other Rank demobilised whilst on U.K. leave, as from 10-1-19	93
	30/19		Nil	93

1/3 LOWLAND
FIELD
AMBULANCE.

Army Form C. 2118.

Sheet 6.

WAR DIARY
INTELLIGENCE SUMMARY.
(Erase heading not required.)

Instructions regarding War Diaries and Intelligence Summaries are contained in F. S. Regs., Part II. and the Staff Manual respectively. Title pages will be prepared in manuscript.

Place	Date	Hour	Summary of Events and Information	Remarks and references to Appendices
MONS.	3/1/19		Decorations.	
			Lieut. Colonel JAMES YOUNG awarded D.S.O.	
			T/S.M. WELDON awarded M.S.M.	
	2-2-19			
				James Young
				Lieut Colonel
				R.A.M.C. (T)
				O.C. 1/3rd Lowland Field Ambulance

Army Form C. 2118.

WAR DIARY
or
INTELLIGENCE SUMMARY.
(Erase heading not required.)

War Diary
—— of ——
3rd Lowland Field Ambulance, R.A.M.C.

from 1st February 1919 to 28th February 1919.

Volume 4.

Army Form C. 2118.

WAR DIARY
INTELLIGENCE SUMMARY
(Erase heading not required.)

Instructions regarding War Diaries and Intelligence Summaries are contained in F. S. Regs., Part II. and the Staff Manual respectively. Title pages will be prepared in manuscript.

Place	Date	Hour	Summary of Events and Information	Remarks and references to Appendices
MONS	1/2/19		Strength:- Officers 4 O. Ranks R.A.M.C. 149	Horses – Riding 2 L.D. 16 H.D. 18
	2/2/19		Nil	
	3/2/19		Strength R.A.M.C. O.Ranks R.A.S.C. 35 O.Ranks R.A.S.C.(M.T.) 12	
	4/2/19		Nil 3 Other Ranks demobilised	
	5/2/19		Nil	
	6/2/19		Nil	
	7/2/19		Strength – Officers Captain D.F. BROWN rejoined for duty from 1/7th High[d]. Light Infy.	
	8/2/19		Strength – R.A.M.C. 3 Other Ranks demobilised	
	9/2/19		Strength – R.A.M.C. 1 Other Rank demobilised	
	10/2/19		Nil	
	11/2/19		Strength – Animals 3 L.D. Animals struck off strength – Handed over to A.V.C. for sale	
	12/2/19		Nil	
	13/2/19		Strength – R.A.M.C. 2 Other Ranks demobilised	
	14/2/19		Nil	

Army Form C. 2118.

WAR DIARY
INTELLIGENCE SUMMARY.
(Erase heading not required.)

Instructions regarding War Diaries and Intelligence Summaries are contained in F. S. Regs., Part II. and the Staff Manual respectively. Title pages will be prepared in manuscript.

Place	Date	Hour	Summary of Events and Information	Remarks and references to Appendices
MONS	15/2/19		Nil	
	16/2/19		Strength - R.A.M.C. 4 Other Ranks demobilised. Lieut-Colonel J. YOUNG, D.S.O. proceeded on 14 days leave U.K.	Rw
	17/2/19		Strength - R.A.S.C. 1 Other Rank demobilised	Rw
	18/2/19		Nil	Rw
	19/2/19		Nil	Rw
	20/2/19		Nil	Rw
	21/2/19		Strength - R.A.M.C. 3 Other Ranks demobilised	Rw
	22/2/19		Nil	Rw
	23/2/19		Strength - R.A.M.C. Major R.G. WALKER, M.C. rejoined from leave U.K.	Rw
	24/2/19		Strength - R.A.M.C. 3 Other Ranks demobilised	Rw
	25/2/19		Nil	Rw
	26/2/19		Strength - Officers. Captain D.F. BROWN proceeded on 14 days leave U.K.	Rw
			Strength - R.A.M.C. 1 Other Rank demobilised off leave.	Rw
	27/2/19		Nil	Rw

Army Form C. 2118.

WAR DIARY
INTELLIGENCE SUMMARY.
(Erase heading not required.)

Place	Date	Hour	Summary of Events and Information	Remarks and references to Appendices
MONS	28/2/19		Strength - Officers 5. Horses Riding 6 O. Ranks R.A.M.C. 127 L.D. 11 O. Ranks R.A.S.C. 34 H.D. 16 O. Ranks R.A.S.C.(M.T.) 12. Rw Strength - Officers Captain & R.M.O. C.E.W. COE rejoined from leave U.K. Rw	
	28/2/19.		{signature} Major Lieut-Colonel (absent on Leave) O.C. 1/3rd Lowland Field Ambulance	

Army Form C. 2118.

WAR DIARY

INTELLIGENCE SUMMARY
(Erase heading not required)

Vol 12
1402551

War Diary
of
13th Lowland Field Ambulance, R.A.M.C.
from 1st March 1919 to 31st March 1919
Volume 4

WAR DIARY
INTELLIGENCE SUMMARY
(Erase heading not required)

Army Form C. 2118.

Place	Date	Hour	Summary of Events and Information	Remarks and references to Appendices
Meerut	1/3/19		Strength 201 Other Ranks reported. Unit from 22nd Sanitary Section	
"			Strength Officers R.A.M.C. 5 Horses 6 Riding	
			O.Ranks R.A.M.C. 138 11 L.D.	
			O.Ranks R.A.S.C.(M.T.) 36 10 H.D.	
			O.Ranks R.A.S.C.(M.T.) 12	
			R.A.M.C.	
"	2/3/19		Strength 1 Other Rank proceeded on 41 days leave to U.K.	Pw
"	3/3/19		Nil	Pw
"	4/3/19		Strength — Animals 5 H.D. struck off strength, handed over to R.A.V.C. for sale	Pw
"	5/3/19		Nil	Pw
"	6/3/19		Nil	Pw
"	7/3/19		Nil	Pw
"			R.A.M.C. 7 Other Ranks demobilized	
"	8/3/19		Strength R.A.S.C. (M.T.) 5 Other Ranks demobilized	Pw
"			Nil	Pw
"	9/3/19		Nil	Pw
"	10/3/19		Strength R.A.M.C. 1 Other Rank rejoined Unit from leave in U.K.	Pw
"	11/3/19		Strength — Animals 2 Riding struck off strength - Landed over to R.A.V.C. for sale	Pw
			2 L.D.	
			2 H.D.	

WAR DIARY
or
INTELLIGENCE SUMMARY.
(Erase heading not required.)

Army Form C. 2118.

Instructions regarding War Diaries and Intelligence Summaries are contained in F. S. Regs., Part II. and the Staff Manual respectively. Title pages will be prepared in manuscript.

Place	Date	Hour	Summary of Events and Information	Remarks and references to Appendices
Diera	11/3/19	Strength RAMC	1 Other Rank evacuated to Hospital	RW
"	13/3/19	"	Nil	RW
"	13/3/19	Strength RAMC	1 Other Rank rejoined Unit from leave in U.K.	RW
"	14/3/19	Strength RAMC	1 Other Rank to be demobilised. 1 Other Rank transferred to Army. Struck off strength. Part II Orders 8-3-19 N400	RW
"		RASC MT	3 Other Ranks demobilised	RW
"	15/3/19	Strength RAMC	Capt. Burton M.B. rejoined Unit from leave in U.K.	RW
"		Strength — struck	1 WO struck off strength and to Base Station en route for Devon	RW
"	16/3/19	Strength RAMC.	3 Other Ranks demobilised	RW
"			1 Other Rank rejoined from leave in U.K. 1 Other Rank rejoined from leave in Drontheim	RW
"	17/3/19	Nil		RW
"	18/3/19	Nil		RW
"	19/3/19	Strength RAMC	1 Other Rank demobilised	RW
"		RASC(MT)	1 Other Rank demobilised	RW
"	20/3/19	Strength RAMC	1 Other Rank rejoined from leave in U.K.	RW
"	21/3/19	Strength + Arrivals	4 Privs struck off strength — Handed over to D.A.P.M. 52 Division	RW

WAR DIARY or INTELLIGENCE SUMMARY

Army Form C. 2118.

Place	Date	Hour	Summary of Events and Information	Remarks and references to Appendices
Nexa	21/3/19		Move - Moved Establishment moved from Nexa to Sognes	RW
Sognes	22/3/19		Strength - RAMC 10 Other Ranks 1 Hospital	RW
	22/3/19		Strength - RAMC 12 Other Ranks left for demobilization	RW
	23/3/19		Strength - Motor Ambulance bars - 1 Ambulance handed over to No 52nd Divn M.T. Workshops	RW
	24/3/19		Strength RASC (MT) 5 Other Ranks - Struck off strength - Attached to 52nd M.T. Workshops	RW
	25/3/19		Nil	RW
	26/3/19		Nil	RW
	27/3/19		Strength. RAMC. 2 Other Ranks left for demobilization	RW
	28/3/19		Strength RAMC. Capt Brown DC posted to Labour Commandant Douai	RW
	29/3/19		Strength. RAMC. 2 Other Ranks returned from Hospital	RW
	29/3/19		Strength RAMC Lt Col Young f OSC demobilized - as from 9th March 1919	RW
	30/3/19		Nil	RW
	31/3/19		Strength RAMC - 3 Other Ranks left for demobilization	RW
			Strength	RW
			Officers 3	
			O. Ranks RAMC 91	
			O. Ranks RASC (MT) 16	
			O. Ranks RASC (MT) 1	

W. Walker Major
O.C. 1/3 Lowland Field Ambulance RAMC(T)

Army Form C. 2118.

WAR DIARY
or
INTELLIGENCE SUMMARY.
(Erase heading not required.)

Vol 13

46/3550

War Diary
of
132nd Lowland Field Ambulance. R.A.M.C.(T)

From 1-4-19 to 30-4-19

(Volume 4)

17 JUL 1919

Army Form C. 2118.

WAR DIARY
or
INTELLIGENCE SUMMARY.
(Erase heading not required.)

Instructions regarding War Diaries and Intelligence Summaries are contained in F. S. Regs., Part II. and the Staff Manual respectively. Title pages will be prepared in manuscript.

Place	Date	Hour	Summary of Events and Information	Remarks and references to Appendices
Soignies	1-4-19		Strength Officers R.A.M.C. 3 Horses – Riding } NIL L.D. H.D.	
"			O.Ranks R.A.M.C. 109	
"			O.Ranks R.A.S.C.(HT) 35	RW
"			O.Ranks R.A.S.C.(MT) 4	RW
"	2-4-19		Nil	RW
"	3-4-19		Strength R.A.M.C. 3 Other Ranks demobilized	RW
"	4-4-19		Nil	RW
"	5-4-19		Nil	RW
"	6-4-19		Strength R.A.M.C – 3 Other Ranks demobilized	RW
"	7-4-19		Strength R.A.S.C.(H.T.) 3 Other Ranks proceeded on 14 days leave to U.K.	RW
"	8-4-19		Strength R.A.M.C. 1 Other Rank to Hospital	RW
"	9-4-19		Strength R.A.M.C. 1 Other Rank struck off strength - posted to Home Estab.	RW
"	10-4-19		Strength R.A.M.C. 3 Other Ranks demobilized	RW
"			Strength R.A.S.C.(H.T.) 1 Other Rank proceeded on 14 days leave to U.K.	RW
"	11-4-19		Strength R.A.S.C.(H.T.) 1 Other Rank returned Unit from 14 days leave.	RW
"	12-4-19		Strength R.A.M.C. 3 Other Ranks demobilized Other Ranks posted to 52nd Divn. M.T. Coy	RW

Army Form C. 2118.

WAR DIARY
or
INTELLIGENCE SUMMARY.
(Erase heading not required.)

Instructions regarding War Diaries and Intelligence Summaries are contained in F. S. Regs., Part II. and the Staff Manual respectively. Title pages will be prepared in manuscript.

Place	Date	Hour	Summary of Events and Information	Remarks and references to Appendices
Sourgues	13-4-19		- Nil -	
"	14-4-19		Strength - R.A.M.C (H.T.) 1 Other Rank reported from hospital	kw
"	15-4-19		Strength - R.A.M.C. 3 Other Ranks demobilized	kw
"	15-4-19		Strength - R.A.S.C (H.T.) 1 Other Rank posted to 52nd Divn. train R.A.S.C (H.T)	kw
"	16-4-19		Strength - R.A.M.C. 5 Other Ranks demobilized	kw
"	16-4-19		Strength - R.A.S.C. (H.T.) 1 Other Rank to hospital	kw
"	17-4-19		Strength - R.A.M.C. 6 Other Ranks demobilized	kw
"	18-4-19		Strength - R.A.M.C. 6 Other Ranks demobilized	kw
"	19-4-19		Strength - Nil -	kw
"	20-4-19		- Nil -	kw
"	21-4-19		Strength R.A.S.C (M.T.) 1 Other Rank posted to 52nd Divn. M.T. Coy	kw
"	22-4-19		- Nil -	kw
"	23-4-19		Strength R.A.M.C. 1 Other Rank proceeded on 14 days leave to U.K.	kw
"	24-4-19		Nil	kw
"	25-4-19		Nil	kw
"	26-4-19		Nil	kw

Army Form C. 2118.

WAR DIARY
or
INTELLIGENCE SUMMARY.
(Erase heading not required.)

Instructions regarding War Diaries and Intelligence Summaries are contained in F. S. Regs., Part II. and the Staff Manual respectively. Title pages will be prepared in manuscript.

Place	Date	Hour	Summary of Events and Information	Remarks and references to Appendices
Sogimo	27/4/19		Nil	lw
"	28/4/19		Strength - R.A.M.C. - 10 Other Ranks proceeded on 14 days leave U.K.	lw
"	29/4/19		Nil	lw
"	30/4/19		Strength. R.A.M.C. - 10 Other Ranks proceeded on 14 days leave U.K.	lw
			Strength R.A.S.C. M.T. 19 Other Ranks demobilized	lw
			Strength Officers - 2	lw
			O.Ranks R.A.M.C. 78	
			O.Ranks R.A.S.C.(M.T.) 4	
			O.Ranks R.A.S.C.(W.T.) 2	lw

Warren Major
O.C. 153rd Lowland Field Ambulance, R.A.M.C.(T)

Army Form C. 2118.

WAR DIARY
or
INTELLIGENCE SUMMARY.
(Erase heading not required.)

Vol 14

1/3rd Lowland Field Ambulance R.A.M.C (T)

War Diary from May 1st to May 31st 1919

Volume No 4.

25 JUL 1919

Army Form C. 2118.

WAR DIARY
or
INTELLIGENCE SUMMARY.
(Erase heading not required.)

Instructions regarding War Diaries and Intelligence Summaries are contained in F. S. Regs., Part II. and the Staff Manual respectively. Title pages will be prepared in manuscript.

Place	Date	Hour	Summary of Events and Information	Remarks and references to Appendices
Surgires	1-5-19		Strength RAMC 2 Officers 69 Other Ranks	Orig
"			RASC (HT) 13 Other Ranks	Do
"			RASC (MT) 2 Other Ranks	Do
"	1-5-19		Strength RASC(HT) T/175244 S.S.M. Brown J. left Unit for Demobilization	Do
"	2-5-19		Nil	Do
"	3-5-19		Nil	Do
"	4-5-19		Nil	Do
"	5-5-19		Nil	Do
"	6-5-19		Nil	Do
"	7-5-19		Nil	Do
"	8-5-19		Nil	Do
"	9-5-19		Nil	Do
"	10-5-19		Nil	Do
"	11-5-19		Strength RAMC 9 Other Ranks left Unit for Demobilization	Do
"	11-5-19		Strength RASC(HT) 2 Other Ranks left Unit for Demobilization	Do
"	12-5-19		Strength RASC (HT) T/7/2191 Sgt Corbin A.H. Granted 14 days leave U.K.	Do
"	13-5-19		Strength - Officers - Capt Ard/Maj D.G. Watson M.C. struck off strength Auth DAC-29/4/19 CR 3729/Mob.	Do
			O.C. 17 Postune Gatheren	

Army Form C. 2118.

WAR DIARY
or
INTELLIGENCE SUMMARY.
(Erase heading not required.)

Instructions regarding War Diaries and Intelligence Summaries are contained in F. S. Regs., Part II. and the Staff Manual respectively. Title pages will be prepared in manuscript.

Place	Date	Hour	Summary of Events and Information	Remarks and references to Appendices
Lourques	14-5-19	Nil		
"	15-5-19	Nil		
"	16-5-19	Strength	R.A.M.C. 320170 Pte Wiseman A. returned from 14 days leave in U.K.	O.i.C
"	17-5-19	Strength	R.A.M.C. 320057 Sgt Whyte J.B. proceeded on 14 days leave to U.K.	O.i.C
"	18-5-19	"	" 315128 Pte Doherty J. proceeded on 14 days leave to U.K.	O.i.C
"	18-5-19	"	" 320070 Sgt Laurent J. returned from 14 days leave to U.K.	O.i.C
"	19-5-19	"	" 315259 Pte McDonald R. proceeded on 14 days leave to U.K.	O.i.C
"	20-5-19	Nil		O.i.C
"	21-5-19	Nil		O.i.C
"	22-5-19	Strength	R.A.M.C. 318259 Pte Green J. returned from 14 days leave in U.K.	O.i.C
"	22-5-19	Strength	R.A.S.C.(M.T.) M2/153041 Pte Renshaw A. posted to 55th Res. M.T. Workshops	O.i.C
"	23-5-19	Strength	R.A.M.C. 330131 Sgt Laurent J. posted to No. 7 Gen.Hosp.	O.i.C
"	24-5-19	do	do 8 Other Ranks left Unit for demobilization	O.i.C
"	25-5-19	Nil		O.i.C
"	26-5-19	Nil		O.i.C
"	27-5-19	Nil		O.i.C

O.C. 1/3 [signature] Lt Col

Army Form C. 2118.

WAR DIARY
or
INTELLIGENCE SUMMARY.
(Erase heading not required.)

Instructions regarding War Diaries and Intelligence Summaries are contained in F. S. Regs., Part II. and the Staff Manual respectively. Title pages will be prepared in manuscript.

Place	Date	Hour	Summary of Events and Information	Remarks and references to Appendices
Boizenne	28-5-19		Nil	A.M.C
"	29-5-19		Nil	A.M.C
"	30-5-19		Nil	A.M.C
"	31-5-19	Strength R.A.S.C. (H.T.)	1/2/2/Lt Left Lambor A/A regimen Unit from 14 days leave in UK	A.M.C
"	31-5-19	Strength R.A.M.C.	1 Officer 42 Other Ranks	A.M.C
		R.A.S.C. (H.T.)	13 Other Ranks	
		R.A.S.C. (M.T.)	1 Other Rank	

O.S. Cole / Capt.
O.C. 1st Lowland Field Ambulance, R.A.M.C.

www.ingramcontent.com/pod-product-compliance
Lightning Source LLC
Chambersburg PA
CBHW080917230426
43668CB00014B/2142